Media Entrepreneurs and the Media Enterprise in the U.S. Congress

The Hampton Press Communication Series
Political Communication

David L. Paletz, Editor

Media Entrepreneurs and the Media Enterprise in the
 United States Congress
 Karen M. Kedrowski

The Politics of Disenchantment: Bush, Clinton, Perot, and the Press
 James Lemert, James M. Bernstein, William R. Elliott, and
 William L. Rosenberg

Glasnost and After: Media and Change in Central and Eastern Europe
 David L. Paletz, Karol Jakubowicz, and Pavao Novosel (eds.)

Political Communication in Action: States, Institutions, Movements,
 Audiences
 David L. Paletz (ed.)

Germany's "Unity Election": Voters and the Media
 Holli A. Semetko and Klaus Schoenbach

forthcoming

Journalism and the Education of Journalists in the
 New East/Central Europe
 Jerome Aumente, Peter Gross, Ray Hiebert, Lisa Schillinger, and
 Owen Johnson

Mediated Women: Representations in Popular Culture
 Marian Meyers (ed.)

Global Communication, Local Cultures, and Intimate Coerseduction
 René Jean Ravault

The Best Laid Plans . . . Strategic Failures in the Modern Presidency
 Mary E. Stuckey

Media Entrepreneurs and the Media Enterprise in the U.S. Congress

Karen M. Kedrowski
Winthrop University

 HAMPTON PRESS, INC.
CRESSKILL, NEW JERSEY

Printed in the United States of America

Library of Congress Cataloging-in-Publication Data

Kedrowski, Karen M.
    Media entrepreneurs and the media enterprise in the U.S. Congress / Karen M. Kedrowski
       p. cm. -- (The Hampton Press communication series)
    Includes bibliographical references and index.
    ISBN 1-57273-012-9 (cloth). -- ISBN 1-57273-013-7 (pbk.)
    1. United States. Congress. 2. Legislators--United States. 3. Communication in politics--United States. 4. Mass media--political aspects--United States. I. Title. II. Series.
JK1140.K43 1996
328.73'07--dc20   95-52810
                                                      CIP

Hampton Press, Inc.
23 Broadway
Cresskill, NJ 07626

Contents

LIST OF TABLES

Acknowledgments

There are many individuals to thank as I complete this process. Any omissions are purely by mistake, not by design. Of course, any errors in the text are mine alone.

First, because this book is based largely on my dissertation, I thank my advisor and chairman, Dr. Gary Copeland, of the Carl Albert Center and the University of Oklahoma. His comments and guidance greatly improved the quality of the final product. I also thank the other members of my committee who provided valuable comments and encouragement: Professors Jon Hale, Allen Hertzke, Larry Hill, and Wilbur Scott.

Second, I thank Professor David Paletz, my editor, and Professor Timothy Cook who reviewed my manuscript. Both provided valuable comments and insights that improved the contents considerably. In addition, Barbara Bernstein and the staff at Hampton Press were a pleasure to work with during the last several months. Emily Sears also deserves special thanks for her proofreading assistance.

Third, I thank my interview subjects and the people who responded to the survey of congressional offices. Obviously, without their help this project would have been impossible. In addition, special thanks go to Amy Ward, Bradley Edgell, Kathy Hennemuth, and Michael Harrington, who served as a pretest group for the survey. Professor Mark Peterson provided many helpful suggestions on the structure of the survey.

Fourth, I wish to acknowledge the support provided to me by the Carl Albert Congressional Studies Center. During my graduate career, they very generously covered many costs of my education and provided opportunities for travel and research that few graduate students around the country can hope to enjoy. In particular, I thank the Center's Director and Curator, Dr. Ronald M. Peters, Jr., and his trustworthy and eminently capable sidekick, LaDonna Sullivan. Carma Nuss and Marsha Clampitt put in yeoman's labor on administering the survey that comprised part of this research.

Fifth, I conducted the bulk of my research while I was an American Political Science Association Congressional Fellow in Washington, DC. I am in debt to the offices of Senator Bob Kerrey and the Congressional Sunbelt Caucus for allowing me to observe their operations and learn from them while I conducted my research. Sunbelt Caucus Co-Chairmen, Representatives Lindsay Thomas and E. Clay Shaw, Jr., willingly lent their names to a cover letter mailed with my survey. Executive Director Dr. Joseph Westphal in many ways acted as a surrogate committee chairperson while I was writing. His encouragement and gentle chiding helped me stay on track during the entire research and writing process.

Sixth, Bob Hunter and Jim Winters helped me wend my way through SAS programming. Danielle Ewen provided information from Washington as needed. Elise Pedersen Moe generously loaned me her word processor and provided proofreading services.

Last, and certainly *not* least, I thank my parents, Clara and Henry Kedrowski and my husband, Timothy Fitzgerald. My parents are consistently supportive of my academic efforts, even when they haven't completely understood exactly what their daughter is doing. I am deeply grateful for Tim's constant encouragement and his steadfast support.

1

Introduction

Senator Bob Kerrey (D-Nebraska) was angry. Clayton Yeutter, who was leaving his post as Secretary of Agriculture to become chairman of the Republican National Committee, stated in a speech before the Rotary Club in Lincoln, Nebraska that opponents of the war in the Persian Gulf would be politically harmed by their vote. Yeutter and Kerrey both hailed from Nebraska, and their antipathy ran deep. Yeutter had named Kerrey in public as a member of Congress who would suffer severe repercussions as a result of his opposition to the Persian Gulf war. Yeutter predicted that the war resolution vote would be a powerful political tool to use against incumbent Democrats in the coming presidential and congressional elections.

Storming into the office the morning after the speech, Kerrey ordered his press secretary to secure a copy of Yeutter's speech and comments so Kerrey could respond. Steve Jarding, Kerrey's press secretary, contacted a number of reporters in Lincoln. Using specially equipped telephones, Jarding taped the speech and the comments from a faceless reporter 1,200 miles away. An American Political Science Association (APSA) Fellow working in the press office was set to the task of transcribing Yeutter's comments for the Senator.

When the Senate went into session later that day, Senator Bob Kerrey rose to respond to Secretary Yeutter's attack on the Senate floor. In carefully measured tones, Kerrey stated: "These remarks are deeply troubling. They attempt to politicize this war and to define victory in terms of electoral gain rather than policy achievements. They trivialize deep misgivings which all Americans have about sending our sons and daughters into combat"(Kerrey 1991).

The episode did not end there. The controversy was covered by a number of news sources, including the *Washington Post*, the *New York Times* and the "McLaughlin Group." Columnist Mary McGrory and the *Washington Post* editorial board weighed in with commentary. However, the coverage was not without some prompting. The only transcript of Yeutter's original comments that existed was in the hands of the Kerrey press operation. Copies of that transcript and Kerrey's floor statement were faxed to dozens of reporters all over the country. Press releases (with supporting materials) were also mailed to interested reporters.

• • •

Representative Jim Traficant's (D-Ohio) hallmark is the "1-minute" speech. At the start of each day's business, members of the House of Representatives may deliver a 1-minute speech on any subject they choose. Often, "1-minutes" are used to announce the introduction of a bill, eulogize a deceased notable, or recognize the accomplishments of a college basketball team. Traficant, however, has daily used this forum to make policy statements. Traficant is a feisty populist whose avocation is to protect fiercely American jobs from what he sees as unfair foreign competition. He has no patience for what he considers government waste, inefficiency, or dishonesty. Traficant is concerned little with social niceties or his colleagues' sensitivities. Traficant uses bawdy humor, bad language, and insults to call attention to maliciousness or incompetence on the part of the administration, the bureaucracy, or even his fellow Democrats.

Traficant reportedly spends hours each day working on his "1 minutes," even missing committee and subcommittee hearings as well as other meetings. Yet, for his efforts, Traficant is frequently rewarded with appearances on the nightly news. Eminently quotable, discussing such items as government studies of "bovine flatulation," Traficant's style and sound bites make great television. But there has been another payoff. The skills he acquired as a result of his daily short oratories translate well into more serious floor statements. More articulate than many of his colleagues, Traficant's "serious" statements are often edited into sound bites on the network news.

• • •

Even though Representative Maxine Waters (D-California) was a only a freshman member of Congress, her face appeared frequently on television in the space of a few days. After four Los Angeles police officers were acquitted in the beating case of Rodney King and violence erupted in the streets of her district, Waters was in great demand as she was the representative of south central Los Angeles at the time. She appeared on morning news shows, "Nightline," as well as evening news and talk shows. As Los Angeles burned and people died, Representative Waters was on television, talking about what was happening in her neighborhood.

Waters knew her district well. Not only did she represent the area in the California state legislature for 14 years, but her home was in the part of the district that was in flames. One district office was nearly burned. From her perspective, the people were lashing out in a desperate attempt to get attention. Her constituents had been without hope, economic opportunity, and justice for decades. In her mind, the violence was a call for help.

In the subsequent weeks, Waters used the media attention focused on south central Los Angeles as an opportunity to talk about the urban problems that afflict many American inner cities—unemployment, a lack of commercial enterprises or industry in the neighborhoods, crime, and hopelessness. Waters used the unrest to define an entire agenda of urban problems. Rarely did she shy away from photo opportunities. One night, Waters was seen on the network news dancing at a street party commemorating the "truce" between several major Los Angeles street gangs. Her efforts bore fruit in the form of an urban aid package that included funds for job training and incentives for businesses to locate in the region. Maxine Waters saw an opportunity in the ashes of her district, and the media were a means to help her achieve her policy goals.

MEDIA ENTREPRENEURS

They are seen on Sunday morning talk shows. They have been ridiculed for their blue shirts and blow-dried hair. Traditionally, they have been condemned as "show horses" who are merely proficient at creating pithy sound bites, but ineffective legislators. They do not eschew reporters; rather they court them. Their numbers have increased noticeably in recent years. It has become obvious that a new breed of legislator is in Congress, and they are impatient to make a mark on public policy.

At first, many of these members operated outside the traditional avenues of power in Congress. In addition to expanding their personal staffs and creating informal groups such as caucuses, many of these members also turned to cultivating the media. Through their efforts with the media, some of these new legislators built national reputations without the benefit of a leadership or high-ranking committee position. These *media entrepreneurs* see the media as an important mechanism to influence the very legislative process in which they are personally engaged.

Kerrey's response to Yeutter's comments are typical of a media entrepreneur. A traditionalist would not have responded to this kind of comment by taking to the floor and launching an aggressive media campaign. A letter of protest would have sufficed. More likely, the comment would have been simply ignored. Certainly, going to the well to speak on a point of personal pique would not have been done.

Instead, Kerrey considered the floor of the Senate an appropriate place to respond to the comments Yeutter made in Lincoln, Nebraska the night before. Clearly, Kerrey's intended audience reached far beyond the handful of Senators lounging on the floor that morning. Through C-SPAN II's coverage of the Senate proceedings, the immediate audience numbered in the millions. Besides the viewing public, many of the important target viewers were located only a few yards away: the reporters located in the Senate press galleries, who monitor floor activities on television monitors while working on their stories.

Furthermore, rather than just waiting to see if any press responded to his statement, the Kerrey staff actively solicited media coverage. The contact with Mary McGrory was initiated by the Kerrey staff after one senior policy staffer commented that "this is something she would really like." Only after repeated calls to her office did McGrory agree to look at anything that was sent over by Kerrey's office.

Although he is in many ways an atypical member of Congress, Traficant typifies the method and the motivation of the media entrepreneur in some very important ways. He started doing "1 minute" speeches in an effort to influence the public policy debate. As Traficant said:

> I was a new member and I found that on very important bills, we would be limited to 1 hour of debate, with 30 minutes for each side. The big shots would use 7 to 10 minutes each, and there simply wasn't enough time for a freshman to come and participate in a debate.
>
> I found though, that during the "1 minutes," I could speak on anything I wanted to for 1 minute. So, I started speaking out on issues that I cared about. But what can you say in 1 minute? I decided that I could say enough to do what I wanted to.[1]

Traficant also typifies media entrepreneurs by his conception of his potential audience. According to Traficant, the intended audience is first and foremost members of Congress. The purpose is to get them to think about serious policy issues. Second, Traficant is trying to reach "the American people out there." In other words, although the purpose of the media enterprise is to influence the policy process in Washington, the public is not irrelevant.[2]

Maxine Waters, like Traficant, is a very junior member of Congress. As such, she does not have access to institutional levers available to senior members to push her policy agenda. However, she was astute enough to take advantage of the opportunities presented to her, and to use them to redefine the entire urban policy debate. As Waters' press secretary recalled:

> The problem was defined as urban poverty, not criminal justice. Representative Waters did play an important role in this process. . . . There has always been an urban consciousness on the Hill. . . . She was able to take the lead in defining a progressive Democratic stance on this issue. And there were many people, both people of color and white people, who have similar feelings.[3]

These questions beg another—What motivates Traficant, Kerrey, Waters, and other media entrepreneurs? There are several possibilities. The short-term goal of the media enterprise is to influence policy in the short run. At the same time, media entrepreneurs want to establish themselves as "players" in the larger sense. They want to be called when the next negotiations come along. Others are quite open about their ambition to seek higher office. Yet most media entrepreneurs have a greater vision of what policy should be—whether it be as general as the fundamental relationship between the state and its citizens, or as narrow as a specific policy area. Concomitantly, they may see themselves as a voice for a group in Congress or a faction of the public. For his part, Traficant sees himself as the leader of a small but growing caucus of discontent—fellow members who hold the same opinions about the course of the country, yet choose not to be vocal. Similarly, Kerrey, as a Vietnam veteran decorated with the Congressional Medal of Honor, can take controversial stands on issues such as the Persian Gulf War or flag burning without having his patriotism questioned. And Waters was able to motivate other members of the Urban Caucus to support a major urban package in response to the unrest in her district.

IDENTIFYING THE MEDIA ENTERPRISE

Representative Newt Gingrich (R-Georgia) understands better than all but a handful of his colleagues how to get national media attention. But all of these efforts—appearances on "This Week with David Brinkley," interviews with *Time* magazine, sound bites on the CBS Evening News—are really different from getting coverage back in the district. Perhaps because of his position in the House Leadership—first as Minority Whip, now as Speaker—the differences between his relationship with the national media and the *Atlanta Constitution* are more stark than in other offices. Gingrich actually employs two press secretaries— one in the personal office, who works exclusively with the local press, and one in his leadership office, who works with the national press corps huddled uncomfortably in the House galleries. The two of them often start out with the same story, but each repackages it differently for his or her particular audience.

Gingrich knows that many commentators think that he got into trouble in his 1990 election bid because he neglected his district. According to one of his press secretaries, Gingrich does not neglect the local reporters or the constituents in his district. The problem is that Gingrich tends to say the same things to every reporter, regardless of which paper or television station he or she works for. Sometimes a message honed for a national reporter simply does not resonate with a local one, and a national story loses its local angle.

• • •

The media enterprise is comprised of activities completely unlike a legislator's media efforts designed to communicate with constituents. The two may spring from the same seed, but they serve distinctly different purposes. The immediate goal of the media enterprise is primarily legislative. It is designed to influence the legislative process or public debate on an issue facing the public agenda. It is designed to reach a small audience of public officials and attentive publics that follow an issue and its legislative progress. These individuals are typically based in the Washington metropolitan area.

The media enterprise can take many forms. It may include interviews or features in television or print media. Op-eds and in-depth interviews with the major print media are coveted. A feature or a "mention" on a network newscast are invaluable, as are appearances on the networks' Sunday morning public affairs talk shows such as "Meet the

Press," or "This Week with David Brinkley." Media entrepreneurs who chair committees or subcommittees can call hearings as another means to attract media attention. Placement is key to the media enterprise. The important newspapers in which an op-ed should appear are those read in the Washington area. Similarly, the nightly newscasts or talk shows enjoy a larger than average audience in the Washington community.

These activities are distinct from members' efforts to reach their constituents. Although in most cases the media enterprise and constituent communications are carried out by the same press secretary, it is important to think of them as distinct activities. Constituent communications are designed to increase the electoral base by claiming credit for legislation and other publicity efforts. The media enterprise is designed to reach policymakers and influence policy development.

All members of Congress engage in some media efforts to reach their constituents. However, only a few aggressively pursue efforts to gain coverage in the national media. This choice is stylistic. For the media entrepreneur, using the media is a commonplace and legitimate way to influence the policy process. It simultaneously augments and provides an alternative to traditional legislative strategies. Media entrepreneurs continue to solicit national media attention, even after they move into formal positions of power. Status as a committee or subcommittee leader can be a platform from which an aggressive media entrepreneur can solicit media attention.

WHAT MAKES THIS STUDY IMPORTANT?

Despite the volumes of literature on the new breed of American politician, the connections between media coverage, the policymaking process, and communicating to the public and constituents alike have not been adequately explored. The purpose of this study is to analyze media entrepreneurs and their attempts to influence the legislative process. This topic was chosen because all of the previous research on Congress and the media has focused overwhelmingly on constituent relations or congressional elections. Certainly, these questions are important, but they ignore what members of Congress do from Tuesday to Thursday—that is to make policy.

This study is justified on several grounds. It is the first attempt to examine how members of Congress use the media to influence the policy process. This dynamic has not been well explored in the past—at least in part because the media enterprise is outweighed by the sheer volume of constituent communications. Nonetheless, it enhances the discipline's understanding of the legislative process. It is also a comprehensive exploration of the policy conversation in the Washington community. Moreover, this phenomenon is not a passing fad. As time passes, more members will adopt the media enterprise as a legitimate strategy to influence public policy.

ENDNOTES

1. Interview, October 1, 1991.
2. Interview, October 1, 1991.
3. Interview with Sabrina Sojourner, Press Secretary to Representative Maxine Waters, August 26, 1992.

2

The Setting and
the Method

Scholars have not ignored the relationship between the media and Congress. In fact, recent major studies of this relationship have surfaced in the last few years. However, these studies tend to focus on members' media relations efforts in general. Consequently, they have found that the bulk of members' media efforts are geared toward communicating with constituents. For example, in his survey of Democratic House press secretaries, Timothy Cook (1989) found that press secretaries rank coverage in local media much higher than coverage in the national media. Cook found overwhelming support for statements such as "We'd rather get in [the hometown paper] than the front page of the *New York Times* any day" (1989, 83), which permeate his analysis. Similarly, in his analysis of press operations in *Live from Capitol Hill!* (1991), Steven Hess found that the majority of members' press activities are geared to enhancing their reputations at home, and their press secretaries are largely homegrown. By contrast, even ambitious efforts to get national media attention go largely unrewarded.

In fact, to Stephen Hess, the very idea that members of Congress might try to use the media to influence their colleagues on policy issues is absurd. As Hess characterized this process: "Trying to use the media to get legislation through Congress is a Rube Goldberg design based on (A) legislator influencing (B) reporter to get information into (C) news outlet so as to convince (D) voters who will put pressure on (E) other legislators" (1986, 103).

Yet both Cook and Hess hint at another reason that members of Congress seek media attention: to influence public policy. In *Live From Capitol Hill!* (1991), Hess noted that the op-ed is not well suited as an electoral strategy. Furthermore, the outlets such as the *Washington Post* or the *New York Times* are not appropriate to reach constituents. Hess concluded, based on interviews with congressional essayists after they published op-eds, that the purpose of these is "to influence policy" (91-92).

Likewise, Cook (1989, 120-125) attempted to understand when members of Congress use the media in the legislative process. He concluded that using the media to set the congressional agenda is particularly important. Getting coverage in the *Washington Post* means that a member has a good shot at getting other members' attention. Similarly, by defining the agenda, members can define the issues in such a way that enables them to become players in the horsetrading that occurs later in the legislative process.

The genesis of this book was to understand how members of Congress use the media to influence policy inside Washington. One should not confuse the volume of members' media attention, which is clearly geared toward local media, with the importance of these efforts. If members of Congress did not think that using the media could influence policy, what motivation do they have to run op-ed articles? What benefit could they get from staying in Washington over the weekend in order to appear on "This Week with David Brinkley," rather than spending time in the district?

Courting the media in an effort to advance policy goals has a long history in Congress. In his classic study of the Senate, Donald Matthews (1973) described the relationship between Senators and reporters in the 1950s. Matthews described how the press is an important source of information to policymakers, in this case Senators, about pending developments in their own chamber. Moreover, Matthews described how Senators cultivate relationships with key reporters to establish themselves as policy experts, qualified to comment on the issues of the day, and how these relationships influence the choice and presentation of the news (1973, 197-217).

This effort is not unique to Senators. In his description of Wright Patman's tenure as Chairman of the House Banking and Currency Committee in the 1960s, Owens (1985) described how Patman used the media to advance his unorthodox and sometimes extreme proposals. He used his position as a committee chairman to stage hearings and to make headline-grabbing statements. Patman and his staff also cultivated relationships with reporters to guide congressional policymaking in a direction he favored. Owens argued that Patman's "extreme advocacy" leadership style, that included aggressive publicity efforts, led to the adoption of several restrictive banking regulation laws that Patman sponsored.

Congressional leaders, especially those from the party that does not control the White House, have long turned to the media to articulate their policy agendas. The Kennedy administration was the first to use televised press conferences regularly. At the time, Democrats controlled both houses of Congress as well as the executive branch. In response to the White House, the minority leadership in Congress hosted over 60 weekly press conferences from 1961 to 1963. These press conferences, known as the "Ev and Charlie Show," for Senate Minority Leader Everett Dirksen (R-Illinois) and House Minority Leader Charles Halleck (R-Indiana), provided the party out of power an opportunity to respond to Democratic proposals, criticize the Kennedy administration, and articulate Republican doctrine and policy alternatives. Dirksen and Halleck addressed about 100 policy issues during this 2-year period (Scheele 1989).

For the purpose of this analysis, *media entrepreneurs* are members of Congress who consider media coverage a legitimate and effective tool to influence public policy. To this end, they often have a high public profile. In this way, media entrepreneurs are distinct from their colleagues who opt to use only traditional insider strategies and do not consider the media an effective policy tool. However, media entrepreneurs are practical politicians. They also are aware of the political realities of Capitol Hill and the power of personal relationships. Media entrepreneurs use the media enterprise to augment, but not replace, traditional means of coalition building.

The media enterprise is the set of activities that media entrepreneurs use to capture the attention of the national media. They include writing op-ed articles; conducting interviews, television, and talk show appearances; conducting hearings; and staging "pseudo events" around some activity or announcement, such as the introduction of a bill, even though these efforts are not always successful. Because its purpose is to influence policy, and often to enhance a member's reputation as a policy heavyweight, the media enterprise is distinct from efforts to communicate with constituents or to get reelected. The journalists targeted by the media enterprise are those who work for outlets with a national audience, such as the television networks, and those who work for outlets with a Washington audience, such as the *National Journal*.

RESEARCH QUESTIONS

This study focuses on four major research questions. The first question is: Who are media entrepreneurs? Because of many dramatic changes in Congress during the 1970s, many members of Congress, even back-benchers in the House, can gain influence in policy areas through many different venues. Norms such as seniority and apprenticeship have weakened. Reforms strengthened subcommittees and limited the number of subcommittee chairmanships a member could hold. As a result, many more members have a subcommittee chairmanship from which to launch the media enterprise (Hinkley 1988, 107, 129-131, 165-166; Rieselbach 1986, 82-83). In addition, committee and subcommittee assignments do not necessarily determine a member's full sphere of interest or expertise. Others may use personal interest or a position on an appropriations subcommittee as a platform from which to become involved in debate (see Stanfeld 1990).

In light of these changes in Congress, media entrepreneurs are likely to be part of a new generation of politicians who are liberal, more ambitious, and anxious to influence the policy process (Ehrenhalt 1991; Hinkley 1988, 158; Loomis 1988). They are often telegenic, articulate, and hard working. The old distinction between *work horses*, who do the serious legislating, and *show horses*, who play to the galleries and the cameras, is no longer true (Cook 1986; Langbien and Sigelman 1989). Rather, there is a growing perception that the members who receive the most media attention are also the most effective members of Congress.

The difference between media entrepreneurs and their colleagues is fundamentally attitudinal first and behavioral second. Media entrepreneurs believe that the media are an important tool to influence policy outcomes. Obviously, members who do not share this belief will not expend the effort to use the media enterprise. One former member of the House of Representatives, Les Aspin (D-Wisconsin), was quite successful in this strategy (Cook 1989, 155-160). Aspin, whose high profile in the media helped him become Chairman of the House Armed Services Committee, described the purpose of his efforts this way:

> What we're pitching for are the serious followers of the subject . . . who read the *Times* and the *Post*. . . . Hell, I don't know how many readers of the *New York Times* understand the stuff, but the *Times* and the *Washington Post* write the stories for aficionados—of the defense business for example. This operation is all aimed at them. . . . You're trying to influence the debate on the subject. You're trying to anticipate where the story is going, but you're also trying to push the story a certain way. (Evans 1981, 28-29)

In addition, media entrepreneurs are also likely to be found among the groups that historically used the media to their advantage: party leaders, committee and subcommittee chairmen, and a select group of Senators (Cook 1989, 130-132, Hess 1986, 1987). These positions offer a potential media entrepreneur a bully pulpit and credibility to comment on issues and to attempt to shape the agenda. Both are extremely helpful in using the media to enterprise.

The second research question is: At which point in the legislative process are media entrepreneurs most likely to approach the media? Previous research indicates that agenda setting and its companion, alternative selection, are the most permeable stages of the policymaking process. Unarguably, items move onto the policy agenda for several reasons. The president may make a speech or statement, which serves as a governmental call to action (Light 1982). Outside events, such as the unrest in Los Angeles in 1991 or the launch of Sputnik, can force attention to urban problems or the space program. Yet agenda setting remains one area in which members of Congress can directly influence the process (Cook 1989, 118-148; Loomis 1988, 74-75).

Once an issue is on the agenda, however it got there, defining alternatives is also important. As E. E. Schattschneider wrote, "the definition of alternatives is the supreme source of power" (1960, 66). Certainly, defining an issue dictates the kind of policy response the issue requires. For example, the unrest in Los Angeles was defined as a lack of economic opportunity in urban areas. Thus, the solution was a jobs program. Despite its roots in the verdict to acquit the police officers accused of brutalizing Rodney King, the problem was not defined as a miscarriage of justice, which would have required an effort to reform the judicial system.

In order to understand the dynamics of the media enterprise, it is helpful to conceive of two distinct agendas: the elite agenda and the mass agenda.[1] In the first case, the specifics of the public policy debate are known only to a few activists and officials. Public opinion provides only very general cues to officials, such as a diffuse support for education. By contrast, items on the mass agenda receive a lot of news coverage and enjoy a high public profile. In this case, public opinion becomes a much more salient variable in determining policy.

The elite agenda is most accessible to the media entrepreneur. The target audience is likely to be small, well educated, politically astute, highly efficacious, and geographically concentrated in the Washington area. An audience with these characteristics is very likely to learn about public issues through the media. Its members' opinions are likely to be shaped by editorials and the amount of coverage an issue receives (MacKuen and Coombs 1981; Shaw and McCombs 1977). Although this audience will probably receive its political information from several news sources, its members are also likely to share one or two key sources of news. As a result, a carefully designed media effort stands to reach a large percentage of the Washington community. The mass agenda can be influenced by the same techniques, but not as easily. The general public is less attentive to news and therefore less easily swayed by media coverage than members of the Washington community.

A related question is: Do media entrepreneurs use the media enterprise later in the process? The traditional picture is that the later stages of the legislative process would be quite impervious to the media enterprise. Committee and subcommittee chairmen tightly control the legislative agenda, whereas the majority part leadership controls the floor agenda. However, members of Congress in positions of political power are also subject to outside pressures, including pressure from media attention. Media entrepreneurs may indeed see the media as another means to capture the attention of legislative leaders later in the process. Moreover, the media enterprise may be used in conjunction with other, more traditional legislative strategies.

The third research question is: Who are the media entrepreneurs trying to reach? I hypothesize that media entrepreneurs attempt to reach their congressional colleagues and other policymakers, either directly or through various intermediaries. The media enterprise is more important today because there are now more actors involved in the process in the Congress. Since the 1970s, Congress has increased the size of committee and subcommittee staff, granted itself more personal staff, and created or expanded research branches such as the Congressional Research Service (CRS), the Office of Technology Assessment (OTA), the Congressional Budget Office (CBO), and the General Accounting Office (GAO) (Fox and Hammond 1977; Hinkley 1988, 88). Estimates of the total number of congressional staff currently hover around 38,000, including employees of these think tanks. Congressional staff are integral actors in the legislative process. They are deeply involved in all stages of the legislative process, save casting floor votes. Staff draft legislation, schedule subcommittee and committee hearings, decide what legislation to cosponsor, negotiate compromise language, meet with executive branch officials, lobbyists, and other attentive publics, and even participate in "staff conferences" with staff from the other chamber that replace formal conference committees. As such they are another valuable audience for the media entrepreneur. Not only do they provide another avenue to reach members of Congress themselves, but they frequently make policy decisions on behalf of members.

There are also more key actors in the executive branch and the Washington community. As the sphere of government influence has grown, so have the number of lobbyists. According to Jeffrey Berry (1989), some 25 percent of all currently registered interest groups have first registered since 1970; 40 percent of all interest groups have registered since 1960. The Washington community includes lobbies for all kinds of trade associations, public interest groups, governments, children, and poor persons. Individual corporations augment umbrella organizations that represent entire industries. Individual states and cities employ their own advocates who complement the efforts of the National Governors' Association and the League of Cities. The executive branch has grown as well. As King and Ragsdale (1988) documented, the president's personal staff and the size of federal agencies have increased dramatically in the last half-century. For example, the White House staff now numbers over 1,000. Similarly, the expansion of federal programs has led to more federal administrators, currently numbering in the tens of thousands.

The concept of a tiny subgovernment has fallen by the wayside. As Heclo (1977) argued, the result is that the traditional typology of the "iron triangle," with its cozy relationship between committee chairmen, interest groups, and federal bureaucrats, is no longer accurate. They have been replaced by "issue networks"—larger, more amorphous, and constantly changing coalitions of interest groups, members of Congress, and various agency and White House officials. These groups may coalesce on one issue but fail to come together on others. Issue networks are another potential audience for the media entrepreneur. As cue givers to policymakers, they provide another means to influence policy.

Given this expansion in Congress and in Washington, communicating personally between all the interested parties is now difficult, if not impossible. Coverage by various media outlets takes on new importance and has become what Stephen Hess has termed, "an interaction of elites" (1981, 119). To the media entrepreneur, forming legislative coalitions is not simply a process of traditional insider strategies. Although individual contacts are still critical to the legislative process, media entrepreneurs want to gain the ear of every staffer, lobbyist, and executive branch official who might influence members' positions. Therefore, effective use of the media to frame issues on the elite agenda is vital in today's Washington. Getting national media attention is still not easy. Yet, many members see the media enterprise as a powerful tool to influence policy, even if they are not able to exploit it themselves.

Reporters themselves are another target audience for the media entrepreneur. If a media entrepreneur's efforts are identified as the "story of the day," coverage in a number of sources raises his or her public profile and enhances his or her credibility. Also, sustained coverage enhances the chances that members of issue networks and policy-

makers will identify the media entrepreneur as a key actor. Media attention lends credibility. As a result, the media entrepreneur can become
part of the horsetrading later in the process.

Aside from reaching actors in the Washington community,
media entrepreneurs cannot ignore other audiences outside the beltway:
constituents, local media, and the general public (outside the constituency). Media entrepreneurs send their messages to the general public in
order to stimulate public interest and constituent support for their ideas.
Absent strong public interest in an issue, media entrepreneurs can assert
strong influence on a member of Congress. Given the fact that reporters
take cues from each other and, in particular, take cues from the national
media, getting favorable *national* media coverage is even more important
for the nascent media entrepreneur.

Influencing public policy through the media is not as convoluted as Hess (1986, 103) described. The importance of constituents
notwithstanding, in the absence of strong public opinion on an issue,
members of Congress seek voting cues from any number of sources,
such as interest groups, staff, party leaders, the administration, and even
the media (Kingdon 1989; Sullivan, Shaw, McAvoy, and Barnum 1993).
For this reason, then, these cue givers are potential targets of the media
enterprise and may bypass Hess's detour through public opinion altogether.

At any rate, media entrepreneurs aim their message at a very
small audience. Rather than trying to communicate to an audience of
millions (an entire state), or several hundred thousand (a congressional
district), the media enterprise is targeted to an audience of perhaps hundreds (the House of Representatives or the Washington press corps),
tens (a committee), or even one (a key chairman). The scope of this activity is dramatically different from the hundreds of millions network television reaches. Yet this effort is important because the target audience is
comprised of other public officials and actors involved in shaping public
policy for the remaining 250 million Americans.

The fourth research question is: Precisely which sources are
important in receiving information about Congress and the legislative
process? Exactly how important are the various parts of the elite press?
Are there any other outlets that are not traditionally considered important to reaching the policymaking audience? If so, what sources are not
important to them? I hypothesize that the most important sources are
not only the national press, such as the major newspapers or the commercial networks, but several sources that cater to a Washington-based
audience. These outlets will be particularly useful in the process of targeting an audience of policy specialists—be they on the Hill, in the
administration, or on K Street.

The effective media entrepreneur knows that he or she only needs to secure coverage in a few media sources in order to reach the individuals concerned with the elite agenda. The *Washington Post* and *Congressional Quarterly* are potentially important sources to reach a Capitol Hill audience (Hess 1986, 111; Robinson and Clancy 1983). Conventional wisdom points to the elite press, such as the *New York Times*, the *Washington Post*, the *Wall Street Journal*, and network television as important outlets. The elite press is also valuable in terms of reaching an educated and politically efficacious audience outside Washington. However, if a media entrepreneur wants to focus his or her efforts within the Washington community, specialized outlets such as the *National Journal*, *Roll Call*, and possibly C-SPAN are important alternatives. Soliciting news coverage through these outlets will reach an audience of political elites, especially congressional staff and various Congress watchers, but not the public outside the Washington area.

The elite press and Sunday morning talk shows (Matlack 1990) such as "Meet the Press" are also important means to reach an audience of other media. Because Sunday is typically a slow news day, comments made by guests on these programs are often reported in Monday's newspapers. Furthermore, new reports appearing first in the *New York Times* or the *Washington Post* provide cues to reporters from around the country.

METHODOLOGY AND CASE STUDIES

Many scholarly studies of the media depend on personal interviews and case study illustrations. Qualitative research methods like these yield a wealth of detail and insight to the academic world. However, these studies are criticized often for their lack of generalizability. This research combines qualitative and quantitative methodological techniques as a way to maximize the strengths of both methods. This study uses semistructured interviews to investigate four legislative case studies and includes a survey of congressional offices to discern their patterns for courting media and consuming information from the media.

SURVEY OF CONGRESSIONAL OFFICES

The survey of congressional offices was administered in Spring 1991. By that time, I had conducted several dozen interviews for the case studies, which helped me identify questions to include in the survey. As I developed drafts of the survey, I solicited comments from several political scientists, and I conducted a pretest of several Hill staff people with whom I was acquainted. The final survey instrument included comments I received from all of these sources.

The survey was designed to elicit data on the four research questions described earlier. The survey was structured with a combination of open-ended and closed questions with many essential questions asked in at least two ways. The bulk of the closed questions used Likert scales in which the respondents were only required to circle a number that corresponded to their answer.

The survey was administered in two waves during the summer of 1991. The surveys were mailed to administrative assistants and chiefs of staff in all House and Senate offices. Administrative assistants were targeted for two reasons. First, it is no secret that members of Congress rarely complete surveys mailed to their offices personally. If surveys are answered at all, it is done by staff. Second, almost without exception, staff mirror the member's philosophy, approach, and values. Administrative assistants, as the top staff people in a congressional office, have the broadest view of what is going on in an office.

Two waves of the survey instrument were mailed to congressional offices. In addition to the survey instrument itself, a letter of introduction signed by me and a postage-paid return envelope were included. (At the time this survey was administered, I was a participant in the American Political Science Association Congressional Fellows program, placed with the Congressional Sunbelt Caucus.) The second wave included a letter of endorsement signed by the Sunbelt Caucus Co-chairmen at the time, Representatives Lindsay Thomas (D-Georgia) and E. Clay Shaw, Jr. (R-Florida). The first wave of the survey was sent to all 535 House and Senate offices; the second wave was mailed to offices that had not responded to the first wave. The first wave was mailed in June 1991. The second wave was sent during Congress's traditional August recess. A copy of the instrument can be found in the Appendix.

In addition to sending the survey to administrative assistants, the bulk of my semistructured interviews were with congressional staff. I consider this approach valid and completely legitimate. For example, much of the literature on congressional staff makes note of their influence and knowledge of the issues in which they specialize (Bisnow 1991; Malbin 1980). Good or bad, the end result is that legislative staff are frequently the arbiters in legislative debate, experts in policy fields, and are deeply involved in the minutiae of legislation. Similarly, press secretaries need to be able to represent the member's positions to the media as an important part of their jobs. However, whenever possible, I conducted interviews with members.

Analysis of Respondents

The survey yielded a 28 percent response rate (N=151).[2] The percentage of respondents was slightly greater from the House of Representatives (29%; N=125) than from the Senate (24%; N=24).[3] The respondents were nearly evenly split between the two waves of the survey. Fifty-two percent of the respondents returned the survey from the first wave; the remaining 48 percent returned the second wave. No significant difference in tone was noted between the respondents of the two waves.[4]

The offices that responded are quite representative of the demographics of the entire Congress. The members from participating offices roughly approximate the partisan, gender, and racial composition of the population. The response set underrepresents the number of party leaders, but approximates the number of committee and subcommittee chairmen and ranking members. The response set also includes a few too many members from the states that comprise the Sunbelt Caucus. None of these differences are statistically significant, although the age and tenure of the members do approach statistical significance (see Tables 2.1 and 2.2).

These results are not terribly surprising. In the course of conducting the survey, I received a number of notes and telephone calls from offices of senior members and party leaders indicating an office policy of not responding to surveys of any sort. Like the members themselves, the staff of more junior members are less busy than the staffs of partisan and committee leaders. Thus, they may have had more time to complete the survey. Furthermore, my analysis shows that younger members use the media more aggressively than older, more senior members. Their interest in the topic of the survey may have motivated their staff to respond to this survey (see also Loomis 1988). Also not surprising is the fact that my response set includes a few too many Southerners. Given my placement with the Sunbelt Caucus and the letter of endorsement included with the survey, it is not surprising that more surveys would be returned from the Caucus delegation (see Table 2.2).

Similarly, analysis of members' ideological scores provided by the Americans for Democratic Action (ADA) and the American Conservative Union (ACU) indicate that the respondents, as a group, work for members who are slightly more conservative than those who did not respond. However, the difference is not statistically significant (see Table 2.2).

Table 2.1. Demographic Comparison of Survey Respondents and the Full Congress.

Variable Name	Full Congress (%) (N = 535)	Respondents (%) (N = 149)
House (of Congress)		
House of Representatives	81.3	83.9
Senate	18.7	16.1
Party		
Republican	40.0	38.9
Democrat	59.8	61.1
Independent	0.2	0.0
Gender		
Male	95.0	94.0
Female	5.0	6.0
Race		
White	92.5	94.0
Black	4.7	4.7
Hispanic	1.9	0.7
Other	0.9	0.7
Region[a]		
Sunbelt	65.6	60.4
Non-sunbelt	34.4	39.6
Leader[b]		
Nonleader	96.6	98.0
Leader	3.4	2.0
Committee Position		
Chairman or ranking member	18.3	12.1
Rank and file member	81.7	87.9
Subcommittee Position		
Chairman or ranking member	53.1	47.7
Rank and file member	46.9	52.3

[a]Region is defined by the states comprising the Congressional Sunbelt Caucus. Member states are Alabama, Arizona, Arkansas, Florida, Georgia, Kentucky, Louisiana, Mississippi, Missouri, New Mexico, North Carolina, Oklahoma, South Carolina, Tennessee, Texas, Virginia, and West Virginia.
[b]Leader is defined as Speaker, Majority or Minority Leader, and Majority or Minority Whip.
Source: Data compiled by author.

Table 2.2. Further Demographic Analysis.

	Nonrespondents Mean ($N = 385$)	Respondents Mean ($N = 149$)
Age*	55.71	54.08
Tenure*	13.11	11.59
ADA Score	51.27	49.94
ACU Score	40.91	41.75

*$p \leq 0.10$
Source: Data compiled by author.

CASE STUDIES

In order to study the media enterprise in more detail, I conducted four legislative case studies: the National Literacy Act, campaign finance reform, the Persian Gulf War debate, and Acquired Immune Deficiency Syndrome (AIDS) policy. The cases were chosen on the basis of three criteria. The first criterion is the level of public attention given to each issue. This way, I am able to document variations between issues on the mass and elite agenda. Both AIDS policy and the Persian Gulf War debate are (or were) highly visible agenda items. By contrast, campaign finance reform receives some attention in newspapers, especially those widely read in Washington, but is absent from television coverage. Illiteracy as a human interest story appears from time to time in both print and broadcast media, but a discussion of policy is conspicuously absent from the news.

The second criterion is the existence and size of an established issue network that is largely responsible for making policy in a given area. This criterion will provide interesting variations between well-established issue networks and those that are poorly developed or loosely structured. For example, the campaign finance reform case study is characterized by the heavy involvement of "professional social movements" (Troyer 1990)—an active elite within the policymaking milieu that boasts some level of grass-roots membership in the country. AIDS policy activists are an odd amalgam of public health and civil rights groups. The adult literacy field is remarkable due to its highly fragmented nature and small number of interest groups. The buildup in the Persian Gulf and the war itself were the dominant news stories that ignited public interest for months (see Figure 2.1).

	Interest Group Involvement	
Level of Public Interest	High	Low
High	AIDS Policy	Persian Gulf War Vote
Low	Campaign Finance Reform	Adult Literacy

Figure 2.1. Case studies

The third criterion is the likelihood of significant development of the issue during my period of investigation. In other words, I wanted to be reasonably certain that Congress would address any issue I studied during the 102nd Congress. The debate over the Persian Gulf War, not to mention the war itself, took place in just six months. Congress passed the first comprehensive bill on adult literacy in history during this period. Both Congress and the Centers for Disease Control grappled with policy regarding testing health care workers and patients for their HIV status. Members of Congress introduce campaign finance reform legislation every Congress. Although these initiatives historically go down to defeat, legislation passed both houses of Congress in both the 101st and 102nd Congresses, even though neither bill became law.

These case studies provide the structure for the qualitative component of my research. I conducted a number of semistructured interviews with members of Congress, congressional staff, and outside groups involved in each case. These interviews focused principally on legislative strategies and if and how the media played a role in the process. In each interview, I asked for names of other people to talk with and for copies of relevant public documents such as speeches, op-ed articles, or committee testimony.

In addition, I interviewed a number of reporters from publications that were important to the process of communication in the Washington community and all of the press secretaries for the House and Senate leadership. These interviews focused on the relationship between the media and Congress more generally and the importance of the media in terms of shaping the terms of the policy debate.

In general, the interviews were conducted off the record, which I believe led to more candid responses. I always entered the interview with approximately six general questions to ask, which provided consistency between interviews. I took notes during the interview, which I transcribed later that same day. I did not reconstruct the interviews verbatim, but I was able to reconstruct the intent quite accurately, and my notes often include exact quotations from the interview subjects. The interviews lasted between 20 minutes and 2 hours.

With a few memorable exceptions, I did not have much difficulty securing interviews. At the time I was conducting most of the interviews, I was participating in the American Political Science Association Congressional Fellows program. I then had access and some status in the Capitol Hill world. I conducted a number of interviews at the staff level initially, which helped me gain access to members later. A full list of interviewees can be found in the Appendix.

The case studies are richly illustrative of the activities of media entrepreneurs and the media enterprise. However, the analysis is more comprehensible if the evidence is placed into the historical context of each case study. Therefore, the following sections are brief descriptions of the issues and recent legislative history in campaign finance reform, the Persian Gulf War debate, AIDS policy, and adult literacy.

CASE STUDY ONE: CAMPAIGN FINANCE REFORM

The issues surrounding campaign finance reform are arcane and complex. According to conventional wisdom, campaign finance reform legislation should be dead upon introduction. The current system benefits incumbents of both parties and leaves challengers handicapped in the race for funds, media coverage, and name recognition. It is counterintuitive to think that a group of incumbent politicians who benefit from the status quo would undergo serious attempts to reform this system. Nonetheless, campaign finance reform is a perennial issue, and scores of bills proposing reforms have been introduced in Congress over the years. Some measures even stand a chance of being enacted.

Issues in the Campaign Finance Reform Debate.

The debate surrounding campaign finance reform is multifaceted; any reform measure must address most of these issues in order to have a chance of passage. Each of these issues has its own set of advocates on the Hill who frequently introduce their own legislation. The campaign finance legislation passed by each house is typically an amalgam of several of these bills.

The current campaign finance system is a product of several reform measures passed in the 1970s, principally the Revenue Act of 1971 and Federal Election Campaign Act of 1971, and its 1974, 1976, and 1979 amendments (Cantor 1989). The Revenue Act established a public financing system for presidential elections. The Federal Election Campaign Act created the Federal Election Commission (FEC), instituted uniform reporting requirements of campaign receipts and expenditures, and established limits on contributions (Cantor and Durbin 1991). This legislation, especially the two original acts and the 1974 amendments to the Federal Election Campaign Act were efforts to decrease the influence of private contributors (be they corporations or individuals) on the electoral system. Individuals were limited to donations of $1,000 to any individual candidate, per election, $5,000 to any other political committee, and an aggregate total of $25,000 per year.

Political Action Committees. Perhaps the most important development from this legislation was the proliferation of Political Action Committees (PACs). These organizations can donate up to $5,000 to a candidate per election. These groups have become the vehicle for corporations, labor unions, various membership associations, and other interests to become involved in the campaign finance system. Multicandidate political committees predate the Federal Election Campaign Act by several decades. However, the 1971 act and its amendments established PACs as a force in the campaign finance system. The growth in PACs and their rate of contribution has been astounding. In the nine years between 1973 and 1982, the number of multicandidate PACs increased from 608 to 3,525, an increase of over 500 percent. The greatest increase has been in the number of corporate PACs, which increased from 14.6 percent of the total number of registered PACs to 43.6 percent. By contrast, labor PACs declined from 33.1 percent of the total registered PACs to 10.5 percent (Sabato 1984, 5-13).

Cost of Political Campaigns. The second issue surrounding the current campaign finance debate is the dramatic rise in campaign costs. Since 1976, the aggregate cost of congressional and senatorial campaigns increased fourfold, whereas the cost of living in the same period only doubled. Similarly, the campaign cost of average winning candidates during the same time frame increased from $87,200 in 1976 to $393,000 in 1988, whereas the cost of the average winning Senate campaign rose from $609,100 to $3.7 million during the same period (Cantor and Durbin 1991).

There are several reasons given for what some critics consider a disturbing increase in campaign expenditures. First, the original act and the 1974 amendments limited both donor contributions and candidate spending. However, in 1976, the Supreme Court ruled in *Buckley v. Valeo* that involuntary expenditure limits violate an individual candidate's right to free speech. As a result, a vehicle for financing campaigns was created without any concomitant restraints on spending for these elections.

Second, the increasing cost of campaigns is frequently credited to the rising cost of media, especially broadcast media. Candidates frequently perceive that advertising, particularly television advertising, is the only way to reach a wide, diverse constituency in an age in which individualized politics have replaced party machines. In Senate races in particular, media expenditures have become remarkable. For example, in the 1986 California Senate race between Ed Zschau and Alan Cranston, the candidates spent over $13 million on media buys and production costs. In 1988, 65 percent of all Senate candidates reported spending over $250,000 on media expenses alone. One pundit estimated that 55 percent of a candidate's budget in a "competitive race" might be devoted to advertising (Hoff and Bernstein 1988, 10-14).

The data for House campaigns are not as telling. The same study indicated that most House candidates spent less than $10,000 on television advertising (Hoff and Bernstein 1988, 12; see also Goldenberg and Traugott, 1987). Although these authors argue that the reason for the relatively low investment in television air time is that House candidates cannot afford television time, others argue that television is a poor medium to reach congressional district residents. Television markets rarely correspond with congressional districts boundaries, which means that candidates' commercials would be wasted on a large number of viewers who do not live in the district (Campbell, Alford, and Henry, 1984). Nonetheless, the perception that the cost of media has contributed to the rising cost of political campaigns is powerful.

Bundling. A third issue in the campaign finance reform debate concerns a practice called *bundling*. Considered by its critics to be another way special interests can influence the political system, *bundling* is a process whereby an independent agent, be it a private individual, a PAC, or a professional fundraiser, collects campaign donations from other groups or individuals and submits these checks in a "bundle" to a candidate. In this way, the intermediary is able to contribute to a candidate an amount far in excess of what is otherwise legally permissible. For example, a group of high-ranking executives from a single corporation may bundle their contributions. Or chief executive officers of several companies in the same industry may pool their checks. The intended result is that the recipient will understand the source of the funds just as if the contribution came from a PAC, and a delivery of fifty $1,000 checks will carry much more weight than a single PAC donation of only $5,000 (Cantor and Durbin 1991; Common Cause 1990).

Because bundling often happens with individual contributions, watchdog groups are particularly upset by this practice. Because the FEC does not require that the employers of individual contributors be disclosed, it is frequently difficult to ascertain the "special interest" nature of these contributions. Similarly, these same donors may make contributions in the names of their family members, which also serves to "hide" the special interest behind the money.

Soft Money. Perhaps the most difficult part of the current campaign system to understand, *soft money* refers to funds that may influence the outcome of federal races, but would be illegal if spent directly on behalf of candidates vying for federal office. For example, some states permit large corporate, individual, and labor union donations for activities such as "get out the vote" drives or voter registration. According to Common Cause (1990), these contributions can run as high as $100,000. These activities, be they voter drives or political commercials railing against political parties (Drew 1983, 14-18), will inevitably help federal candidates in addition to state and local candidates.

Independent Expenditures. Particularly bothersome to political incumbents, *independent expenditures* are monies spent by "an individual or group to support or defeat a candidate *which is made without consultation with, or the cooperation of, any candidate or campaign*" (Sabato 1984, 96; emphasis in original). Truly independent expenditures have no limits placed on them under federal law. Although few PACs engage in independent expenditures, the perceived success of the National Conservative Political Action Committee (NCPAC) in 1980, when it targeted six liberal incumbent Senators for defeat (four of whom lost their bids for reelection), keeps this issue alive. This phenomenon has several important ramifications. First, opponents charge that it increases the cost of political campaigns as the charges lodged by these outside groups must be answered. Second, independent expenditures allow some candidates to skirt state spending limits because the outside group funds advertising and other activities on behalf of its favored candidates. Third, many critics charge that independent expenditures are not, in fact, independent. Coordination between the independent organization and the candidate it supports may be present. Consultation and coordination are illegal, but difficult to prove (Cantor and Durbin 1991; Sabato 1984, 96-105).

Public Disinterest and Suspicion of Politics. Many critics of the current campaign finance system charge that the current system gives special interests too much influence over the political system—that is, PACs essentially "buy" votes in Congress through their contributions (Sabato 1987). Furthermore, the pressure to accumulate large war chests in order to discourage challengers disenfranchises most citizens because they are unable to compete financially with wealthy individuals and PACs. This perception, critics charge, has contributed to the deep-seated cynicism and apathy on the part of the citizenry. As a result, the average voter not only fails to contribute to political candidates, but often abstains from voting on election day as well (see, for example, Pease 1991).

Suggested Reforms. In response to these problems, activists have suggested a panoply of reforms. At the beginning of the 102nd Congress, over 40 bills were introduced into the House of Representatives and over 10 were introduced into the Senate. A number of the provisions included in these proposals were incorporated into the final bills passed by the House and the Senate (Cantor 1991). Concerns about limiting the influence of special interest money (be it PAC money, soft money, or bundling) and the rising cost of campaigns are universal. However, the centerpiece of the debate focuses on whether or not public financing should be instituted for congressional elections. Advocated by the "good government" group Common Cause, these proposals are usually coupled with some form of voluntary spending limits, media subsidies, and the limitation or elimination of PACs, bundling, and soft money (Cantor 1991; Gejdenson 1991; Sabato 1987).

CASE STUDY TWO: THE PERSIAN GULF WAR VOTE

On January 12, 1991, both houses of the United States Congress approved resolutions authorizing the use of military force in order to force Iraq to withdraw its invasion force from neighboring Kuwait. This vote was the climax of five months of debate between the legislative and executive branches of government, as well as within Congress itself, regarding the appropriate response to this crisis in the Middle East.

The vote to authorize use of force was unusual for many reasons. First, it was the first vote of the 102nd Congress. About 10 percent of the House of Representatives were freshmen, who were still setting up their offices and hiring staff while contemplating their positions. Second, the Democratic party leadership considered this resolution "a vote of conscience." The Democratic leadership placed no pressure on members and promised no recriminations against those who voted to authorize force. Third, all subjects interviewed on this topic considered this vote a "declaration of war." As such, it was the first vote of its kind since World War II. Even if it cannot be considered a formal declaration of war, the specter of Vietnam and the Gulf of Tonkin Resolution, which was used to justify the United States' increasing involvement in that conflict, weighed heavily on members' minds. Importantly, prior to the vote on the final resolution authorizing the use of force, congressional debate developed cautiously and thoughtfully. Members of Congress considered the political realities they faced and remained sensitive to national security issues.

The Iraqi Invasion of Kuwait

On August 2, 1990, Iraq invaded its tiny, wealthy neighbor, Kuwait. The invasion had both economic and territorial origins. The territorial origins of the dispute had its roots in the region's colonial history. After its liberation from England, Iraq was left with only one seaport, which it shares with Iran. The Iraqi leader Saddam Hussein sought to protect access to its seaport by controlling two Kuwaiti islands, Bubiyan and Warbah, that block Iraq's access to the Persian Gulf. The ruling family of Kuwait did not wish to surrender control of these islands, which angered Hussein. In addition, Iraq and Kuwait were constantly at odds over control of the Rumalia oil field, which the two countries share (Yant 1991, 67-68).

Most importantly, the dispute was economic. Severely in debt and trying to rebuild its infrastructure after its protracted war with Iran, Iraq was suffering economic difficulties from low world oil prices. Facing a $100 billion foreign debt and an anemic economy, Hussein and others blamed Kuwaiti overproduction for deflated oil prices. Iraq pressured Kuwait to cut back production in order to increase oil prices worldwide. When Kuwait resisted, Iraq invaded its neighbor on August 2, 1990. Within a week, Iraq announced that it annexed Kuwait, making it Iraq's 19th province.

The American response was immediate. There was widespread concern that Saudi Arabia and its rich oil fields would be threatened next by Iraqi aggression. On August 3, President Bush first imposed economic sanctions against Iraq. The sanctions prohibited all trade with Iraq and froze Iraqi assets in the United States. The European Community joined the United States on August 4 (Yett 1991). On August 7, Bush dispatched the first American troops to Saudi Arabia. Within a month, troop strength reached 50,000. Congress quickly passed legislation that codified the executive order imposing sanctions into law (Doherty 1990a). On October 1, 1990, both houses passed resolutions supporting the military deployment in the Gulf, but did not authorize the use of force (Yett 1991). During these months, the United States worked through the United Nations to build an international coalition to oppose Hussein both economically and militarily.

By October, American forces numbered 200,000. The day after the midterm congressional elections—November 8, 1990—President

Bush announced his intentions to nearly double the size of the American force in Saudi Arabia, providing allied forces with an "offensive option" (Yett 1991). Meanwhile, as both Iraqi and coalition forces gathered in the desert, the United Nations and the United States continued to negotiate unsuccessfully with Iraq. After Saddam Hussein failed to comply with a January 15, 1991 deadline to withdraw completely from Kuwait, the coalition forces attacked Baghdad. Within 100 days, a ceasefire was declared and peace negotiations commenced.

Issues in the Persian Gulf Policy Debate

Congressional criticism and opposition to administration policies evolved over time and changed in response to events in the Middle East. President Bush's initial response—economic sanctions plus a small deployment of troops—enjoyed widespread, bipartisan support. For example, the resolution supporting sanctions passed the House of Representatives by 416-0 (Doherty 1990a). Democratic leaders consistently voiced support for the administration. For example, in a September 1, 1990 press conference, House Speaker Tom Foley (D-Washington) stated: "The president was personally commended by Democrats and Republicans, Senators and House members, across the board for his own particular efforts in bringing together an international effort to isolate Saddam Hussein and to bring economic pressure to bear to end this crisis" (*Congressional Quarterly Weekly Report* 1990, 2801).

Senate Majority Leader George Mitchell (D-Maine) agreed:

> I think the president has made the right decision in sending American forces to Saudi Arabia to deter an invasion of Saudi Arabia by Iraq and to organize, through the United Nations, economic sanctions to be universally and internationally applied in an effort to compel the Iraqi withdrawal from Kuwait. And today the president restated that as American policy, and it is a policy I support. (*Congressional Quarterly Weekly Report* 1990, 2802)

As time passed, congressional support for economic sanctions and building an international coalition against Iraq did not wane. However, other aspects of the Gulf policy were cause for concern. Specifically, some members of Congress balked at selling additional arms to Saudi Arabia. Others were distressed by the cancellation of Egypt's $7 billion military debt in exchange for securing Egyptian participation in the coalition. Similarly, disputes erupted over which branch of government had authority to appropriate the "burden sharing" donations from other countries (Doherty 1990b).

The confused nature of executive-legislative authority in war making was also brought to bear during the months preceding the January vote. By law, the president is required to consult with Congress during a foreign policy crisis and inform Congress in a timely manner of any military action. Precisely what consultation means and who should be involved is a matter of some dispute. Likewise, there is no commonly accepted definition of *timely*. No amount of time is specified, nor is there any distinction between consultation *before* or *after* a policy decision, such as a military strike, is implemented (Doherty 1990c).

Added to this stew is the debate about the War Powers Act. Enacted in response to the Vietnam experience, the War Powers Act gives Congress the power to limit military involvement to 60 days, with a possible 30-day extension. In the context of the Persian Gulf crisis, there was widespread concern that after starting the War Powers clock, American options to deal with Iraq would be severely limited. Furthermore, no president has ever acknowledged the constitutionality of the War Powers Act. Asserting a direct challenge to the executive under the War Powers Act could lead to a court case that Congress could lose. In either case, an extended, vituperative debate over the use of force could have been misconstrued by Hussein as weakening American resolve (Doherty 1990d).

Both issues deal with the fundamental question surrounding the constitutional role of each branch of government in war making. It was within this context that members of Congress of both parties pressured the administration to allow Congress to vote on authorizing the use of force in the Persian Gulf. Senate Majority Leader George Mitchell (D-Maine) was quoted frequently as saying, "If there is to be a war in the Persian Gulf or anywhere, it requires a formal act of Congress to commit to it" (as quoted in Doherty 1990e).

In response to this same concern, some 44 members of the House of Representatives and one Senator, led by Representative Ron Dellums (D-California), filed a lawsuit in United States Federal Court, charging that the President did not have a right to attack Iraq without a declaration of war by Congress. This suit received considerable media coverage, but in mid-December 1990 a federal judge declined to rule on the case because Congress had not yet dealt with the issue, continuing the court's tradition of remaining outside political disputes between the legislative and executive branches (Yett 1991).

Once it became clear that Congress would debate and vote on resolutions regarding the use of force in the Persian Gulf, the content of the debate turned again. This time, debate centered around whether or not to authorize the immediate use of force or to postpone the authorization in order to give sanctions more time to work. With Bush's request for this debate, the constitutional question was diffused for the time being. In the end, the resolutions authorizing the use of force passed both the House and the Senate. The tally in the Senate was 52-47, whereas the vote in the House was 250-183. The divided Congress mirrored the weak feelings of support registered in public opinion polls immediately prior to the vote. According to a *Congressional Quarterly* analysis, the winning coalition was comprised of Republicans and conservative Democrats, typically from the South. Age and seniority were also important, as younger and less senior members voted more solidly with the president (R. Cook, Elving, and the CQ Research Staff 1991).

CASE STUDY THREE: DEFINING AIDS ISSUES

Acquired Immune Deficiency Syndrome (AIDS) is a disease transmitted either through sexual intercourse or through blood or blood products. This disease, which first captured the attention of the public health community in 1980, attacks the body's immune system. If an infected person does not die of the disease itself, which also attacks the nervous system, he or she is likely to die of any number of opportunistic infections that healthy humans can easily resist. The disease may incubate for years, but once AIDS develops, it is 100 percent fatal. Unlike some other diseases in which some carriers become immune to infection, thus far, every person exposed to the virus has eventually developed the disease.

Since it appeared, some 128,000 Americans have died, and over 1 million persons are infected with HIV virus. Approximately 40,000 AIDS patients die annually (Johnson 1992; Lynch 1992), making AIDS the 11th most common cause of death in the United States. Despite its rising morbidity, cancer and heart disease still claim many more victims. However, there are important demographic variations; for example, AIDS is the second leading cause of death among men aged 25 to 44 and the fifth leading cause of death for women of the same age (Cunningham 1992).

As mentioned earlier, AIDS is transmitted through sexual intercourse or the exchange of blood or blood products. AIDS may be transmitted through both heterosexual and homosexual intercourse; yet unlike other countries in which the disease is equally prevalent in both genders, in the United States, AIDS is unusually prevalent among homosexual males. Intravenous (IV) drug users who share needles also suffer disproportionately from the disease. Numerous AIDS victims have contracted the disease through blood transfusions, use of contaminated blood products, *in utero* infection, and heterosexual intercourse. Yet homosexual men and IV drug users still comprise the majority of cases in

the United States. These two groups fall well outside the American mainstream. Doubtless this fact has contributed to the many acts of violence
and civil rights violations AIDS patients have suffered in the last decade.

Also because of the heavy concentration of AIDS among IV drug
users and homosexual men, AIDS policy has developed some interesting
permutations not found in the discussion of other diseases in this country. For example, how can traditional public health precautions be rec-
onciled with a patient's right to privacy, especially if that patient does
not want his homosexual lifestyle made public? Do public health concerns about the spread of the disease outweigh the legal ramifications of
distributing needles to illegal drug users? Are AIDS activists correct in
their assertion that AIDS does not receive adequate attention from policymakers because of the fact that the disease's victims fall outside mainstream America?

Patient Testing and Privacy

The standard public health approach to arresting the spread of sexually
transmitted diseases (STDs) is that when an infected person seeks treatment, he or she is interviewed and asked to name all his or her sexual
contacts. These contacts are then notified by public health officials, tested, and, if necessary, treated and interviewed. All of *their* contacts are in
turn contacted, treated, and interviewed as appropriate. Furthermore,
some states require STD screening in other circumstances, such as when
applying for marriage licenses. When resources match the prevalence of
disease, this approach is very effective in preventing massive outbreaks
of STDs.

Testing, however, is a contentious issue in the case of AIDS.
Historically, the homosexual community and other AIDS activists have
opposed AIDS testing. As a result of past bigotry and discrimination,
homosexual activists are reluctant to endorse any activity that might allow
additional harassment from the heterosexual majority. Furthermore, public fear of the disease has led to discrimination against AIDS victims,
regardless of how they had contracted the disease. The experiences of
AIDS victims bear this out. Individuals with AIDS and their families have
faced recrimination from neighbors and coworkers. Others have lost their
jobs and health insurance coverage when they had been diagnosed with
AIDS. Thus, maintaining individual confidentiality has become the primary concern of activists and public health officials alike.

Early in the epidemic, too, there was some question about the
usefulness of early testing. There were no drugs available to delay the
onset of AIDS. Medication could treat only the various opportunistic
infections that accompany full-blown AIDS. Aside from preventing fur-

ther spread of the disease, mandatory testing seemed pointless—and would only unnecessarily and cruelly inform many people of a painful, early death. As AIDS researchers learned more about how AIDS is spread, some policymakers began advocating an aggressive voluntary testing program. With the development of the drug AZT, which can delay the onset of AIDS, some activists advocated early testing in order to get seropositive individuals into treatment. However, many mandatory testing proposals still are opposed rigorously as a potential violation of civil rights.

Nonetheless, there was strong evidence that voluntary testing did not work. A study conducted in an Albuquerque, New Mexico STD clinic revealed that the rate of HIV infection was five times higher among the group that did not submit to voluntary testing for HIV than the group that did (Americans for a Sound AIDS Policy 1991). During interviews for this research, this study was cited by both liberals and conservatives alike. Conservatives cited it as evidence of the need for mandatory testing. Liberal activists asserted that this result was due to fear of reprisal should the subjects test positive. As a Democratic House subcommittee staff member stated:

> [Senator Jesse] Helms and [former Representative Bill] Dannemeyer have tried to force people into testing in order to punish them somehow. As a result, people won't come in until they are ill and symptomatic. They are afraid to come in because of the conservative battle cry to stop people. . .
>
> There have been breaches of confidentiality. The state of Illinois has just announced that it is going to search its roles of those who tested positive for health care workers. Well that just means that health care workers will stop coming in to be tested. Using epidemiology and testing and punishment have disarmed the public health community.[6]

Evidence does exist that people will go to some length to avoid being tested involuntarily. In 1988, Illinois implemented a mandatory HIV test for all marriage license applicants. The law required only that applicants take the test and be informed of the results; only those testing positive on two separate AIDS tests would be classified as seropositive and reported to the state health department. In the one year of its implementation, some 156,000 applicants were tested; 26 were found HIV positive. At the same time, there was a sharp drop in the number of marriages in Illinois and a concomitant increase in the number of marriages in Wisconsin and other neighboring states. During 1988, the marriage rate per 1,000 people dropped from 8.3 to 6.7. Both the cost of the test and a fear of a positive test result seem to be reasons for the exodus (McKilip 1991; Walsh 1991).

Yet conservatives charge that mandatory testing and partner notification are the only ways to reach the populations at risk of AIDS and to stop the spread of disease. According to Americans for a Sound AIDS Policy (ASAP), voluntary testing, even with the most rigorous privacy protections, simply do not reach the groups highest at risk. On the contrary, the people most likely to volunteer for testing are those least at risk of infection. In addition, uniformity between states will eliminate the kind of problem Illinois experienced with its marriage license requirement (Americans for a Sound AIDS Policy 1991; Republican Study Committee 1990).

Furthermore, conservatives argue, the seriousness of the AIDS disease means that the strictest interpretation of the doctor-patient confidentiality and the privacy rights of AIDS/HIV victims cannot be followed. Given that the most common means of transmission involves direct personal contact with others (i.e., sexual relations and needle sharing), it is incumbent on the infected individual to take precautions to prevent transmission. All too frequently, AIDS patients may be indifferent to this risk and continue to infect his or her contacts (Larher, Charrel, Enel, Manuel, Reviron, Auquier, and San Marco 1991). Under current law and medical ethics, physicians may not even inform an AIDS patient's spouse of the patient's seropositive status, much less conduct any further contact tracing. Conservatives assert that this kind of public health risk is simply too much to tolerate.

This difference of opinion transcends traditional political ideology. Rather, the positions adopted by political conservatives such as former Representative William Dannemeyer (R-California) reflect a more complex set of attitudes held by the general public. In general, the public favors stronger AIDS laws than do the activists. Furthermore, an American Civil Liberties Union (ACLU) study found that discrimination against people infected with AIDS and those in groups at risk of AIDS has increased even as the public becomes more educated about how the disease is transmitted (Hilts 1990).

Testing and Health Care Professionals

The well-publicized case of Kimberly Bergalis, a Florida woman who contracted AIDS from her dentist, Dr. David Acer, brought the debate surrounding testing and confidentiality to a new level. Bergalis was one of five patients infected by Acer; they are the only documented cases this type of transmission (Johnson 1991). Rather than defending the rights of groups outside the mainstream, suddenly the group under suspicion was health care workers: doctors, nurses, dentists, and so forth—people respected for their careers of caring for the ill.

Opponents to mandatory testing of health care workers cite several reasons for their position. First, they assert that mandatory testing would be an invasion of privacy for health care workers. Once again, they argue, this policy proscribes testing as punishment rather than as a step toward treatment or prevention. Second, they argue that the chances of this kind of transmission are minuscule. Only 7,000 health care workers have AIDS; another 1,500 health care workers are HIV positive. In fact, the chances of a health care worker contracting AIDS in a professional setting are much, much higher than the chances of a seropositive health care worker transmitting the virus to his or her patients (Johnson 1991).

These opponents voice other concerns as well. If health care workers are prohibited from practicing medicine if they are HIV positive, or if their seropositive status is made public, experts fear that health care workers would be even more reluctant to treat AIDS patients for fear of contracting the disease themselves. Furthermore, mandatory testing of health care workers could lead to the first steps of sanctioned discrimination against people with AIDS or HIV. Given that seropositivity is included in the definition of *disabled* under the Americans with Disabilities Act, opponents see the imposition of mandatory testing as a chink in that landmark legislation and a potential step backward in the AIDS movement (Schatz and Novick 1991).

However, the concerns about medical workers transcend transmission through simple exposure to blood. Given the fact that AIDS can attack the brain and central nervous system, there is an additional concern that a health care worker may not have the mental faculties to make appropriate decisions about treating patients. Kimberly Bergalis stated that she did not blame her dentist for transmitting AIDS to her; she believed that Acer was incapable of understanding his actions. Rather, Bergalis believed that the health care community needs to impose and enforce guidelines for HIV-infected health care workers who may not be capable of rational judgment (Bergalis 1991; Helms 1991).

Bergalis was not alone. Public opinion favors strict laws regulating doctors and dentists with AIDS. A 1991 Gallup poll found that 95 percent of the survey respondents believed that surgeons should be required by law to inform their patients of their HIV status; 94 percent favored the same policy for all physicians and dentists (Grandy 1991; Helms 1991).

In 1991, Senator Jesse Helms (R-North Carolina) effectively capitalized on these sentiments and introduced a set of amendments on the floor of the Senate. These amendments did not require mandatory testing. However, health care workers who know they have AIDS or HIV and who perform "invasive" medical procedures without informing their patients of their seropositive status would be subject to a $10,000 fine and a 10-year jail term (Helms 1991). The debate occurred at the time that the American Medical Association and the Centers for Disease Control were developing guidelines on testing health care workers. After a highly publicized debate, the Senate agreed to the Helms amendment by a vote of 81-18 (Helms 1991).

The House debate on the same issue included a well-publicized appearance by Kimberly Bergalis before the Subcommittee on Health and the Environment of the Energy and Commerce Committee, chaired by Representative Henry Waxman (D-California). Following her testimony and the testimony of her angry father, the House of Representatives eventually defeated the resolution (Culhane 1991). The debate and the intense media scrutiny it generated did lead the Centers for Disease Control (CDC) to issue more stringent guidelines regarding health care workers than previously expected. The final CDC guidelines recommend informing patients of an HIV risk before invasive procedures are performed, and also state that infected workers should not perform risky procedures without outside advice. (Culhane 1991; McKinney 1991). Even these guidelines were unacceptable to some activists. In the words of Dr. Ruth Finkelstein of the National AIDS Council:

> Essentially, the consequences will be that health care workers who perform invasive procedures and are HIV positive will not be able to practice. This is not warranted by public health evidence. It is not sound public health policy. . . . The CDC, which we have relied on to not give in to the mass hysteria, chose to listen to the minority instead of the majority. (McKinney 1991, 46)

Federal Funding for AIDS

A perennial issue in the AIDS debate surrounds the amount of funding that the federal government should devote to AIDS testing and research. AIDS activists and public policymakers point to a history of neglect and paltry funding for AIDS research and prevention activities during the early years of the epidemic. In his book, *And the Band Played On*, Randy Shilts (1987) painted a compelling portrait of the Reagan administration as indifferent to AIDS and hostile to its victims. Administration officials routinely requested small amounts for AIDS research, and agencies frequently did not spend all the money appropriated by Congress (363-364, 398, 466, 492-493). Furthermore, AIDS activists frequently cite the fact that Ronald Reagan never mentioned AIDS in any public speech until 1987. Even then, he never once mentioned homosexual men as one group of victims of the disease (Shilts 1987, 595-596).

Despite opposition from both the Reagan and Bush Administrations, AIDS funding has increased dramatically. However, AIDS activists and sympathetic public officials still thought that funding levels were too low and that the Bush administration was indifferent to the disease. For example, even though President Bush's fiscal year 1993 budget request included a small increase in federal AIDS funding in real dollars ($51 million), activists charged that the increase was seen only when entitlements such as Medicaid were included. They assert that these entitlements are not typically included in funding calculations for other diseases; consequently, the amount of money requested for AIDS research actually represents a funding cut after accounting for inflation (AIDS Action Council 1992).

On the other hand, some activists argue that AIDS has become "a privileged disease" (Krauthammer 1990). The $2 billion spent annually by the federal government on AIDS research and prevention is more than the appropriations for cancer, heart disease, diabetes, or Alzheimer's disease. Yet all of these other diseases claim many more lives each year than does AIDS. Although Americans perceive AIDS as the country's number one health problem (*American Medical News* 1990), only 128,000 people have died of AIDS in the last decade. At the same time, some 730,000 Americans will die of heart disease in one year alone. Another 300,000 will die of diabetes, and more than half a million will die of cancer (Johnson 1992).

Opponents and activists alike credit the high level of AIDS funding to the efficacy of AIDS activist groups (Cunningham 1992; Fumento 1990, 1992; Helms 1991; *The New Republic* 1990). Obviously, they disagree on the appropriateness of current funding levels. Advocates argue that the debate should not be defined as "AIDS versus Another Disease" but "AIDS versus Defense Spending" or "Health Care versus Other Expenditures." Furthermore, advocates argue, further research on AIDS has important applications in terms of understanding other immune system disorders and STDs (Cunningham 1992). Opponents, such as Charles Krauthammer, note that over 90 percent of all AIDS patients contracted the disease through drug abuse or homosexual activity, which is

> some voluntary action. . . . You don't get AIDS the way you used to get TB, by having someone on the trolley cough in your face. You don't get it the way you get, say, brain cancer, which is through some act of God that we don't understand at all.
>
> AIDS is in the last class of diseases whose origins we understand quite well. It is behaviorally induced and behaviorally preventable. In that sense, it is in the same moral class as lung cancer, the majority of whose victims get it through voluntary behavior, well known to be highly dangerous. (Krauthammer 1990, 80)

One theory explaining activists' success in securing federal funds is again a definitional issue. In order to place AIDS on the federal agenda, at least in terms of appropriations, AIDS had to be sold as a disease that anyone could contract. In many ways, this is certainly the case. In Africa, where experts believe the disease originated, AIDS is a heterosexual disease, and incidence among women is rising faster than among men. Nonetheless, in the United States, the overwhelming number of AIDS victims contracted the disease through homosexual activity or IV drug use, and the victims have been overwhelmingly male. The degree that AIDS is becoming a "heterosexual disease" in the United States is due largely to the rising number of infections among the female sexual partners of IV drug users (Americans for a Sound AIDS Policy 1992).

Both sides on the AIDS debate are sharply critical of media coverage of this disease. First, Randy Shilts (1987) argued that the media were completely uninterested in AIDS when it affected only homosexual men. It was not until there were "innocent" victims such as Ryan White, who did not contract the disease through homosexual intercourse or drug use, or a "famous" victim such as Rock Hudson that the media gave AIDS the coverage that it warranted (see also Shaw 1987a, 1987b). Concomitantly, Michael Fumento in his book, *The Myth of Heterosexual AIDS* (1987), argued that the AIDS community kept predicting the impending breakthrough of a heterosexual epidemic of AIDS in the United States in order to secure funding for research and to stimulate interest in what was otherwise considered a "gay disease." Fumento argues that they grossly exaggerated the risk of contracting the disease for most heterosexuals. The media, for their part, were more than willing to print this inaccurate information. However, both Fumento and Shilts argued that AIDS simply was not considered newsworthy until it moved from the fringes of society to pose a threat to the mainstream. Once this transition was accomplished, the interest of the public and elected officials was sufficiently piqued to lead to increased funding and research.

CASE STUDY FOUR: THE NATIONAL LITERACY ACT

On July 25, 1991, President Bush signed the National Literacy Act (P.L. 102-73) into law. This action culminated three years of effort on the part of literacy activists and a few key members of the House and Senate (and their staffs) who shepherded the legislation through the 101st and 102nd Congresses. Interestingly enough, the National Literacy Act was a solidly bipartisan bill. It passed the Senate with a vote of 99-0; the final House vote was almost as lopsided.

In terms of understanding the media in the legislative process, the National Literacy Act provides a valuable countercase. The National Literacy Act is a perfect example of a technical piece of legislation that will have a dramatic impact on millions of adult literacy students nationwide. In terms of upgrading the American workforce to make it more competitive with its peers, the potential ramifications of this legislation are notable. Yet it remains largely invisible outside a small community of literacy professionals and the Washington issue network.

History of the National Literacy Act

The first major piece of legislation to address adult basic education was the Adult Education Act, passed in 1966. This legislation established adult general education courses equivalent to a high school diploma. These programs were modestly funded through a combination of federal, state, and local taxes and administered through local school districts.

Aside from these programs, adult literacy efforts were largely unrecognized by policymakers and the general public alike. The United States perceived itself as a land of universal literacy and unlimited educational opportunity. Perhaps the only exceptions to this rule were foreign-born immigrants who do not speak English natively. The prospect of large numbers of adults who were unable to read, write, and compute beyond the second- or third-grade level was unfathomable. As a result, adult literacy programs nationwide tended to be private, nonprofit organizations, staffed almost exclusively by volunteers. These volunteers usually received little or no educational training and depended on materials developed by one or two volunteer literacy organizations.

The literacy field faced a number of other problems. First, the community was, and remains, highly fragmented. Teachers and tutors often are not aware of other programs in their own areas or states, which means that students cannot move easily from basic literacy programs into more advanced training. There are few agencies that provide information about additional learning opportunities to tutors and students. Second, the literacy community has little or no ability to recruit students. Standard efforts to reach students with newspaper announcements or printed ads, for example, are fruitless. Illiterate adults do not buy newspapers, and they may not be able to decipher a billboard. As a result, estimates are that only about 2 percent of the adult illiterate population receive training. Once students are in a program, retention is difficult. The typical adult literacy student has both a job and a family. Transportation, child care, and family responsibilities can be insurmountable barriers to the literacy student (see, for example, Kedrowski 1987).

Third, until very recently, the literacy community was not organized at all into any national associations and had no lobbying group to represent them. As a result, the needs of adult literacy went unheard and unrecognized in Washington. As a result of these myriad problems, literacy activists often are demoralized and lack completely any sense of political efficacy.

By the mid-1980s, the situation began to change slowly. There was a growing recognition that adult illiteracy was a widespread problem. Barbara Bush, the spouse of then Vice President George Bush, helped publicize the issue. ABC and PBS began a joint public service effort—Project Literacy U.S. (PLUS)—to raise awareness of the problem and to recruit adults into literacy programs. Last, there was a growing perception that one factor contributing to the decline of American industrial competitiveness was a failure of the American educational system. Nothing embodied its shortcomings more than the example of an adult—often a high school graduate—who could not read.

Interest in developing a major piece of literacy legislation began in both the House of Representatives and the Senate in 1988, although the efforts were independent of each other. Senator Paul Simon (D-Illinois) was the first lawmaker who became interested in a major piece of adult literacy legislation. After his 1988 presidential campaign, as Simon was going through some correspondence that had accumulated during his absence, Simon happened upon a letter from Jonathan Kozol, the author of *Illiterate America* (1985). Kozol suggested that it was time for Simon to sponsor a major piece of literacy legislation. Simon had sponsored smaller literacy programs in the past—programs that were wrapped into larger pieces of legislation such as the Stuart B. McKinney Homeless Assistance Act or the VISTA reauthorization. In response to the request from Kozol, Simon approached his committee staff and, in July 1989, introduced S. 1310. This bill was an omnibus literacy bill that attempted to address the myriad problems in the literacy field more systematically.

The process on the House side was much different. The House of Representatives did not have a member with a long-standing history of support for literacy like Simon on the Senate side. Rather, the impetus for the legislation came from a public interest group, the Southport Institute for Policy Analysis (SIPA). Several years earlier, the SIPA had been approached by the Business Coalition for Effective Literacy (BCEL), a nonprofit literacy network chaired by Harold McGraw, former Chairman of McGraw-Hill. Mr. McGraw was interested in an in-depth look at the federal role in literacy and the problems faced by the field. After some initial inquiries, the SIPA took on this project, in part because its staff believed that:

[Literacy] was an issue of importance. In many ways, too, it was a microcosm of all human resource issues. It was ripe for the plucking. We needed to pull the politics together in the federal policy area. I saw it as an easy victory . . . In addition, it was a bipartisan issue, and it was a motherhood issue. There were not really any losers with the right kind of formula.[7]

The SIPA produced a report entitled *Jump Start: The Federal Role in Literacy Policy*, published in December 1988. This monograph is a compilation of a number of papers from literacy activists that assessed the problems faced by the literacy field: fragmentation, an overreliance on volunteer tutors, an inability to recruit and retain adult students, and a general lack of funds. The report was greeted with a good deal of favorable reaction from literacy professionals, Congress, and the Departments of Education and Labor. Rather than simply becoming part of the milieu that might eventually lead to substantive legislation, the staff at SIPA then realized that "our recommendations might be enacted into law in the near term, rather than the long term."[8]

The staff of the SIPA then began looking for a House sponsor for what was essentially "their" bill; by this time, Simon had already introduced S. 1310. Their eventual choice was Representative Tom Sawyer (D-Ohio). Sawyer is a former teacher and at the time was a member of the House Education and Labor Committee. In addition, Sawyer was genuinely interested in the bill, and he wanted to build a reputation for himself on Capitol Hill. As a result, Sawyer became the principal sponsor of H.R. 3123 in 1989.

In the process of conducting their study, the SIPA recognized the problems facing the literacy community—including the fact that there was no coherent literacy lobby on Capitol Hill. Thus, the SIPA spearheaded the lobbying campaign for the National Literacy Act. They worked most closely with the House staff, but they also tracked activities on the Senate side. The SIPA staff drafted the various versions of the bill and worked to eliminate differences with Simon's draft. They created a network of literacy activists at the grassroots level, which they used for various letter-writing campaigns during the legislative process. Last, the SIPA staff conducted a public relations campaign specifically geared toward reaching these literacy activists in the field in order to educate them about the provisions of the act and to organize them.

In addition, the Business Coalition for Effective Literacy (BCEL) coordinated the activities of an informal "business lobby for literacy." This group was comprised of 13 chief executive officers of major corporations, who signed a number of letters to members of Congress and senators at various parts of the process. These efforts were particularly effective in generating strong bipartisan support for the bill. It also represented an unprecedented level of involvement in education policy on the part of the American business community. In addition, BCEL used its newsletter as the principal means of communication within the literacy community. Its quarterly newsletter reaches some 24,000 business contacts and literacy professionals. For three years running, their newsletter was largely devoted to the National Literacy Act and its progress in Congress.

In mid-1990, the National Literacy Act eventually passed the House of Representatives as part of a larger education bill, H.R. 5115. Likewise, S. 1310 had been incorporated into an omnibus education bill on the Senate side. At this point, the National Literacy Act became the victim of election eve politicking. Senator Jesse Helms (R-North Carolina), facing a tough reelection battle against Harvey Gantt, allegedly placed a "hold"[9] against the education act. The bill, poised for a floor vote, contained a provision for the National Teacher Standards Board, Gantt's brainchild. Helms did not want this legislation passed, which would have handed his opponent an important victory. As a result, the act died as the Congress adjourned at the end of the 101st Congress in October 1990.

Senate and House versions of the National Literacy Act were reintroduced immediately when Congress was sworn in for the 102nd Congress. The House version of the bill, H.R. 750, passed the House in March 1991. There was virtually no opposition—any changes in the legislation from the version sponsored by the 101st Congress were purely technical clarifications made in consultation with the Departments of Education and Labor. The Senate bill, S. 2, faced another round of difficulties. Once again wrapped into a larger education reform measure, the bipartisan nature of the National Literacy Act made it a target for a number of more controversial items. The hope was that the popularity of the National Literacy Act and the momentum behind it would lead the Senate to pass the bill—and other proposals as well.

Once again, a senator placed a "hold" against the bill. This time, Senator Jeff Bingaman (D-New Mexico) allegedly wanted to include a provision for a "national report card" into the legislation. The bill remained "at the desk" for months without any movement. The lobbying efforts coordinated by BCEL and the SIPA eventually resulted in the National Literacy Act being split from the remainder of S. 2 and passed independently. The remainder of S. 2 was held at the desk until the final hours of the 102nd Congress.

The National Literacy Act authorized $400 million for literacy programs at the federal level, which increased the appropriation for adult literacy by some $300 million. The legislation vastly increased the level of appropriations and scale of various existing literacy programs, such as adult basic education, demonstration projects, and specific programs for prisoners and commercial truck drivers. In addition, it contained new money for a national literacy research institute and state and regional literacy centers.

SUMMARY

Although scholars have not focused extensively on how members of Congress use the media to influence policy, previous studies hint at the existence of both media entrepreneurs and the media enterprise. However, using the media as a policy tool has become more prevalent in recent years, as the number of potentially important actors has increased, both in Congress and in the Washington community. The purpose of this research is to probe the dynamics of how media entrepreneurs use the media to influence public policy—which includes reaching other members of Congress and other policymakers and opinion leaders in Washington.

ENDNOTES

1. The concept of several distinct agendas is common in the agenda-setting literature. In their seminal work, Cobb and Elder (1983, 85-88) divided the policy agenda by the level of public attention given an issue. Implicit in their analysis is that an issue must be important to the public before it will be taken up by policymakers. The agenda-setting process is not this linear. Therefore, I conceive of parallel agendas, with some items on the elite agenda and others on the mass agenda.
2. The survey instruments included a numerical code on the front page that identified the respondent's office. Two respondents cut these codes off their instruments and thus are not included in this analysis.
3. Like many studies of the Senate, this response rate has a "small N" problem. This circumstance is not a major problem because most analysis will be of all the responses in the aggregate. Analysis of any differences between the two houses of Congress are done with appropriate care.
4. Two offices did, however, return surveys from both waves. One office seemed to take the same amount of care in their responses to both surveys. The other took a decidedly humorous approach to the second survey. Responses to questions such as "intended audience" generated responses such as "Martians" and "Klingons." In

both cases, the responses to the instrument sent in the first wave were analyzed.

5. Over the decade since its appearance, AIDS has developed its own lexicon. Acquired Immune Deficiency Syndrome (AIDS) is the disease. It is caused by the Human Immunodeficiency Virus (HIV). The blood test commonly used for AIDS actually looks for antibodies to the HIV virus. Antibodies indicate that a person has been exposed to the virus that causes AIDS, but has not necessarily developed the disease. The term for testing positive for HIV is *seropositivity* or *seropositive status*. The nature of HIV is such that antibodies may not appear in the blood for 6 to 18 months after exposure. A seropositive person may not develop AIDS for years after HIV antibodies are detected.

6. Interview, March 9, 1992. This interviewee agreed to speak only on the condition of anonymity.

7. Interview with Dr. Forrest Chisman, President. May 29, 1991.

8. Chisman Interview, May 29, 1991.

9. Under Senate rules, a Senator may anonymously place a "hold" against a bill if the Senator has some concerns about the legislation. The bill will then be "held at the desk," until the hold is lifted. Technically, the Majority Leader can bring a bill to the floor even when a Senator has a "hold" against it. But as the Senate's workload has increased, the disruptions filibusters can cause are even greater. As a result, "holds" have become practically absolute. Any Senator can halt the progress of a bill by placing a "hold" against it because of the threat of a filibuster that a hold implies (Sinclair 1989, 130-131).

3

Who Are The Media Entrepreneurs

Even though more and more members of Congress appear on "Meet the Press" and more and more op-ed articles with congressional bylines make their way into the *Washington Post*, it is still true that some members shun media attention. Media entrepreneurs are clearly a distinct breed on Capitol Hill—a subculture characterized by their instinct to go through the media as they react to political developments. They try to reach other members of Congress through public venues, instead of, or in addition to, conversations on the House floor, in committee meetings, or on the basketball court.

This chapter answers the first research question posed in this study: Who are the media entrepreneurs? It also analyzes what obstacles members have to overcome to translate their interest in media attention into a successful media enterprise, and how these efforts can be maintained successfully. This portion of the analysis uses survey data to identify the demographic characteristics common to potential media entrepreneurs and to estimate how many members of Congress are possible media entrepreneurs. In addition, this analysis draws on case study analysis to illustrate examples of successful and unsuccessful media enterprise efforts.

In addition, this analysis shows that there is a large cadre of potential media entrepreneurs wandering the halls of Congress. Yet, when media entrepreneurs do try to engage the media enterprise, their success is not necessarily guaranteed. Rather, it depends on three major variables: the member's ability to establish him- or herself as a credible source, the media entrepreneur's personal style, and the effectiveness of the strategy employed to reach fellow policymakers.

THE MEDIA ENTREPRENEURS

Research on the generational shift in American politics predicts that media entrepreneurs will be young, ambitious, and liberal. As Ehrenhalt (1991) indicated, because government service at almost any level requires a full-time commitment, candidates who are likely to run for public office are people who like government and are willing to forego high incomes in the private sector. Typically these candidates are liberal Democrats, rather than Republicans, with a laissez-faire approach to government.

Media entrepreneurs fit this mold. Because one purpose of their efforts is to influence policy, they are likely to have a greater sense of efficacy in both the government's ability to serve the public good and the media to influence policymakers and the public. In this analysis I use an attitudinal definition to identify media entrepreneurs. Before members use the media to influence policy, they must consider some utility to the exercise. If at least some members of Congress did not hold this belief, this research would stop here. No member would expend the effort to get media coverage. Moreover, using an attitudinal definition to identify media entrepreneurs opens up the possibility that many members are receptive to using media strategies and are waiting for an opportune moment to use the media enterprise.

In order to identify media entrepreneurs, I combined responses to four questions on the survey instrument to identify potential media entrepreneurs. These questions were designed to measure the respondents' perceived importance of media coverage in the Washington community. Respondents chose from five possible responses to each question, from "strongly agree" to "strongly disagree." In response to all four questions, large majorities of the respondents agreed that using the media was an effective mechanism to influence the policy debate in the Washington community and in Congress itself. The first question inquired whether members of Congress purposely solicit media attention in order to stimulate discussion of their policy proposals in Washington. The response was overwhelmingly favorable: 81.4 percent of the respondents replied either "agree" or "strongly agree," whereas only 11.9 percent responded "disagree" or "strongly disagree" (see Table 3.1).

Other questions narrowed the audience to other members of Congress and the executive branch specifically, and the responses here are more muted. Two-thirds (67%) of the respondents agreed that using the media was an effective tool to convince other members of Congress; two-thirds (66%) agreed that media coverage piques executive branch interest as well. Yet only 18.6 percent and 17.7 percent, respectively, registered any disagreement (see Table 3.1).

The fourth question in this section asked if media exposure *was not* an effective means to influence the Congressional agenda. The responses remained consistent: 73 percent of the respondents indicated "disagree" or "strongly disagree." Interestingly, only 12 percent of the respondents circled "agree," and no one circled "strongly agree," (see Table 3.1).

The aggregate responses to these questions provide an important vehicle for identifying media entrepreneurs. Certainly, members will not engage the media enterprise if they do not think it is important or an effective means to reach fellow policymakers. Furthermore, media entrepreneurship is an episodic activity, dependent on a number of outside forces. By asking questions about perceptions of media influence, the analysis can include potential entrepreneurs who have not yet aggressively engaged in this kind of activity or who are not actively engaged in the current policy debate. Yet they provide a pool of potential entrepreneurs should their positions shift or the agenda change.

For this purpose, I created a new variable to measure attitude toward the media from the responses to these four questions. After accounting for the difference in the wording of Question 2, I calculated the mean responses into the new variable. The new variable was constructed so that scores were positively correlated with attitude toward media strategies. These attitude scores had a normal bell-curve distribution, with a range of values from 1.75 to 5.25. The variable was used in this form for regression analysis (see Table 3.2).[1]

In order to conduct statistical analysis appropriate to ordinal level data,[2] the respondents were divided into two groups: media entrepreneurs and their low-profile counterparts. I divided the media entrepreneurs into three categories. The first category includes all respondents whose aggregate attitude score was 4.0 or higher. This score reflects an "average" answer of "agree" on all four questions comprising the attitude variable. I call this group the potential *pool of media entrepreneurs*, although it is unlikely that all of its members do, or will, engage the media enterprise. However, they are favorably disposed to this

Table 3.1. Questions on Attitude Toward the Media.

Question 1: Members of Congress—in both the House and Senate often solicit media exposure (i.e., interviews, talk show appearances, op-eds, press releases, etc.) as a way to stimulate discussion about national policy proposals in Washington.

Strongly disagree	1.3 %
Disagree	10.6 %
Neither agree nor disagree	6.6 %
Agree	58.9 %
Strongly agree	22.5 %
TOTAL (N = 151)	100.0 %

Question 2: Soliciting media exposure *is not* a particularly effective way to put an issue on the congressional agenda.

Strongly disagree	25.2 %
Disagree	47.7 %
Neither agree nor disagree	15.2 %
Agree	11.9 %
Strongly agree	0.0 %
TOTAL (N = 151)	100.0 %

Question 3: Media exposure is an effective way to convince other legislators in both chambers to support policy proposals.

Strongly disagree	1.3 %
Disagree	17.3 %
Neither agree nor disagree	14.6 %
Agree	58.7 %
Strongly agree	8.0 %
TOTAL (N = 150)	99.8 %

Question 4: Media exposure is an effective way to stimulate discussion on policy alternatives and issues among executive branch officials.

Strongly disagree	0.7 %
Disagree	17.0 %
Neither agree nor disagree	16.3 %
Agree	59.8 %
Strongly agree	6.1 %
TOTAL (N = 147)	99.9 %

Source: Data compiled by author.

Table 3.2. Frequency Distribution of Media Attitude Scale.

Attitude Scale Value	Percentage	N
1.75	0.7	1
2.00	2.0	3
2.25	3.3	5
2.50	3.3	5
2.75	2.6	4
3.00	4.6	7
3.25	11.3	17
3.50	7.9	12
3.75	10.6	16
4.00	25.2	38
4.25	13.9	21
4.50	6.6	10
4.75	2.6	4
5.00	4.6	7
5.25	0.7	1
Total:	100.0	151

Source: Data compiled by author.

approach. The second group are those respondents who had an aggregate attitude score of 4.25 and above. This score corresponds to answering "strongly agree" on at least one item and answering "agree" to the other three. I call this group the *likely media entrepreneurs*. The last group, which I call the *hard-core media entrepreneurs*, consists of the respondents who had an aggregate score of 4.5 and above, which roughly approximates to two "strongly agree" responses and two "agree" responses. The pool of media entrepreneurs actually comprises a majority of the survey respondents (53.6%). This result indicates that the media are *widely* considered a useful tool to influence policy in the Washington community. The next strictest definition of media entrepreneurs—the likely media entrepreneurs—are still a formidable force. They account for more than a quarter of the total number of respondents. The hard-core media entrepreneurs account for 14.6 percent of the respondents (see Table 3.3).

Regression analysis unearths some interesting demographic patterns in the respondents' attitudes toward using the media although the model is not strongly predictive. Age, party affiliation, and ideology are all statistically significant variables. Respondents from the offices of young members, Democrats, and liberals view the media more favor-

Table 3.3. Media Entrepreneur Classifications (Frequencies).

Respondent Group	Percentage	N
I. Pool of Media Entrepreneurs		
Comparison Group (Score < 4.0)	46.4	70
Media Entrepreneurs (Score $\geq$4.0)	53.6	81
II. Likely Media Entrepreneurs		
Comparison Group (Score < 4.25)	59.6	108
Media Entrepreneurs (Score $\geq$ 4.25)	28.5	43
III. Hard-core Media Entrepreneurs		
Comparison Group (Score < 4.50)	73.5	129
Media Entrepreneurs (Score $\geq$ 4.50)	14.6	22

Source: Data compiled by author.

ably than do respondents for older members, Republicans, and conservatives. Tenure in office was the only variable that was not statistically significant at the 0.05 level (see Table 3.4). Even though age and tenure were strongly correlated ($r= 0.56183$; $p = 0.0001$), I concur with the results of the regression analysis: Media entrepreneurs are younger, but not necessarily junior, members of Congress. This finding fits with the picture of an aggressive young generation of politicians who wish to influence policy through many means (Ehrenhalt 1991; Loomis 1988). There is also ample evidence that media entrepreneurs do not abandon media strategies as they accrue tenure and move into leadership positions. Rather, their new position provides a bully pulpit from which to attract more media attention. If this study were repeated in several

Table 3.4. Regression Analysis of Attitude Toward the Media Enterprise, by Demographic Variables.

Variable Name	Parameter Estimate	Standard Error	p
Intercept	4.5676	0.3998	0.0001
Age	-0.0181	0.0077	0.0203
Tenure	0.0110	0.0075	0.1446
Party	-0.5167	0.2032	0.0122
ADA91[a]	0.0074	0.0029	0.0131
$R^2 = 0.0866$			

[a]Member's ADA score in 1991.

Source: Data compiled by author.

years, after many senior members of Congress retire, I predict that the relationship between age and attitude would remain statistically significant, whereas the correlation between age and tenure would decrease.

Furthermore, there is a weak regional component to this relationship. Hard-core media entrepreneurs, who have the greatest sense of media efficacy, are less likely to be from the South than from other parts of the country. Interestingly enough, this relationship can be seen in two different regional analyses. The first used a dichotomous independent variable that divides respondents into those from the Sunbelt Caucus states and those from other states. The second used the Census Bureau's classification that divides the country into four regions: northeast, midwest, west, and south. In both cases, chi-square analysis found that hard-core media entrepreneurs are less likely to hail from Dixie. Given that the respondents overrepresent members from the South, this finding might actually mute some of the relationships reported later in this analysis (see Table 3.5).

Table 3.5. Chi-Square Analysis of Media Entrepreneurs by Region.

Type of Media Entrepreneur	Definition of Region	p
Pool of Media Entrepreneurs	Sunbelt/Non-Sunbelt[a]	0.435
Pool of Media Entrepreneurs	Census Definition[b]	0.692
Likely Media Entrepreneurs	Sunbelt/Non-Sunbelt	0.137
Likely Media Entrepreneurs	Census Definition	0.268
Hard-core Media Entrepreneurs	Sunbelt/Non-Sunbelt	0.026
Hard-core Media Entrepreneurs	Census Definition	0.077

[a]The Sunbelt states are the states that comprise the Congressional Sunbelt Caucus: Alabama, Arizona, Arkansas, Florida, Georgia, Kentucky, Louisiana, Mississippi, Missouri, New Mexico, North Carolina, Oklahoma, South Carolina, Tennessee, Texas, Virginia, and West Virginia.

[b]This variable uses the Census Bureau classification of four major regions in the country: West, Midwest, South, and Northeast. The states comprising each region are: **West**—Alaska, Arizona, California, Colorado, Hawaii, Idaho, Montana, Nevada, New Mexico, Oregon, Utah, Washington, and Wyoming. **Midwest**—Illinois, Indiana, Iowa, Kansas, Michigan, Minnesota, Missouri, Nebraska, North Dakota, Ohio, South Dakota, and Wisconsin. **South**—Alabama, Arkansas, Delaware, District of Columbia, Florida, Georgia, Kentucky, Louisiana, Maryland, Mississippi, North Carolina, Oklahoma, South Carolina, Tennessee, Texas, Virginia, and West Virginia. **Northeast**—Connecticut, Maine, Massachusetts, New Hampshire, New Jersey, New York, Pennsylvania, Rhode Island, and Vermont.

Source: Data compiled by author.

Importantly, there is no statistically significant difference between House members and Senators and their attitudes toward the media enterprise. The literature on Congress and the media points to the fact that Senators historically receive more media attention than do House members (Hess 1986). Senators come by this coverage more easily. They are courted by their local media, and a few enjoy status as "originals," called on to comment on any number of public issues. However, one necessary element of a successful media enterprise is credibility. Therefore, the House, with its emphasis on specialization, is fertile soil for media entrepreneurs. Foote's (1991) finding that the House surpassed the Senate in overall television coverage in 1990 may be evidence of media entrepreneurs' success in that chamber.

These results can be used to construct a prototypical media entrepreneur. He or she is likely to be a young, liberal Democrat representing a district outside the deep South, serving in either the House or the Senate.[3] However, this analysis has its limitations. This model successfully predicts only 13 percent of the total variation in attitude toward the media. Although it does produce some weak support for Ehrenhalt's (1991) analysis, the more important finding is that media entrepreneurs can be found across demographic groups. It is important to note that this phenomenon is not determinative. Young, liberal Democrats may adopt a quiet approach to public policy. Others may maintain only local media relations. Similarly, it is possible that media entrepreneurs may be conservative, Southern, Republican, and old. Furthermore, there is no evidence, for example, that full committee or subcommittee chairmen engage the media enterprise to any greater or lesser degree than those members who lack these political tools. Therefore, this finding provides evidence that the media enterprise is used by members irrespective of their institutional stature. It is not simply a tool used by impatient, young, junior members who lack the means to influence policy more directly—only to abandon media strategies when they become subcommittee chairmen. Nor is the media enterprise the sole domain of committee chairmen and party leaders. Rather, the media enterprise transcends seniority and formal position.

Lastly, it is important to note that although this analysis has not generated any strong models to predict who the media entrepreneurs are, this chapter and those that follow do indicate that media entrepreneurs (in all three categories used in this analysis) are a distinct breed in Congress. They perceive the media's effectiveness differently. They evaluate their colleagues in Congress differently. Media entrepreneurs consume news differently. And they approach the policymaking process very differently from their colleagues.

STRATEGY AND STYLE: PATHWAYS TO ENTREPRENEURSHIP

The demographic characteristics of media entrepreneurs yield a few insights about these members. However, they do not lend much insight into the motivations of media entrepreneurs. Nor do they reveal the factors that lead to success for some and failure to others. This section turns to the case study data to examine how media entrepreneurs achieve success. Most members make a conscious decision to court the media, but their success depends on their ability to establish themselves as credible sources.

Stumbling On Entrepreneurship

When he was in Congress, former Representative Mike Synar (D-Oklahoma) had an unusual relationship with the *New York Times*. Synar was one of the members of Congress they frequently quoted on any number of issues, including energy, campaign finance reform, the environment, and federal land use issues. Synar described the development of the relationship this way:

> A reporter named Steve Roberts [of the *New York Times*] was sitting on an airplane next to Cleta Deatherage [at the time an Oklahoma state politician]. Roberts told her he was planning to do a feature on another person, and Cleta told him that no, he ought to feature a guy named Mike Synar. Then I got to know Keith Schneider who covers energy issues and the editorial boards through the campaign finance reform issue. The *Times* has enough reporters to specialize, and when they print a story in the morning, it will be on the national news that night.[4]

Synar's final comment in the preceding quotation indicates that, even though he did not seek out the relationship with the *New York Times* himself, he saw the benefit of maintaining this kind of important relationship with them over time. Certainly, the kind of coverage that Synar received in this eastern, metropolitan journalistic giant did not help him to a great degree in his Southern, rural, poor, predominantly conservative district—a fact that Synar readily admits:

> I have traditionally given the Oklahoma papers the same stuff I feed the *New York Times*. They generally don't pick it up, but I don't want them to feel like second class citizens. But there is a lack of coverage on those issues. They just aren't interested in it.[5]

Therefore, the principal benefit Synar stood to receive from this relationship was the prestige that comes from an appearance in the *New York Times*, a newspaper that was widely circulated among elites in the country. Repeated mentions will penetrate the issue networks in which Synar was active, enhancing his credibility and ability to influence policy.

Synar's relationship was not unusual. As Nancy Travor, congressional correspondent for *Time* magazine, related:

> It's not unusual for me to place a call to an office and talk to an aide in the morning and have the call returned by the member in the afternoon. And I am not talking about some little member from North Dakota here. I mean Newt Gingrich, the [then] House Minority Leader. And we're on a first-name basis. I call him Newt and he calls me Nancy.[6]

Another reporter noted the same tendency and worried that it might jeopardize journalistic independence:

> We do live in a hot house here. So many media personalities have actual status here in Washington. Reporters simply don't enjoy the same ranking elsewhere in the country. But here, they're on par with members of Congress and Cabinet members. . . . It's an unhealthy phenomenon. I know that some reporters regularly socialize with the people they cover, and that's not good. I guess it happens everywhere, but not the extent that it does here.[7]

More typical is the case of Representative Newt Gingrich (R-Georgia), who made a conscious decision to pursue media attention. As a member of the Conservative Opportunity Society, Gingrich was one of several members of Congress who made use of "special orders" broadcast on C-SPAN to lambaste the folly of liberal Democrats.

Reaching In from Outside

Two Senators who opposed the use of force in the Persian Gulf War provide striking examples of media entrepreneurship as a strategy employed by an outsider attempting to influence policy. Both Bob Kerrey (D-Nebraska) and Paul Wellstone (D-Minnesota) are junior midwestern Senators. At the time of the January 1991 vote, Kerrey had just completed his first two years in the Senate and Wellstone had just taken his oath of office. He carried the distinction of being the only freshman Senator who defeated an incumbent in the 1990 midterm elections. Both Kerrey and Wellstone sought media attention to explain their positions. Yet they experienced widely varying degrees of success. Kerrey enhanced an already solid reputation. Wellstone rendered himself impotent.

Bob Kerrey is the prototype of a media entrepreneur: an articulate, photogenic, moderate-to-liberal Democrat. Kerrey first came into the national spotlight during the flag-burning debate that followed the 1989 Supreme Court decision that protected flag-burning as "free speech." Kerrey, a Vietnam veteran who won the Congressional Medal of Honor and lost part of his leg in a war injury, was able to criticize efforts to ban flag burning without calling into question his own patriotism. Likewise, Kerrey opposed the military buildup in the Persian Gulf. Not only did he argue that the United States did not need to enter into another conflict like Vietnam, Kerrey continually asserted that Bush's real motivation behind the troop deployment was to protect oil fields, not to free Kuwait, unseat Hussein, or install democratic forms of government in the region.

Kerrey articulated his views consistently on national television and in other meetings with reporters. He was not only widely quoted by the press, but Kerrey appeared on a number of occasions on "NBC Nightly News" with Senator Robert Dole (R-Kansas), then the Senate Minority Leader. "The Bob and Bob Show" was great television. It included two war veterans who suffered severe wounds in the course of their service, debating whether or not the United States was justified in entering yet another war. Kerrey also articulated his views through floor statements and speeches before the Democratic Caucus.

What was Kerrey's motivation? In the words of his press secretary:

> The decision to become vocal about his opposition to the President's policy was a personal one. It was not based upon media concerns. It was based upon his own war decision and experience with a government that had lied and treated the troops badly during the Vietnam War. And you will remember that at the time, there were 20,000 to 30,000 projected individual casualties. So, Kerrey wanted to voice his reservations about the policy.[8]

As Kerrey himself characterized it:

> I came to the decision that the reasons we were going to war were not good enough. "Preserving our way of life" means that we can continue to consume petroleum products. Economic arguments were also insufficient reasons to go to war. And I came to the conclusion that the only good reasons to use force were the traditional reasons and values that we have fought for before.[9]

When asked who Kerrey intended to reach with his statements, the Senator and his aides listed three audiences: other members of Congress, the administration, and the public. An outside strategy was considered the most effective for two reasons. According to one aide, "Kerrey instantly decided to be a vocal critic of the policy. It was a gut reaction on his part." Equally important, the aide went on to state was that Kerrey ranked 94th out of 100 in seniority. He lacked an institutional mechanism such as a committee chairmanship to use as a platform for his position. Furthermore, a public strategy stood to reach as many people as possible.

Kerrey himself added another important reason for his success in articulating his opposition. He saw the Persian Gulf War debate as a fairly atypical instance. In his words:

> The media are demand driven, and this kind of war-and-peace issue was really fairly simple. In other issues, like health care, education, or agriculture, I need to present a complicated picture . . . and listen to the response. . . . This was more similar to other sorts of emotional issues.[10]

Kerrey later demonstrated another trait common to many media entrepreneurs: ambition for higher office. Kerrey made an unsuccessful bid to become the Democratic presidential nominee in 1992. Doubtless Kerrey speculated that taking a high profile in this debate stood to enhance his visibility as he positioned himself for the 1992 campaign effort. Likewise, Kerrey came off well on television. He was articulate and forceful on the medium. Favorable impressions like these are also helpful when establishing oneself as a presidential contender.

Senator Paul Wellstone (D-Minnesota) also fits the general profile of a media entrepreneur. A baby boomer who became politically active as a result of the civil rights and antiwar movements of the 1960s, Wellstone still carries much of the fire that characterized that era. As a scholar, Wellstone specialized in studying grassroots political movements and the origins of social problems, such as rural poverty. When he was elected, many observers predicted that Wellstone would become the most liberal member of the Senate (Schwartz 1991). Yet Wellstone had much less success with the media enterprise than Kerrey. Wellstone had difficulty with the media, especially television. He is an exuberant public speaker who is effective in person, but somewhat overwhelming on television. Moreover, Wellstone is not telegenic, with his small stature, unruly hair, and ill-fitting suits. However, the primary reason that Wellstone failed at the media enterprise is that he failed to establish himself as a credible expert on foreign policy.

During the initial congressional debate, Wellstone was still a candidate for office, running a poorly financed campaign against incumbent Republican Rudy Boschwitz, who possessed a $7 million war chest. The campaign focused on issues such as farm policy, health care, and the budget debacle that kept Boschwitz in Washington, rather than at home, campaigning for reelection (Truehart 1990). The Persian Gulf crisis did not appear on Wellstone's agenda until after the election. Wellstone learned during his Senate orientation that the administration seemed intent on going to war. Motivated by this knowledge, Wellstone returned to Minnesota where he hosted a series of "town meetings" to discuss with his constituents the possibility of going to war.

By his own admission, Wellstone was far removed from the initial debate. He was unable to offer any evaluations of others who opposed the war, like Senators Sam Nunn (D-Georgia) or Bob Kerrey. Rather, as Wellstone characterized it, "before the vote I really couldn't tell you [about the debate]. I wasn't there. It all happened so quickly."[11] After he returned from Minnesota, Wellstone joined in the war debate. However, his tactics became increasingly controversial. He repeatedly cornered President Bush at a White House function where he voiced his opposition about going to war.[12] He played a tape of the comments of some Minnesotans who opposed the war to Vice President Dan Quayle. Although these events happened in the midst of reporters, the event that came closest to a press conference was Wellstone's trip to the Vietnam Veterans' Memorial. After he placed a bouquet of flowers near the engraved name of a veteran from Wellstone's home town, Wellstone restated his opposition to going to war in the Gulf. Wellstone was roundly attacked for exploiting the memorial for current political purposes.[13]

Wellstone characterized his activities in this way:

> I had a sense of urgency because of the immediacy of the vote. Once I was in Washington, I made more of an attempt to communicate with the country at large. I still had a real sense of urgency. I was afraid of the terrible loss of life and the sense that there was no purpose to the war. As it is, there *was* a great loss of life, only it was Iraqi casualties, not American. I was "on fire" about the issue, and it was on purpose.[14]

Wellstone's press coverage improved after the debate on the resolution to authorize the use of force. His floor statement was widely quoted in debate summaries that appeared in various newspapers around the country. As the war progressed, Wellstone was one of the few members of Congress who remained vocally opposed to the war effort, even in the face of allied domination over Iraq. By contrast, most of the other members adopted Kerrey's approach, which was to "oppose the war but support the troops." At this point, Wellstone adopted a more conventional approach to the media enterprise, with op-ed articles in the *New York Times* and the *Christian Science Monitor* (Wellstone 1991a, 1991b). As a result of his continuing opposition, Wellstone appeared on several television news programs to debate Persian Gulf policy.

Wellstone was the lone voice crying in the desert, and he did not relish this position. Wellstone described the experience in this way:

> Once the military activity began, after the bombing started, general-ly speaking there was a conventional wisdom that you should not speak out against the war. I was the only one who would. I would appear on talk shows and be the only opponent. I distinctly remem-ber one panel on MacNeil-Lehrer where it was supposed to be two and two. But I couldn't figure out who the other war opponent was. I was the only one who would appear, and I would have welcomed the help.[15]

One commentator remarked during this period that Senator Wellstone needed to learn the finer points of "gadfly politics" (Merry 1991). A well-respected Senate reporter agreed:

> Wellstone was all charged up about the war. I think his approach was a result of being the new kid and being an outsider. And it appears that his extreme approach was a product of his own lack of experience. It, too, has hurt him here and back at home.[16]

Wellstone's early activities undermined his initial credibility as a war opponent. Not only did he burst onto the scene at the eleventh hour, Wellstone's reputation was further undermined by a number of other incidents; for example, he called Jesse Helms a racist. His decrepit green campaign bus broke down on Capitol Hill, blocking a half dozen covet-ed parking spaces, and Wellstone eschewed senatorial tradition by refusing to allow his colleague, David Durenburger (R-Minnesota), to stand by him as Wellstone took his oath of office.

Wellstone, however, was a quick student of the media enter-prise. Over time, Wellstone learned the value of floor statements, op-ed articles, interviews, and news show appearances. As a result of the Persian Gulf conflict, Wellstone settled down to become a student of Judaism and Middle Eastern history. As a result, Wellstone stands to carry more credibility should he choose to speak out on Middle East pol-icy in the future—credibility Kerrey possessed at the outset and enhanced after this experience.

Reaching Out From Inside

Media entrepreneurship is not solely the bailiwick of outsiders trying to penetrate the legislative machinery. The media skills developed prior to entering positions of political power are easily adapted to these new circumstances. Once again, the debate on the Persian Gulf War provides some fascinating examples of high-ranking officials in Congress using the media to articulate their positions in a public manner. At the time, former Representative Les Aspin (D-Wisconsin) and Senator Sam Nunn (D-Georgia) were the two chairmen of the Armed Services Committees. The two legislators varied dramatically in style and approach to their offices and, in the case of the Gulf War, stood on opposite sides of the debate. The cautious Nunn opposed the authorization of the use of force. The more flamboyant Aspin sided with the administration. They both used their positions as a means to publicize their positions and garner support from their colleagues as the congressional vote approached.

Senator Sam Nunn is a 22-year veteran of the Senate. Nunn is the grandnephew of one former Georgia Senator, Carl Vinson, and succeeded another former Georgia Senator, Richard Russell, as chairman of the Armed Services Committee. Nunn is a conservative Democrat whose instinct is to use insider strategies to affect policy rather than to engage the media. Furthermore, Nunn is considered a nonpartisan legislator who is well versed in all aspects of military policy. Nunn's first foray into a well-publicized national debate was his opposition to the nomination of John Tower as Secretary of Defense under George Bush (Duncan 1989).

In the case of Desert Storm, Nunn used his position to conduct a series of hearings on the effectiveness of the Desert Shield operation and the potential political repercussions of going to war in the Persian Gulf. Over a period of weeks, a long parade of military experts, including former Chairman of the Joint Chiefs of Staff, Admiral William Crowe, testified before Nunn's committee. They all questioned the wisdom of a military action and noted the success of the United Nations sanctions against Iraq. Secretary of Defense Dick Cheney and other administration officials also testified. In one exchange, Cheney asserted that "there is no guarantee . . . that sanctions will force him out of Kuwait. It might, but there is not certainty there." Nunn's response became of the most often-quoted phrases of the debate, "If we go to war, we're never going to know whether they would work, are we? That's the point" (Doherty 1990f). According to Charles Harmon, Nunn's Administrative Assistant, "[this was] a pretty strong statement for the normally cautious and moderate Sam Nunn. He just doesn't make statements like that unless he feels very strongly about it."[17]

Nunn's decision to conduct hearings was not motivated by a desire to receive media attention. Rather, they were principally motivated by the desire to examine dispassionately the administration's decisions regarding the Gulf crisis. The media attention they received was simply a result of their historical importance. As Harmon recalled:

> It happened when we learned about the operation [to deploy additional troops]. That indicated there was a clear change of emphasis when we doubled troop strength. His [Nunn's] most quoted statement is: "we were justified to be there in August. We were justified to do what the President wanted. We were justified to attack Saddam, with appropriate congressional approval. *But is it wise?*"
>
> Sam Nunn believes in building a record. He makes personal contacts. He does not use an outsider strategy. Instead, he calls hearings and he amasses testimony. And he makes a floor speech . . . they are all factual and aimed toward building a case for his position.[18]

Intentions aside, Nunn did receive ample media attention and was cast as an administration critic as the Gulf War debate developed. Nunn worked on a personal level, contacting fellow Senators individually. Yet he also engaged in some activities typical of the media enterprise. First, Nunn became a visible and oft-quoted opponent to administration policy. He was an original co-sponsor of the Senate resolution introduced by George Mitchell that opposed the use of force. Third, Nunn wrote two op-ed articles for the *Washington Post*, elucidating his opinions on the Gulf crisis. The first was published in November 1990, and the second appeared just two days before the Senate vote (Nunn, 1990, 1991).

Postmortems concluded that Nunn's presence on Capitol Hill has waned in the wake of the Gulf War. His visible opposition to the administration policy in what turned into a very successful war effort seemed to have diminished his effectiveness on Capitol Hill (Barone and Ujifusa 1991; Towell 1991). The insider who went outside despite his normal instincts may have enjoyed the limelight, but may have suffered politically as a consequence.

Former Representative Les Aspin (D-Wisconsin) is a familiar face and accessible voice to Capitol Hill reporters. Aspin is known for his success in garnering media attention, particularly on defense issues. Aspin was one of the first members to establish his credibility through the media enterprise. As *The Almanac of American Politics* recorded it:

> Aspin started off in the House as a gadfly, a minority of one on Armed Services, issuing as many as 60 press releases a month attacking high Pentagon spending and wasteful projects and getting

plenty of ink in the process. . . . By 1983, Aspin was the *de facto* leader in the House on military issues, supporting the nuclear freeze resolution in debate and the Scowcroft Commission recommendations for the MX missile. (Barone and Ujifusa 1991, 1341-1342)

Aspin was the beneficiary of a coup in the Democratic Caucus to replace the aging Representative Melvin Price (D-Illinois) as Chairman of the House Armed Services Committee. His legislative skills in this endeavor are well documented elsewhere (Heymann 1987; Loomis 1988, 214-217). What is relevant to this analysis is that Aspin brought with him his skills and proclivity to use the media to direct the debate on military issues.

Aspin was busy during the days preceding the Persian Gulf War vote. Like Nunn, he wrote two op-ed articles for the *Washington Post* (Aspin 1990, 1991). But unlike Nunn, Aspin did not shun media appearances. References to Aspin's appearances on public affairs talk shows such as "Meet the Press," "John McLaughlin's One on One," and "Larry King Live" pepper the written record of this period (see, for example, Doherty 1990f; Swoboda 1990).

Like its Senate counterpart, the House Armed Services Committee held hearings on the Gulf Crisis in the waning months of 1990. In a conscious effort to shape congressional debate in a way distinct from Senator Nunn's efforts, Aspin's hearings focused on the possible tactical points of the war, rather than its potential political ramifications. Unlike Nunn, Aspin then used these hearings and other conversations as a basis for a set of position papers analyzing the Gulf crisis, outlining policy options, and advocating specific positions. Aspin's position on the Gulf resolution was quite complex. He favored the resolutions authorizing the use of force, yet he advocated pursuing a diplomatic solution for as long as possible. However, Aspin argued that a diplomatic solution would have to take a hard line against Iraqi aggression. He (1991, A17) wrote: "The model is the Cuban missile crisis of 1962 . . . Then as now, there was no backing down on the basic demand. The missiles had to go then and Iraq has to leave Kuwait now. Compliance of 75 or 80 percent would not do."

One of the position papers released in late December echoed this argument. It cautioned that a diplomatic solution must not concede any part of the basic issue—Iraqi withdrawal from Kuwait—to Saddam Hussein (Pincus 1990) The last paper in the series received the most publicity. In this paper, Aspin used data from Pentagon sources to outline the probable military campaign and projected approximately 3,000 American casualties. Clearly designed to influence his congressional colleagues, Aspin was quoted as stating: "It's the first time we've been able to know in advance how a war would likely be conducted. And it's the first time Congress and the nation can make a decision on war based on this kind of information"(Moore 1991, A15).

This last report led to a storm of criticism because of its prediction of some 3,000 American casualties. Mary McGrory (1991) led the charge in her column "Calculating Callous Aspin." McGrory's charges ran the gamut from calling Aspin "boyish" to maligning Aspin's proficiency in dealing with her colleagues in the media. In her comparison to the more reticent Nunn, McGrory wrote:

> Nunn's influence on matters of war and peace is legendary. He runs the Senate on those issues and he has a hard-core following of at least 20 in the House. This is an affront to Aspin, who feels he should shape the debate. He is much more accomplished than Nunn in the media—Nunn scorns the 20-second sound bite, but is treated with deference. (1991, A2)

Aspin and his like-minded Democratic colleagues created a coalition that authorized the use of force in the Gulf. Aspin's predictions of a quick war with few American casualties was borne out in the historical record. There is nothing like being on the winning side to enhance one's reputation. Although Nunn had to defend his position against the authorization during the highly successful military campaign, Aspin found his position enhanced by his accurate predictions. Postmortems of Aspin's involvement in the Gulf War debate characterized him as "the new Sam Nunn" (as quoted in Towell 1991; see also Barone and Ujifusa 1991). Aspin, of course, later served as Secretary of Defense in the Clinton administration.

Although Nunn's reputation in the Washington community may have suffered briefly because of his opposition to the administration, nonetheless, he did succeed in the media enterprise. Sam Nunn's position defined and legitimated the position of those voting against the authorization to use force. Rather than eliminating the use of force as an option, Nunn's contingent was able to argue that sanctions should be given more time. Force was *not* ruled out. Both his position and Kerrey's opposition provided political cover for other senators who lacked either Kerrey's status as a veteran or Nunn's status as Chairman of the Armed Services Committee.

Aspin's success was similar. As a "hawkish" Democrat, he articulated a position for like-minded Democrats who wanted to justify a vote to use force, especially in light of the party leadership's opposition, quiet though it was. In addition, it is clear that years of experience with the media enterprise have made Aspin an astute operator. He clearly searched for means to distinguish his committee's hearings from those held by Nunn's committee. In addition, the hearings provided less of a platform for Aspin's position than did the position papers he released shortly before the final vote.

Avoiding Press Coverage

It is critically important to remember that a lot of policy still gets made in the old-fashioned way. One such example is the National Literacy Act. This case provides valuable insights into the way the media enterprise is peripheral to the legislative process. The media were not completely ignored by the people involved with this legislation; they were incidental to the business at hand.

In many ways, Representative Thomas Sawyer (D-Ohio) fits the mold of a potential media entrepreneur. The 8-year veteran from Akron has a liberal voting record. He is photogenic, articulate, and his name— Tom Sawyer—is memorable (Barone and Ujifusa 1991, 985-987). Furthermore, Sawyer has earned a strong legislative reputation in both of his committee assignments: Post Office and Civil Service and Education and Labor. Yet Sawyer has not established himself as a media entrepreneur, perhaps in part because he does not hold a seat on a high-profile committee. His legislative efforts have been notable, yet the national media have failed to feature Sawyer in any way.

Sawyer was the principal House sponsor of the National Literacy Act, passed in 1991. Despite some effort on the part of Sawyer, Paul Simon (D-Illinois), his Senate counterpart, and the literacy community, there was negligible press coverage of the legislation as it churned through the congressional machinery. As Sara Platt Davis, Sawyer's Legislative Director, recalled:

> We did the standard stuff. First, we went all over the country giving speeches. We held a press conference here in Washington when we introduced the bill. We also held hearings and sent out a Dear Colleague [letter to members]. . .
>
> [The Washington media] covered it, but they only covered it as a story that already happened. They did not cover the dynamics of how the bill developed. The bill was caught in a deep and undeserved political struggle in the last Congress [the 101st] that was completely ignored in the press. *Congressional Quarterly* covered that only cursorily. They really were not helpful at all.[19]

Notably, however, when the bill in the 101st Congress fell victim to a "hold" in the Senate, neither Sawyer and his allies in the Congress, Simon, nor the literacy community aggressively tried to publicize the issue. No major press conferences were held or public statements issued. One literacy activist, who insisted on anonymity, remembered these events with frustration:

> There was no way to get the literacy titles out of S. 2. When we were trying to separate the bills, we approached the editorial boards of the *New York Times* and the *Chicago Tribune*. Mitchell and Kennedy were sitting on the bill. Frankly, if you took the literacy act out of the bill, there wasn't much left of substance in the education reform package. We wanted to get the major newspapers to say something. We met with them, provided them with background information. But nothing came of it. They didn't decide to do an editorial on it.[20]

At another point in the process, Education Secretary Lauro Cavazos threatened that the Bush administration would veto the literacy bill. Cavazos asserted that the goals of the National Literacy Act would contradict other literacy efforts and intrude on various prerogatives of the President and Secretary of Education. Those active in drafting the bill generally thought the objections were groundless. But Cavazos did stonewall the Literacy Act for a time. As Forrest Chisman of the SIPA remembered it:

> [T]here was virtually no hard news reporting of the process . . . the issues, the problems, the substance and the politics were all missed.
>
> I thought for sure we would get coverage of the Cavazos stuff. I spoke before the National Governors' Association [NGA], and there was press all around. When I told them about Cavazos, the audience erupted. . . . But nobody, except the literacy press, picked up the story.[21]

Thus, the opportunity for any potential press coverage of the legislation or literacy policy more generally was lost. First, aside from some "standard" activities when the legislation was introduced, Sawyer did not engage in any other component of the media enterprise. The staff did not make any efforts to sell the legislative story to the media. Literacy activists also did not pursue a coordinated media strategy. The speech before the NGA and the contact with editorial boards were ad hoc and lacked any follow-up efforts. The story certainly had newsworthy components. "Innocent Victim of Partisan Politics" or "Administration and Congress Clash" come to mind as potential headlines. Nonetheless, Sawyer and the literacy activists chose a low-profile strategy over taking their case public.

Granted, it would have been a tough sell. Reporters do not find adult literacy a top priority. One major Washington reporter confessed in an interview on another matter that he had never heard of the National Literacy Act.[22] Even after a brief description of its legislative history, the reporter was still hard pressed to find much he considered "newsworthy" in the story. This problem is common to education and job training issues generally. In his analysis of then Senator Dan Quayle's stewardship of the Job Training Partnership Act, Fenno (1989) found that Quayle received very little attention from the national or state media for his efforts on the bill.

Furthermore, activists and congressional staff alike were skeptical that media attention would have enhanced the National Literacy Act's chances of passing in the 101st Congress. In the words of one lobbyist:

> The bill wouldn't have passed if the media had paid more attention to the issue. The bill was killed because the literacy act was incorporated into an omnibus bill. That bill had some other controversial aspects that were unrelated to literacy. It was those things that prevented the bill from coming to the floor. And the media would not have been able to fix them.[23]

Sawyer's decision to pursue low-profile strategies to get his legislation passed seems to be a stylistic choice. In addition to his service on literacy, Sawyer, who is the former chairman of the the Census and Population subcommittee of the now defunct Committee on Post Office and Civil Service, had built a strong reputation on Census issues based on his subcommittee's scrutiny of the 1990 Census. Sawyer did not receive or solicit widespread coverage in the national media on these issues. Sawyer chose quiet effectiveness over the media enterprise. Even low-profile committee assignments could provide a bully pulpit for the ambitious media entrepreneur.

Sawyer is not alone in his choice. One reporter, while remarking on the general availability of members of Congress, noted that subcommittee chairmen of the House Appropriations Committee (the so-called "College of Cardinals") were, as a group, close mouthed. As a result, despite their power on the Hill, these members are largely invisible to the media. This reporter was not able to correctly identify former Representative Jamie Whitten's position on the committee at the time (as full committee chairman) or the state he represented (Mississippi).[24] Whitten, in fact, had only one appearance on network television news during the entire 101st Congress. This finding stands in sharp contrast to his fellow committee chairmen Les Aspin (69 appearances), Dan Rostenkowski (D-Illinois, 64 appearances), and John Dingell (D-Michigan, 37 appearances; Foote 1991).

Nor was Whitten alone among committee chairmen. Representative Dante Fascell (D-Florida), chairman of the House Foreign Affairs Committee, adopted a very low profile in the debate on the Persian Gulf resolutions. Yet he and his committee were responsible for drafting the resolutions that the full House debated and voted on in January 1991. It would have been a simple feat to plant stories about committee deliberations or probable resolution language. Yet Fascell did not aggressively pursue these kinds of activities. The vacuum left by Fascell was filled by two committee members noted for their foreign policy experience—Lee Hamilton (D-Indiana) and Steven Solarz (D-New York), both of whom were ranked among the 50 most visible members of the 101st Congress (Foote 1991).

ANALYSIS AND IMPLICATIONS

So who *are* the media entrepreneurs? These disparate data provide several important insights into the nature of media entrepreneurs. First, the survey data indicate that the pool of potential media entrepreneurs is quite large. It actually accounts for over half of the survey respondents. Given that southern members have a lower sense of media efficacy, and that the respondents slightly overrepresent southern members, it is not too much to generalize that fully half the current Congress can be classified in the pool of media entrepreneurs. However, the members who are most likely to engage the media enterprise are a substantially smaller subset of the population. Just over one-fourth of the respondents fall into the category of likely media entrepreneurs, and about one-seventh of the respondents can be considered hard-core media entrepreneurs.

Statistically speaking, there is weak evidence that media entrepreneurs fit the mold of a new generation of liberal politicians who differ from their predecessors in a number of ways. They are more likely to be young, liberal, nonsouthern Democrats. Yet this relationship is weak. It is important to remember that media entrepreneurs can easily transcend boundaries of age, ideology, and position. Media entrepreneurs do represent a distinctly different group of members in Congress. As further analysis demonstrates, they consistently court and consume media differently than their non-media-oriented peers. They also see the purpose of the media enterprise in a different way and evaluate some of their colleagues differently. Media entrepreneurs can best be identified by their sense of efficacy toward the media and the media's usefulness in Washington. As such they differ fundamentally from their low-profile colleagues.

Certainly there is a difference between believing that the media are a powerful policy tool and translating those beliefs into the media enterprise. It is difficult to get media attention; developing the media enterprise is clearly a stylistic choice. A member may aggressively pursue media attention, like Les Aspin did throughout his career. Or he or she may stumble on it and see its long-term utility, like Mike Synar. And, importantly, Tom Sawyer provides a good example of the stylistic choice to be a low-profile operator.

Second, the media enterprise is not the domain of members who otherwise lack any means to influence policy through traditional ways. Media entrepreneurs will use whatever tools they have at their disposal. These tools include position, rank, background (such as veteran status), personal relationships with journalists, or a willingness to act as a "gadfly." All are potential means to attract press attention.

Third, the media enterprise is risky and not always successful. Credibility is at the core of a successful media enterprise. Without it, members will not be taken seriously by journalists, who are the gatekeepers to publicity, or by other members of the Washington community. Paul Wellstone's reputation certainly suffered as a result of his initial attempts to influence the Gulf War debate. Nunn's reputation suffered—if only temporarily—because he came down on the "wrong" side of the Gulf debate. He was not evaluated on his level of success in shaping the debate on the Persian Gulf, but on the substance of this argument. Similarly, the modest efforts to generate press coverage by Sawyer and the literacy lobbies yielded no notable coverage.

ENDNOTES

1. Calculating a new variable to measure attitude toward the media enterprise is valid. On the survey, one question attempted to measure how many members actually attempted to use the media to influence policy (Question 17: Does your member consciously solicit national or Washington-based media attention for the purpose of attracting support for specific legislation? Responses: Frequently, Occasionally, Rarely, Never). Questions 1 through 4 all correlate with Question 17 in the anticipated direction, and all four are statistically significant (Question 1: $r = .4318$, $p = .0001$; Question 2: $r = -.0355$, $p = .0001$; Question 3: $r = .2409$, $p = .0036$; Question 4: $r = .2572$ $p = .0019$).

2. Most of the statistics reported here will be difference of means tests and other statistics appropriate for ordinal-level data. Although some scaling techniques are appropriate for regression analysis, these data, generated from Likert scales, do not fall in that category. I am not willing to make the assumptions necessary to run

regression using ordinal-level data. For example, I am not at all sure that the distances between the values for each variable are equal; certainly the strength of opinion reported between persons will vary. My "strongly agree" may be much weaker than someone else's "strongly agree."

Regression analysis is also not appropriate for theoretical reasons. Understanding legislative behavior is difficult. The patterns are complex, and I argue that using the media is only one component of this process. Regression analysis is designed to predict behavior, whereas the difference of means tests are used to describe phenomena, not to predict legislative behavior accurately. Alone, the media enterprise does not predict much. But we as scholars must recognize its role in order to understand and describe the *complete* process.

The results of the regression analysis reinforce these concerns. The "attitude" variable is significant for the same variables I reported using the difference of means tests. However, the predictive power of the regression equation was often anemic. The predictive capacity of the models did not improve noticeably by adding additional variables to the equations, such as party, ADA score, gender, race, house, and so on.

Nonetheless, regression did yield some interesting results from time to time. I will report results of regression analysis when they are theoretically important or when I use interval-level data, such as age, ideology, or tenure.

3. There were no statistically significant differences in terms of race or gender. However, this may be due to the highly skewed nature of the data. The population of members of Congress is composed overwhelmingly of white males. It would be very interesting to repeat this study if the demographics of Congress ever approach those of the population as a whole.
4. Interview, July 29, 1991.
5. Interview, July 29, 1991.
6. Interview, March 16, 1992.
7. Interview, April 21, 1992.
8. Interview, September 18, 1991.
9. Interview, March 1, 1991.
10. Interview, March 1, 1991.
11. Interview, September 19, 1991.
12. Bush then turned to an aide and said, "Who is this chicken——?" (Rosellini 1991).
13. Wellstone's staff later denied that the trip to the memorial was a press conference. Rather, they asserted that it was a personal visit, and Wellstone did not expect to be accompanied by a dozen reporters. The press secretary refused to provide a transcript of the event, stating that one was not available. ("New Senator Pleads for Peace" 1991).

14. Interview, September 19, 1991. Emphasis is Wellstone's.
15. Interview, September 19, 1991.
16. Interview, May 7, 1991.
17. Interview, January 23, 1991.
18. Interview, January 23, 1991.
19. Interview, May 13, 1991.
20. Interview, July 17, 1991.
21. Interview, May 29, 1991.
22. Interview, December 6, 1991.
23. Interview, July 9, 1992.
24. Interview, March 16, 1992.

4

Setting the Agenda and Defining Alternatives

This chapter focuses primarily on the second research question posed in this study: When do media entrepreneurs use the media enterprise? If the purpose of the media enterprise is to influence the policymaking process, then the potential effectiveness of the media enterprise will vary depending on the stage of the policy process. This chapter shows that the agenda-setting and alternative selection stages of the policy process clearly provide the most opportunity for the media entrepreneur to influence the media enterprise. Survey data augment interview data generated from case studies and conversations with the press secretaries to the congressional leadership.

PUBLIC OPINION AND AGENDA SETTING: THE ELITE AND THE MASS AGENDAS

The dynamics of the media enterprise will vary depending on the newsworthiness of a particular issue. The biases of journalism lead reporters to seek out stories that have an important human interest element, contain an element of drama, and have factions with points of view that are easily communicated. In addition, especially in the age of television, "news" must possess compelling visuals to accompany the story (see Bennett 1988).

The level of media coverage will, in turn, shape public opinion on an issue. Public opinion often has a strong influence on policymakers. It provides a general guide on public policy. At the same time, public opinion can also constrain policymakers from making policy decisions that are ultimately unpopular, but may have a desirable outcome—such as banning smoking or lowering the speed limit (both would save lives) (Kingdon 1984, 69). Yet, even if the public is not particularly captivated by an issue, every issue has a network of activists that are interested in the policy. These activists want to be informed of policy developments and seek to influence the process.

To understand how the dynamics of the media enterprise vary in light of these differences between public opinion and activists' interest, it is helpful to divide the policy agenda into two separate agendas: the elite agenda and the mass agenda. The elite agenda is comprised of policy problems in which the public has only cursory knowledge and weakly held opinions about the policy and how it should look. Only the Washington-based issue networks and a few well-organized grassroots organizations will be concerned with these policies and their legislative specifics. The mass agenda is comprised of policy problems in which the public has a high level of knowledge and strong opinions about the course public policy should take. Not only are the Washington-based issue networks interested in policy, but the public at large is more likely to hear about and react to politicians' positions on these issues.

Issues, of course, may appear on both the elite and the mass agendas. But issues may take very different forms in each. For example, health care reform is an issue that is clearly on the mass political agenda. The public wants everyone covered. The elite agenda includes a debate about how to cover everyone and when. Should everyone be covered through an employer mandate, an individual mandate, or government insurance? Should the length of the phase be five years, ten years, or some other interval?

The case studies examined for this research fall neatly into these two categories. The Persian Gulf crisis and AIDS policy are both high-visibility cases. The possibility of war dominated news coverage prior to the vote to authorize force and public interest in the developing crisis was very high. Similarly, various public opinion polls show that Americans consider AIDS as the United States' foremost health problem. The prevalence of the disease has been covered widely in recent years.

In addition, news coverage of violence and other problems confronted by AIDS patients and public education efforts have raised public knowledge about the disease. By contrast, campaign finance reform and adult literacy policy have never made the list of the public's chief policy concerns. The public in both cases fails to understand the complexity of the policy issues or the exact nature of the problems.

Media entrepreneurs' efforts to set the agenda are checked by public opinion. Specifically, media entrepreneurs stand to be much more successful in terms of setting the elite agenda than influencing the mass agenda. When public opinion is intense and embraces specific policy proposals, public opinion defines and limits the parameters of the policy debate. Media entrepreneurs can either use public opinion as a springboard to advance their own policy goals, or they may be constrained by public opinion. Justifying a decision that runs contrary to strongly held public opinion requires very careful marketing with a heavy dose of media activity.

Policies that make their way onto the elite agenda provide media entrepreneurs far greater opportunities to shape the amount and content of public discourse; however, members must make a more sustained effort to seize these opportunities. If media entrepreneurs fail to take advantage of the opportunity to enter and dominate a policy debate, someone else, such as an interest group or the administration will. Without a timely entrance into the policy debate, media entrepreneurs will be forced into a reactive position—in which they will have to justify their proposals in terms that someone else has devised. For example, if the reason for the decline of American competitiveness is defined as a failure of the education system, it would be difficult to argue that upgrading factories would improve the skill level of the labor force.

This section examines the four case studies upon which this research is based in terms of the role of the media and the agenda-setting process. In the case of testing health care workers for HIV or AIDS, public opinion served as a constraint on political liberals and the public health community and a springboard for political conservatives who wanted to shape public policy in a way normally denied them. Similarly, the Persian Gulf War debate was defined by the administration's reaction to historical events in the Middle East, public opinion in the United States, and the fact that the debate was being conducted before an international audience that included, among others, Saddam Hussein.

By contrast, the elite agenda items held much more opportunity for the media entrepreneur. Campaign finance reform in particular has been the subject of many competing efforts in defining the problem and the solution. However, because most members are latecomers to the policy debate, they have not been able to control fully the agenda-setting process. Instead, they compete unsuccessfully with a special interest organization—Common Cause. Likewise, adult literacy was a wide open policy field as late as 1989. Simon in the Senate seized the opportunity to initiate the policy debate through the media enterprise. Specific policy prescriptions, however, were determined in private. Meanwhile, media strategies took a backseat in the House process where the debate was defined at all stages by alternatives offered by another interest group—the SIPA.

The Mass Agenda: Policy Definition and AIDS

AIDS policy, as a mass agenda item, is an excellent example of both the power public opinion has in terms of boosting a media entrepreneur and constraining the parameters of public debate for those who disagree with public opinion. All the interview subjects who discussed AIDS believed that the importance of media coverage in the battle against AIDS placed this disease in a unique position. Since the first cases of "gay pneumonia" were chronicled by the Centers for Disease Control (CDC) in 1981, news coverage of AIDS has gone through a series of fits and starts. Network news coverage of most diseases generally parallels the incidence of the disease. As the number of cases increases, so does network coverage; likewise, coverage wanes if the disease is brought under control. Not so with AIDS. Prior to 1987, when former President Reagan and then Vice President Bush made their first AIDS policy speeches, network news coverage of the disease was characterized by peaks and valleys that corresponded instead to discoveries that seemed to foreshadow the epidemic's spread to the "general population." The sharpest peak accompanied Rock Hudson's diagnosis and death from the disease (Colby and Cook 1991; Shaw 1987). AIDS did not become a permanent part of the news agenda, with regular updates on research and findings, until the administration gave an official response to the AIDS epidemic (Colby and Cook 1991).

In the last five years, AIDS has been the subject of a great deal of media attention, yet this scrutiny has served two conflicting purposes. On the one hand, media coverage contributed to a sense of mass hysteria that did not reflect what was known then (or now) about the real threat of the disease. The media not only reported the public's at times hysterical response to AIDS, but they helped spread some of the misinformation about AIDS and its transmission. The most notable example was the publicity surrounding the research conducted by noted human sexuality experts, Masters and Johnson, that suggested AIDS could be transmitted through casual contact (Fumento 1990). By contrast, the media was the source of most public education efforts regarding transmission and prevention of the disease. Not only were public information efforts carried out through newspapers, but public service announcements were aired widely as well. As a result, American adults have a high degree of information about AIDS and its transmission. One study conducted in 1989 found three-fourths of the respondents knew that AIDS destroyed a victim's immune system, and 80 percent knew that the virus could be transmitted through sexual intercourse. At the same time, the study also revealed that many adults had inaccurate perceptions of the way AIDS is transmitted. For example, over 50 percent of the adults surveyed thought that AIDS could be transmitted by restaurant cooks handling food, through coughing or sneezing, or via mosquitos and other insects (Hardy 1990).

Perhaps as a result of these many misconceptions, the public takes a hard line toward AIDS patients. Public opinion polls show that some of the general public advocates quarantines or assigning identification tags to AIDS patients (Bull 1991). Furthermore, the level of public intolerance toward AIDS patients and those testing positive for HIV seems to be increasing rather than decreasing over time.

Various policy actors in the AIDS debate fall along unusual cleavages. Liberal Democrats who chaired the appropriate congressional committees in the 102nd Congress, Representative Henry Waxman (D-California) and Senator Edward Kennedy (D-Massachusetts), historically have agreed with the policies recommended by the Republican political appointees in the public health community. Their policy prescriptions advocate voluntary testing and concern for civil liberties. Contact tracing is only done with the permission of the person with HIV or AIDS. Conservative Republicans in Congress, such as former Representative William Dannemeyer (R-California) and Senator Jesse Helms (R-North Carolina), have thus been forced into the unusual position of opposing both the Democratic leaders in Congress and officials of Republican administrations, but advocating policies supported by the public.

Democratic congressional leaders, such as Representative Henry Waxman, who has chaired the Health and Environment Subcommittee of the House Energy and Commerce Committee, found themselves in a delicate position when designing policy. One Waxman aide stated that their strategy was to build a case based on public health considerations first and to confront civil liberties considerations second. Therefore, policy was built on a foundation of expert opinion, which becomes the basis for justifying policy decisions to the public. In his words: "Mr. Waxman has always said that if it comes down to a choice between civil rights and public health, he would have to support public health considerations. And that has gotten him into trouble with some activists."[1]

An American Civil Liberties Union (ACLU) lawyer involved in this issue agreed. The ACLU founded its AIDS project because of the discussion of quarantines and other efforts to contain the disease that would violate civil liberties of people with HIV or AIDS. He characterized the ACLU's involvement in this way: "It's our opinion that AIDS shouldn't be a civil liberties issue. It should be a public health issue. So you should do what you need to do in terms of maintaining public health."[2]

This intellectual approach solidifies the coalition within the issue networks of public health officials, subcommittee members, and activists. However, it is difficult to sell to the general public. As the Democratic staffer related:

> The media have always treated Dannemeyer and Waxman as equals, even though Dannemeyer can't find the public health people to back him up. For example, when we face an economic crisis, people don't turn to Dannemeyer and listen to him talk about the gold standard—which is his position on economic recovery—because there are no experts who agree. Yet you see the media bending over backwards to see how they could help him.

> [W]hen you see Dannemeyer and Waxman together talking about AIDS, the public health community will always support Waxman's position and no one will defer to Dannemeyer's side. That's because Henry has chosen to defer to the advice of the experts.[3]

Because of the chasm between public opinion and elite opinion regarding the proper course of AIDS policy, ambitious entrepreneurs such as Dannemeyer or Helms could capitalize on public opinion in order to force a change in public policy. The case of Kimberly Bergalis and the debate surrounding testing health care workers is an important example.

Helms is a particularly astute media strategist, yet his press operation is decidedly low key. Helms does not employ a press secretary, only a press assistant. But before he came to Washington, Helms was a conservative newspaper columnist and television commentator. His experience as a journalist no doubt gives Helms a distinct advantage over others in terms of timing his initiatives to make them newsworthy. As an assistant to Helms related:

> We got a lot of play on [this] issue. We used the media's attention to the issue to our advantage. We timed our amendments to coincide with the media coverage of the CDC guidelines. You can't often see Helms holding up the front page of *Newsweek* and say, "this is what I mean."

We knocked the AIDS establishment in the Senate and in Washington off balance. People favored our position in overwhelming numbers. Polls showed that 90 percent of the people sided with us. We defined it as a public health issue, not a civil rights issue. We moved beyond the perception of victimhood in the AIDS community.[4]

Tom Brandt of the National Commission on AIDS remembered the events this way:

The Helms amendments were not passed, but they did result in the CDC guidelines being rewritten. Kimberly Bergalis got a lot of attention, more than what the advocates would have liked. The apogee was when she came to Congress and presented her case. Reporters traveled with her on the train, and they filed their stories from stops along the way. It was almost a 1930s-style campaign train. The press entourage waiting for her at Union Station had me thinking that nothing like that had happened since Lindbergh.[5]

Brandt also acknowledged that Bergalis's was an unusual story, yet he saw the media's attention to it as a testimony to the evenhanded way that media attention has developed over time. In his words: "Editors certainly could have spiked the Bergalis story as an anomaly. But it's easy to understand how they won't make that judgment. And it hasn't sent them into a hysterical response."[6]

Yet again, Bergalis's case typifies the difficulty Waxman and like-minded members of Congress have in selling policy positions that run contrary to public opinion. After her testimony, members of Congress universally expressed their sympathy to Bergalis and her family, yet had to justify their opposition to their public policy proposals. It is a difficult, complex argument to communicate, even in the best of circumstances; in this case, the glare of media coverage truncated and distorted the debate. In the two days of hearings Waxman's subcommittee held, two television cameras were present for the first day of testimony. Thirty-three were present for the second day when Bergalis appeared. Testimony from other AIDS patients and health care workers followed Bergalis's appearance, and the messages from policymakers who disagreed with Bergalis's policy recommendations were eclipsed by her personal tragedy.

Former Representative J. Roy Rowland (D-Georgia) was one of the two medical doctors serving in Congress at the time. He was also a member of the Health and Environment Subcommittee. He characterized the difficulty policy makers face in this way:

I think we need to address this issue solely from a scientific stand-
point. But we also need to deal with discrimination and confidentiality concerns that make this disease unique. . .

My colleagues on the committee are certainly aware of the level of
misinformation out there. And they do not wish to be adversely
affected politically.[7]

Public opinion in this case provided an opportunity for two
media entrepreneurs to shape the debate and, hence, the outcome of
public policy on AIDS. Senator Helms capitalized on public support for
strict testing and criminal penalties for health care workers with AIDS or
HIV, and not only managed a victory in the Senate, but changed the
shape of the CDC guidelines regarding HIV-infected health care workers. Similarly, Representative Dannemeyer capitalized on the media
attention and public opinion to force Chairman Waxman to hear
Kimberly Bergalis make her case before Congress, which helped keep
pressure on the CDC. Furthermore, Waxman and his colleagues were
placed in the uncomfortable position of telling Bergalis, under the glare
of public attention, that because she was an exception to cannons of
medical knowledge, her proposals would be opposed.

In this case, Helms, with assistance from Dannemeyer, used
public fear of being infected with AIDS by a health care worker as a
launch pad for his very successful media campaign to influence policy
regarding testing these workers. They forced the traditional AIDS policymaking coalition to justify unpopular and complex policies to a fright-
ened and skeptical public. The power of strong public opinion and its
constraining influences are both aptly demonstrated by this case.

The Mass Agenda and the Persian Gulf War Debate

In the debate preceding the vote to authorize the use of force in the
Persian Gulf, public opinion was an imperfect guide and a constraint on
potential media entrepreneurs. Congressional debate was curbed further
by events as they developed in the Middle East, the administration
responses to them, and the fact that the American policy debate was
monitored closely by an international audience. From moment to
moment, our allies, the United Nations, various Gulf states, and Saddam
Hussein in Iraq scrutinized the congressional debate. There was widespread awareness among members of Congress that the congressional
debate on the use of force could be too easily misinterpreted as weakening American resolve (Doherty 1990g).

Events overtook congressional initiative first when Iraq invaded Kuwait, and again later when the Bush administration decided to commit troops to the region. As time passed and the United States seemed bound for war, members of Congress had essentially two options in defining alternatives in the debate. First, a group of members successfully defined the action as being a *war*—not a *police action* or some other term that would have allowed the administration to sidestep the congressional vote on the resolutions altogether. Second, once the decision to consult Congress was made, congressional debate then primarily focused on *when* force should be authorized—in the near term or after allowing sanctions some time to work—even though there was still a small cadre of members who opposed the use of force under any circumstances. In both cases, the questions were fairly clear-cut; there were not a lot of conflicting ideas being put forth by disparate groups.

Nonetheless, national and international scrutiny of the debate did not squelch the media enterprise. First, a proliferation of op-ed articles bearing congressional by-lines appeared during these months. Between the initial Iraqi invasion in August 1990 and the conclusion of the war in February 1991, there were 13 op-ed articles written by members of Congress or senators that appeared in either the *New York Times* or the *Washington Post*.[8] Most of these thought pieces focused on consulting Congress on whether or not to use force. However, some members used this opportunity to discuss other issues. For example, former Senator Lloyd Bentsen (D-Texas) argued for a coherent energy policy. Former Senator Jim Sasser (D-Tennessee), then Chairman of the Senate Budget Committee, discussed the potential economic ramifications of the costs of Operations Desert Shield and Desert Storm. Representative Sonny Montgomery (D-Mississippi), then Chairman of the House Veterans' Affairs Committee, used this platform to argue against the reinstatement of the draft (Bentsen 1990; Montgomery 1990; Sasser 1990).

Second, the members and leadership of both parties used the media to put pressure on the administration to consult Congress before using force. For example, in *Congressional Quarterly* alone, members of Congress, especially Senate Majority Leader George Mitchell (D-Maine), were quoted from their television appearances on "Meet the Press," "Face the Nation," "MacNeil/Lehrer NewsHour," and CNN (see, for example, Doherty 1990f, 1990h, 1990i; Liebert 1990).

Third, one faction of war opponents received media attention simply because their actions filled a vacuum in the policy debate. Led by Representative Ron Dellums (D-California), this group of some 50 members of Congress first filed a federal court suit against the administration to force it to consult Congress before commencing military action.[9] After it became apparent that Congress was going to vote on the resolutions,

Dellums and his counterparts became the unofficial whip organization opposed to the use of force, because the Democratic party leadership stepped away from what they considered a "vote of conscience." Likewise, the activities of Democrats who favored the use of force, such as former Representative Dave McCurdy (D-Oklahoma) and former Representative Steven Solarz (D-New York), became noteworthy as they too created a whip organization for their faction.

These members frequently received press coverage simply because their actions were newsworthy. They did little to generate media attention. One good example was Representative Henry Gonzales (D-Texas), who introduced a resolution to impeach Bush as a result of his Gulf policies. As one aide recalled, Gonzales's office did not design an aggressive media strategy:

> It all happened very quickly. We did talk to one reporter about the calls we have received voicing support. . . . I would have liked to have handled it better, to get the best results. But so far, we have been getting a lot of calls . . . and we have been doing a lot of faxing to reporters.[10]

An aide to Representative Steven Solarz agreed. In his words:

> The media sought the office. It was a natural story, sort of a "man bites dog" thing. Here you had a liberal Democrat who has a very good reputation on foreign affairs who bucked his party leadership, and as it turns out, his constituency as well, to side with the President. Solarz was sought out by every major national TV station, all the major news stations, "Nightline," all the major clips. There were simply too many interviews to grant. Solarz will not shy away from selling a story, but in this case, he simply didn't have to.[11]

These divisions between congressional factions reflected how public opinion was divided prior to the January vote. Public opinion polls taken from August through December 1990 found solid support for the Persian Gulf policy. However, support for the potential use of force was not strong. Most polls showed that Americans favored using diplomatic pressure and economic sanctions before committing to force, although the results varied depending on how the questions were worded. Regardless, a solid 20 to 30 percent consistently opposed the current policy and the use of force (Idelson 1991). The final debate and discussion eventually reflected the conflicts found in public opinion itself.

The actions and decisions of Congress in this case were limited in at least two important ways. First, throughout the crisis, Congress had little control over the agenda. Events precluded much congressional involvement. Nor did Congress have much opportunity to define the issue in any way distinct from the administration. Nonetheless, the media enterprise was helpful in the effort to convince the Bush administration to allow Congress to vote on the use of force. In this way, Congress carried credibility as a separate but equal branch of government with clear constitutional authority. Second, members of Congress were constrained by the public nature of the debate and the extremely equivocal and uncertain nature of public opinion. With the exception of Gonzales's aborted impeachment resolution, no member of Congress advocated any position that did not have a modicum of support publicly—it is important to remember that it was not until *after* the overwhelming early success of the military campaign did public opinion solidify in favor of administration policy. As a result, many members of Congress received copious amounts of press coverage for their efforts without a sophisticated and well-executed media enterprise. Simply because the stakes were so high and their actions were so newsworthy, several members, such as Stephen Solarz, Ron Dellums, and Henry Gonzales received press attention, even without coordinated media strategies.

It is impossible to determine the degree that congressional debate may have been constrained by international attention instead of public opinion. However, there are several possibilities. First, the Democratic leaders in Congress repeatedly stated their strong support for the use of sanctions, the administration's efforts to build an international coalition, and initial troop commitments. Second, the debate really hinged around *when* to use force rather than whether or not force should be used at all. Third, the content of the congressional floor debate, broadcast widely by C-SPAN and CNN, included repeated statements of support for the current policy and the dedication of American troops in the Gulf. All of the messages had clear applications in the context of international as well as national politics.

The Elite Agenda and Campaign Finance Reform

In many ways, campaign finance reform typifies an elite agenda item. Whereas public opinion polls show that the public favors some form of campaign finance reform, when public opinion poll respondents are asked to name the most serious issues facing the United States, campaign finance reform is never mentioned (Shinn 1991). Furthermore, most congressional offices interviewed for this study reported that campaign finance is not an important issue to their constituents, although Fred Wertheimer of Common Cause and other activists have argued that general voter angst and cynicism toward politics are due in no small part to the public's perception of corruption and special interest dominance. It is more than likely that the general public lacks a clear understanding of policy options and proposed solutions.

Nonetheless, campaign finance reform is a perennial issue in Congress. The process of alternative selection is largely uninhibited by public opinion. For example, by the end of the first session of the 102nd Congress, some 67 bills were introduced into the House and Senate dealing with campaign finance reform. Their specific proposals varied widely—from banning PACs completely to limiting them in other cases. Some included tax breaks; others called for public financing and spending limits (Cantor 1991). Such myriad proposals are testimony to the wide open nature of the alternative selection process in campaign finance reform.

Members of Congress active in the campaign finance reform debate follow a fairly standard path in their attempts to influence the debate. First, after introducing legislation, members typically hold a news conference to advertise the provisions in their particular legislation. Afterwards, many publish op-ed articles in various news sources. For example, in the 101st and 102nd Congresses, op-eds on campaign finance reform were authored by Senator Mitch McConnell (R-Kentucky) and former Representative Don Pease (D-Ohio), among others (McConnell 1991; Pease 1991). Representatives Al Swift (D-Washington) and Sam Gejdensen (D-Connecticut), past chairmen of the House Task Force on Campaign Finance Reform, also received a fair amount of publicity in connection with the Task Force's work. Former representatives Mike Synar (D-Oklahoma), Dan Glickman (D-Kansas), and Representative David Obey (D-Wisconsin) were also frequently mentioned.

Despite all of this activity, members of Congress have some difficulty framing the debate surrounding campaign finance reform. First, public opinion understanding is limited by the data on campaign finance available to reporters. Documents produced by the FEC and analyzed by various public interest groups and investigative reporters focus on PAC contributions. Tracing individual contributions, bundling, and independent expenditures is much more difficult. As a result, press coverage and the public's understanding of the issues is skewed toward PACs and away from other issues. For example, opinion polls show that the public favors eliminating PACs—without necessarily recognizing that PACs themselves were the result of reform.[12] Interestingly, public opinion polls do register opposition to Common Cause's favorite solution: public financing. Polls indicate that barely 20 percent of the populace cares to institute public financing of congressional elections, especially if it would result in increased taxes (Donovan 1992; Shin 1991).[13]

Second, the public interest lobbying organization—Common Cause—leads a cottage industry of "good government" groups that focus attention on campaign finance issues.[14] Common Cause began a campaign finance monitoring project in 1972, shortly after the first campaign finance reform measure was passed. For the last two decades, Common Cause has analyzed and distributed campaign finance information based on Federal Election Commission (FEC) reports.

Common Cause overtly set out to define the issues surrounding campaign finance legislation; its preferred solution is public financing of congressional campaigns. Fred Wertheimer, President of Common Cause, characterized it:

> We have set out to define the solution. We basically believe that you need this solution. The President, the Congress, the Supreme Court—every time we have looked at this issue, this is the solution we come up with. . . . It's hard to do a serious study of the problem without reaching this conclusion.[15]

Steven Stockmeyer, Executive Vice President of the National Association of Business Political Action Committees (NABPAC), the principal pro-PAC lobbying organization on Capitol Hill (Matlack 1991), agreed:

> Without question, it is Common Cause and a thorough effort over the years. It is a political organization and they have research skills that are first rate. They also had the field to themselves and no counterpoints of view being expressed. . . . There was no one fighting back. And after 15 years of the common drum beat, their answer, as a result, has become the answer. They have dominated the field.[16]

As a staff member representing one of the Democrats considered a "liberal" legislator on this issue put it: "Congress is certainly not framing the issue. Any defense of PACs is seen as a defense of special interests. And pushing for any kind of public financing is seen [by Republicans] as a raid on the public treasury. So Congress is not framing the issue."[17] Certainly one could add that the public is not framing the issue either.

Common Cause has been very successful in directing the course of the debate. But, during the early interviews conducted for this research, there was a great deal of bitterness associated with Common Cause's activities at the end of the 101st Congress. At that time, the Senate had passed a bill that more or less satisfied Common Cause. However, the public interest groups considered the House legislation "weak" and cynical. As one activist claimed, "the spending limits were so high that most members did not spend that much money in their campaigns."[18] Because it carried high spending limits and included no public financing mechanisms, Common Cause began a successful media campaign to kill the House bill.[19] From that point onward, it became apparent that any bill that stood a chance of success must include public financing and other provisions acceptable to Common Cause.

If there is any one member who was successful in framing the debate on campaign finance reform it was former Senator David Boren (D-Oklahoma). Boren's credibility on this issue stemmed in part from his long involvement with the issue. About two years before Boren's first reelection campaign in 1984, he attended a retreat held by the Democratic party on planning the next election. As a former staff aide remembered it:

> Boren went on this retreat, and there was one session on how to play the PAC game. . . . Boren came away from the retreat feeling almost dirty about the money game. Even though he didn't take any PAC money in any of his elections, the money chase seemed so much more sophisticated that it had only four years before. So, Boren compiled some FEC records and found a growing reliance on PAC money from his colleagues. . . . In 1983, Boren introduced his first bill on campaign finance reform.[20]

Common Cause and Senator Boren formed an alliance by 1985. Since then, Common Cause has consistently supported Senate versions of the campaign finance bills. The Senate bills have become the standard against which the House bills are compared. Furthermore, Common Cause and David Boren's office worked closely in designing legislative strategy. As Senator Boren characterized the relationship:

> At times, Common Cause has gone after individual Senators, and that has led to a backlash, and it has jeopardized their effectiveness. I remember one time, they attacked Senator Cohen from Maine. He's a Republican, but I spoke on the floor in his defense and condemned the actions of Common Cause. That way, members remain sympathetic of me. . .
>
> In the process of negotiation, it's strategic for them to take an extreme position. . . . It's useful to me. If I'm trying to move someone from one extreme to the center, it's useful to have someone very vocal on the other extreme.[21]

As a result, Boren and Common Cause shared a mutually beneficial relationship. Common Cause was able to play the heavy—attacking individual Senators and intimating that they are under the sway of special interests. By contrast, Boren was able to look reasonable and sympathetic. As a result, the two were able to work toward a common goal of passing campaign finance reform legislation. Common Cause typically uses a media campaign to apply pressure to legislators. One notorious tactic is their habit of purchasing full-page advertisements in major newspapers around the country to attack various members for their campaign finance practices (Alston 1989).

Noticeably absent from this debate are those who favor most or all of the current system. Senator Mitch McConnell (R-Kentucky) is the most recognizable opponent to reform and public financing of any form—including both the existing presidential system and any proposals forwarded by Common Cause. He and other advocates such as Steven Stockmeyer of NABPAC argue that the public spending limits that accompany public financing proposals violate candidates' free speech. Likewise, eliminating PACs would jeopardize the rights of free association and free speech for those who contribute to them (Matlack 1991; McConnell 1991a, 1991b).

In interviews for this research, Mr. Stockmeyer and a spokesperson for Senator McConnell both expressed extreme frustration with the media coverage of their side of the issue. Although both Stockmeyer and McConnell have authored op-ed pieces, they asserted that they are rarely called on by the press to make appearances or to be interviewed. In fact, a former Senate staff member involved in this issue stated that McConnell's reputation had been enhanced because of the coverage McConnell received in *Roll Call* (a newspaper that covers Congress and enjoys wide circulation in Washington), and that *Roll Call's* reputation improved as well. As this activist stated: "McConnell only got calls from *Roll Call*, and McConnell was the only guy who would return their phone calls."[22] Chuck Alston, a reporter from *Congressional Quarterly*, agreed: "Senator Mitch McConnell has a specific point of view that he has fought tooth and nail to get expressed. And it's a valid, alternative point of view to Common Cause, but he has a tough time getting any credibility."[23]

McConnell's problem is that he has put forth a position that falls outside the area in which the issue has been defined. Common Cause has convinced the media that the current campaign finance system has problems. Therefore, the media are looking for *solutions*. Someone who argues that everything is fine simply does not have any standing. This situation is in marked contrast to the experiences of Senator Helms and former Representative Dannemeyer on AIDS policy. Although their position was not credible to the public health community, the force of public opinion behind their positions lent them some standing. By contrast, in campaign finance reform, the general public's perception of government corruption has been translated into reporters' minds in such a way that McConnell is left out in the cold.

In short, more and more members are engaging the media enterprise in an effort to shape the debate surrounding campaign finance reform. Even though it is clearly an elite agenda item, with little public interest in the specifics of campaign finance reform, media entrepreneurs still face serious difficulties in setting the agenda and defining the problem and its solution. Most of these problems surface because of the success Common Cause has enjoyed in defining the problem and its solution. Advocating a stand such as McConnell's—that the current system does not need reform—flies in the face of the public's perception of corrupt politicians and congressional ineptitude. Similarly, advocating reforms that do not include the Common Cause solution—public financing—are regarded as efforts to avoid real reform and to maintain the current system that benefits incumbents and allows them to grow rich and powerful because of special interest money.

The Elite Agenda and Adult Literacy Policy

The case of adult literacy policy continues to be an excellent example of policymaking without a media spotlight. But as in the case of campaign finance reform, activists utilizing selected media played an important role in bringing the issue to the attention of Congress and shaping the policy alternatives. Literacy activists approached both Senator Paul Simon (D-Illinois) and Representative Tom Sawyer (D-Ohio) with the idea for a literacy bill. The seed was planted in Simon's head by Jonathan Kozol, the reformer who had publicized a number of problems in the field of education, such as adult illiteracy. Similarly, it was the SIPA and the Business Coalition for Effective Literacy (BCEL) who approached Sawyer with a proposal for a House bill.

Simon took the impetus on himself to design the substance of the Senate bill and at the outset behaved like a quintessential media entrepreneur; he staged a "pseudo event."[24] Simon used his position as Chairman of the Employment and Productivity Subcommittee of the Senate Labor and Human Resources Committee to generate legislation and press coverage of the issue. In May 1989, Simon's subcommittee held a series of hearings on illiteracy; the findings of these hearings became the basis of the Senate bill in the 101st Congress. These hearings followed the classic formula for media attention to a congressional hearing. Testifying were literacy experts, including Forrest Chisman of the SIPA, prominent literacy advocates, such as Harold McGraw and Wally "Famous" Amos, and Gloria Wattles, a literacy student from Illinois. The crowning event, however, was the testimony of Dexter Manley, who was at the time a defensive end for the Washington Redskins. In a made-for-media-coverage moment, Dexter Manley stumbled through his prepared statement, describing an educational career of failure and frustration. During his testimony, this epitome of machismo broke into tears in front of the television cameras and was embraced by Wally Amos while he continued. A source close to Senator Simon remembers the event this way:

> From what I hear, that day was the biggest event in Simon's political history. And that's tough on a domestic issue. The hearing was covered absolutely all over. It was terribly dramatic testimony. Here was Manley, as tough and cocky as they come. In front of 20 television cameras, he froze and started to cry. Famous Amos, who markets himself as a personality, was there and came up and put his arm around Manley. It was incredible. You could not have staged it nearly so well.[25]

Thus Simon engaged the media enterprise for the purpose of putting the problem of adult literacy on the elite agenda (if not temporarily on the mass agenda as well). However, at that point, Simon's media efforts stopped. Designing the policy specifics was done by Simon's subcommittee staff who operated without any pressure from media coverage. This choice was astute. Whereas Simon could have generated more media attention for himself, he also would have run the risk of getting another member interested in the area and becoming involved in defining competing alternatives. By keeping a low profile, Simon helped keep the field relatively clear of competing proposals.

There are several reasons that other potential media entrepreneurs failed to enter the debate. Literacy remains the domain of activists and specialists. It does not provide much opportunity to generate a lot of national media attention. Furthermore, on the Senate side, Simon controlled the legislative machinery; any competing proposals were likely to be dead on arrival. For their part, Republicans were largely uninvolved in education issues. For those Republicans who were interested in education, the lack of enthusiasm from their colleagues is a constant source of frustration. Therefore, it is not surprising that Republicans failed to get involved in the issue at all. Thus, the agenda was set with the aid of the media, but framing the policy itself occurred in private.

The history in the House was even more subdued. As a junior member of the Education and Labor Committee, Sawyer was not in a position to conduct hearings in the House. Instead, the SIPA essentially brought a full piece of legislation to Sawyer and his staff, based on the findings in the SIPA's report, *Jump Start*. In fact, the SIPA staff admitted on several occasions that they wrote all versions of the House bill, save the final "staff conference" between the House and Senate staff members involved in the legislation. Any debate on the fine points of the legislation occurred within the literacy community. As a House staff member recalled the process:

> This is a perfect example of Congress not setting the agenda. They came to us with clear-cut legislative language based on their experience at the local level. I often proposed something that sounded like it would work well, but my literacy contacts would come back and say, "no, that won't work in the field." The bill really evolved in the last couple of years that way.[26]

The literacy lobbies approached the Senate in much the same way. After some early successes focused to improving what one activist called, "a really awful Senate bill,"[27] Simon and his staff became less receptive to the alternatives being presented by the literacy community. The final result was the compromise legislation worked out at the staff level between the House and the Senate.

In the final analysis, the SIPA and its allies were extremely successful in passing a bill they essentially designed. One reason for this success was that there were no significant battles to frame policy in any other way. The "alternatives" that were generated were simply the differences between two fairly similar Democratic proposals. There were no administration or Republican counterproposals on the table. Likewise, there was no attempt to argue that addressing illiteracy was *not* the responsibility of the federal government. Just as there was no controversy or battle for the media to report, there was also little reason for members of Congress, or others, to pursue aggressively more media attention.

The policy debate surrounding the National Literacy Act was a completely elite phenomenon. There was no massive grassroots letter-writing campaign from irate constituents. Instead, the letters that were generated came from either the ad-hoc business lobby coordinated by BCEL or literacy professionals in the field. Both groups were stakeholders who stood to benefit from the legislation. Furthermore, the legislation was not picked up in media outlets that would reach a vast majority of Americans.

Debate within the Washington community of literacy activists followed very traditional paths. The issue network did not follow the *Washington Post* or even *Congressional Quarterly* to monitor the progress of the bill. Instead, activists depended on personal communication—telephone calls and face-to-face meetings—to get information. In addition, they sought some information from the trade press, such as *Report on Literacy Programs* or *Education Week*. Generally, however, this case is a testimony to the small number of people actually involved in drafting and moving the legislation. All totaled, the number of key people involved in literacy policy—including interest groups, the Senate, and the House—was under one dozen.

The adult literacy policy area was wide open to both Senator Simon and Representative Sawyer. Both members had the opportunity to shape the policy agenda without much interference from other members, the media, or the public. Simon used his position as a subcommittee chairman first to set the agenda through the media, but then he devised specific policy alternatives in private. Sawyer did not employ any media tactics of the same scale when his bill was introduced. Nor did he aggressively pursue his policy alternatives in the media.

As in the case of campaign finance reform, problem definition and alternative selection were heavily influenced by public interest groups. In this case, the SIPA actually handed Representative Sawyer a bill. In addition, they lobbied Simon and his staff heavily in an attempt to get the Senate bill in line with the House version. Yet when Simon's staff resisted further pressure, neither Sawyer nor the literacy lobbies were able to generate outside pressure to get Simon to compromise. The lack of media attention and public interest in the policy area failed to either guide or constrain legislators and activists involved in literacy policy.

Simon's media efforts, however, were sufficient to raise awareness of the bill and to generate bipartisan support for both the House and the Senate versions of the bill. The coalitions were maintained by modest levels of new spending proposed in the legislation. The degree of media coverage, unfortunately, was not sufficient to rescue the bill from falling victim to partisan politicking at the end of the 101st Congress.

FRAMING THE DEBATE: THE PRESS SECRETARY'S JOB AND REPORTERS' REACTIONS

> Spin is a fact of life here. And these attempts are not properly reported. We are too much the object of spinners. It is convenient and easy. . . . We take what we are spoon fed, and the public is disserved. They don't get a clear picture of what is happening in Washington. For example, we don't cover the agencies, but the government really happens at the regulatory level. We report on the charade.[28]

> The media are an important tool to respond to the White House and congressional Republicans. . . . My goal in this office is to do the best job possible at making sure the reporting of Congress and the leadership is accurate and objective. I have learned that when dealing with the political opposition, you have to counter their attacks in order to achieve balance. You can't just let the story play itself out. You will be swamped by those who are seeking the media.[29]

• • •

Actually calling attention to a public problem—agenda setting—is only the initial step in shaping the policy debate. Framing the issues is equally important to this process. Media entrepreneurs also use the media to influence the way public problems are defined. After all, the definition of the problem dictates the eventual solution. However, once a member calls attention to an issue, a number of other factors can take over, and the final solution can be much different than what the member originally intended. A good example of the importance of controlling how the debate is framed is the case of former Representative Don Pease (D-Ohio) and the Federal Supplemental Compensation (FSC) program. Timothy Cook recounted how Pease had to recast his message about the FSC to make it attractive to reporters. The result, according to Cook, may have "invited political remedies Pease found less effective than his own. Successfully setting an agenda through a press strategy does not guarantee that favored solutions will become the front runners" (1989, 147).

Cook's case study shows that Pease succeeded in getting the FSC on the congressional agenda, but he lost control of how the issue is defined. In many ways, framing the debate, or *spin* as its known in the Washington lexicon, is the cornerstone of congressional involvement in the agenda-setting process. Because public issues can come onto the public agenda in so many ways—through media attention, presidential statements, historical events—members of Congress frequently are left to react to events and interpret them for their own policy goals. Thus, *spin* is a central part of the conversation in the Washington community. My interviews with press secretaries and reporters reinforce this notion. However, as the previous quotations illustrate, the opinions about spin vary dramatically depending on whether one is "spinning" or "being spun." Press secretaries see the process as getting the word out, whereas reporters sometimes feel manipulated and at times resentful.

Interpreting Events–A Press Secretary's Job

This analysis is based on interviews conducted with press secretaries of the majority and minority party leadership in both chambers of Congress. The congressional leadership is a good place to look to understand the media enterprise and its relationship to alternative selection. Leaders are in the media spotlight; they receive a lot of coverage by virtue of their position. Therefore, they exaggerate, rather than only typify, the media enterprise. Furthermore, the leadership of the party out of the White House is elevated to the position of "loyal opposition." The

Democratic leadership played this role under recent Republican administrations. Republican leaders play it today.

Both Democratic and Republican press secretaries indicated that framing issues, or putting a "spin"[30] on the political debate, is part of what they do. However, the leadership press secretaries vary widely in their approaches to their jobs and the degree to which they consider framing issues a part of their jobs. The differences mirror the differences between the leaders' styles. For example, Tony Blankley, press secretary to then House Minority Whip Newt Gingrich, said:

> [I]n the capacity as Press Secretary, it [spin] is about 90 percent of my job. I do give some background information, but mostly I engage in an effort to frame issues and to portray Gingrich's perceptions to the media. With the exception of small amounts of hard information, most reporters are working off the same bank of data. It is not hard to get information. So most of my job is analyzing and explaining.[31]

A staff person working for Gingrich's counterpart at the time, then Majority Leader Richard Gephardt (D-Missouri), concurred:

> That is virtually all I do. We work in an environment where Congress has a bad reputation. There is a media bias against Congress. We have a very Republican press apparatus. We are always in a race for interpretation to show that the Democratic role is different.[32]

On the other end of the spectrum at the time were former Speaker Foley and former Minority Leader Michel. Their press secretaries asserted that, although "spin" happens, they do not see it as a vital part of their jobs. According to Press Secretary Jeff Biggs, Foley carried into the Speakership his low-key, "almost judicial" approach to policy and a commitment to bipartisanship, which has led him to be less strident with the media. In Biggs's characterization, "Foley is not good at one-liners and sound bites like some people around here."[33]

Furthermore, Biggs was skeptical of overt attempts at agenda setting and alternative selection on the part of members of Congress. As he stated:

> Controlling the agenda is important, but less so than the principals think. Since World War II, divided government has been the rule, rather than the exception. That gives both branches (and both parties) effective vetoes. Being Speaker then requires collaboration with the executive.

A good example is the [1990] budget agreement. There was unanimity with the executive. If we had approached the agenda in terms of hard-edged interpretation, we would not have done it and it probably wouldn't have been effective. It's really hard for the Congress to control the "spin" on issues.[34]

Biggs's counterpart in then Minority Leader Bob Michel's office articulated a similar, low-key perspective:

I . . . don't think you can underestimate the role of personality and the media. My boss is really only oriented to Illinois. He doesn't seek higher office. . . . We do work hard at framing issues. We work on legislative accomplishment, too. We really do concentrate on getting things done rather than coming up with issues to run for president. And for a large degree, our issues come from the White House.[35]

The same variations between low-key and aggressive approaches to spin occur on the Senate side as well. For example, then Minority Leader Bob Dole (R-Kansas) was the single most visible member of the 101st Congress (Foote 1991). Walt Riker, Dole's Press Secretary, described "spin" this way:

It's pretty much what you do all day long. "Spin" means you are reflecting a point of view. You need to persuade people to understand. Again, spin means you're competing with another spin. It's part of participating in a political debate. When you are our number [meaning Republicans] it's even harder. So, you have to be tough and confrontational. The reporters don't like it, but we have to do our job.[36]

Dole's Democratic counterpart in the 101st Congress, Majority Leader George Mitchell (D-Maine), took a low-key approach like Speaker Foley. According to Diane Dewhirst, Mitchell's press secretary:

I guess I don't believe that spin actually exists. I give reporters more credit than that. The news doesn't dramatically change based upon what you may say. Reporters have too many sources and are too smart for that.

I do want to see Democrats in a good light and Congress in a strong position. If the Democrats are successful in pushing a problem, they will get credit for it. If they fight among each other, or make a stupid decision, or shoot themselves in the foot, it will be a bad spin. You want to emphasize the good point you want to make, then you will get a good spin.[37]

Perhaps the most surprising reaction was that from the press secretary to then Senate Minority Whip Alan Simpson (R-Wyoming). Simpson has a reputation for approachability and solid relationships with reporters, and he is also featured in Stephen Hess's analysis of the Senate and the press, *The Ultimate Insiders* (1986). As Hess wrote, "Alan Simpson obviously loves journalists. Nothing seems to give him as much pleasure as to argue with a reporter who disagrees with him" (1986, 46). Furthermore, Hess gave Simpson credit for having a very shrewd, analytical approach to press coverage, noting Simpson's desire to receive favorable coverage from several columnists in order to pass a particular piece of legislation (1986, 46).

By contrast, Stan Cannon, Simpson's press secretary, sounded more like a press secretary for a low-profile member of the House of Representatives, rather than a Senate leader, when characterizing his position:[38]

> Let me say that the most important part of this job is to serve the Senator from Wyoming. If I get a call from the *Pine Bluff Herald* and the *New York Times*, the weekly from Wyoming wins. That's the reason we're here. And with Wyoming being such a small state, we have only one reporter here in Washington . . . so we also serve as a clearinghouse for information back to the state. Al doesn't see leadership as an all-encompassing job. The state comes first.
>
> After saying that, we do try to represent the White House position on things. In the Minority party, it's all that much more important to hold solidarity together. In that situation, we don't try to spin arguments, but make them.[39]

In general, these responses correspond to the generational shift in Congress. On the one hand, both Gingrich and Gephardt are young, ambitious members—members of the media-oriented generation in Congress. They have dealt with the media their entire careers and are very comfortable with it, especially with television. Their press secretaries have a keen sense of how to use the media to get their messages out. Framing the debate—be it through sound bites or more sophisticated speeches—is a vital part of their jobs. On the other hand, both Foley and Michel served long careers in Congress. They carried their old-school philosophy toward the media into their leadership positions.

The interviews with the press secretaries to Gingrich, Gephardt, and then Majority Whip Bonior also reflect a greater understanding of the media influence in politics. Rather than asserting that spin does not exist, or that there is an objective reality that reporters will grasp and transmit, these staff members all understand that there is competition to put out their messages. Without their own efforts to frame issues favorably, the debate will automatically be cast in terms presented by their political adversaries. The media, like nature, abhor a vacuum. Therefore, the astute politician (and press secretary) must offer something to fill this vacuum in order to compete in the policy conversation.

These personality differences also provided both the Democratic and the Republican leadership the opportunity to play "good cop, bad cop." With Gephardt and Gingrich staking out the extreme positions in a public way, Foley and Michel could work out a compromise that made these leaders look bipartisan and reasonable in comparison. In the 104th Congress, the media entrepreneurs have moved to the pinnacles of the leadership ladders. It will be interesting to see how Gephardt and Gingrich will act now.

Demographically, the Senate leaders profiled here are a puzzle. These members reinforce the notion that media entrepreneurship is a personal choice. Dole is the most obvious choice to be characterized as a media entrepreneur; yet he is the oldest of the leaders profiled and has the longest congressional career.[40] By contrast, Mitchell is 10 years Dole's junior and had only served in the Senate since 1980. Yet his press secretary's comments reflect that Mitchell takes a much more passive approach to framing issues and agenda setting than Dole. Simpson remains an enigma. Although no stranger to controversy and the public eye, Simpson clearly believed that his duty as a Republican leader was to close ranks behind the then Republican President when he is not courting the Wyoming press. Simpson's profile is more like Mitchell than Dole; he is two years older than Mitchell and has served in the Senate two years longer.

Nonetheless, Simpson and Mitchell are both about 10 years older than Gingrich and Gephardt, although the length of service in Congress for all four men is nearly identical. If these four cases are any indication, media entrepreneurs are not likely to be found frequently among members over age 50. Dole, of course, stands as proof that media entrepreneurship transcends all demographic considerations.

Reporters' Perspective

Reporters are perhaps even more sensitive to issues surrounding spin than are the press secretaries. After all, they are the primary intended audience for such efforts. The way reporters write or broadcast their stories will influence public and elite opinion and have a huge impact on the policy debate from that point on. Whereas press secretaries were equivocal in their evaluations and perceptions of "spin," the reporters interviewed for this research were generally dissatisfied and suspicious of such efforts.

One veteran Washington reporter had developed an elaborate theory about the unique relationship between the press and policymakers in Washington. One manifestation of what he saw as an unhealthy, close-knit relationship were attempts at "spin." In his words:

> Spin control ranks up with trial balloons and anonymous sources as a third unique factor in the way that the press in Washington work. It's another distinction of newsgathering in Washington.
>
> It happens unceasingly and incandescently. It surrounds all events and lives. Spin control is an incredible and understandable smoke screen used by newsmakers in the beltway, intended to shape how their news is reported by journalists.[41]

Other reporters take a more resigned view of the situation. As Eleanor Clift of *Newsweek* magazine related:

> As a reporter, I have to be aware of the spin a politician is putting on an issue. Let's use the House Bank scandal as an example. . . . Most reporters understand Foley's attempts to put the scandal into perspective. But reporters understand that it won't sell beyond the beltway. . . .
>
> Gingrich and his attempt to use the scandal to get to the Democrats on issues will be discounted equally. . . . Reporters have to put up their own filters when reporting this issue.[42]

James Wooten of ABC News agreed. In his assessment:

> I think it's fair. The media get used all the time. Local TV will be used by local government reformers to frame issues. And it certainly exists on Capitol Hill, and it happens all the time on networks and the presidential campaign. . . .
>
> I don't object to spin or being used. We are dealing with professional people. They realize that you're not there to be a container to pour their perspective onto the American people.[43]

Reporters varied in their approaches to dealing with efforts at spin. Two approaches surfaced as the most common way to deal with spin. The first was to present both sides' interpretations to the American public. In this case, even handedness and equal time substitute for critical analysis and minimize the risk of picking the "wrong" side to report. Of course, there are important variations between media. Television, with its truncated format, is much more dependent on simply repeating points of view than are newsmagazines, in which there is more opportunity for thoughtful and thorough analysis. Similarly, news wires, with their frequent deadlines and clientele that cross the political spectrum, also tend to lean to even-handed reporting over any sort of interpretation by the reporter. News consumers are then left to make their own decisions.

Second, a number of reporters see spin as a product of the staff, not the principal. For example, James Wooten of ABC News, stated that "I deal with members, not staff. It simplifies life and reduces the amount of spin to which I am subjected."[44] Wooten was not alone in his perception that spin is the product of staffs', not members' efforts. This analysis seems incredibly naive and removed from a great deal of reality on Capitol Hill. First, it assumes that members are not capable or do not engage in political spin. On the contrary, the one purpose of the media enterprise is to involve the *member* in the policy debate—not the staff. Second, it fails to recognize the true role of staff on Capitol Hill. Staff do not act autonomously. Rather, they accurately reflect their members' wishes and perceptions. If they do not, the staff member is out of a job. Thus, staff do not "spin" unless their bosses want them to.

Nonetheless, the press's attempts do seem to be paying off if press secretary dissatisfaction with the coverage their members receive is any indication. Press secretaries indicated that their bosses had a very good, very amicable relationship with the national press. However, there was also a marked pattern of discontent with the eventual coverage they do receive. The most aggressive press secretaries characterized their jobs as an unending battle against a better equipped partisan enemy. Furthermore, they were at the time vying for the attention of a press corps that was more receptive to their opposition's message. Numerous Republicans related that they believe the media carry a liberal (i.e., Democratic) bias. Therefore, they thought they had a much more difficult time getting fair or favorable coverage. Democrats, on the other hand, saw themselves as an underdog against the overwhelming media machine of the Republican White House and its congressional Republican allies. They believed they were engaged in a losing battle to communicate their message. The White House bully pulpit is strong. When Democrats gained control of the presidency, Republicans in Congress had even greater obstacles to overcome. They copied Jim Traficant (D-Ohio) and turned to "1 minutes," where they coordinated efforts to criticize the Clinton administration (Gugliotta 1994).

The first lesson here is that attempts at spin are not always successful. Rather, it takes a concerted, coordinated, and consistent effort in order to capture the media's attention and to compete against the same efforts generated by others. Without these attempts to frame issues, however, only one side of the story and one interpretation will be presented. Policy alternatives will be determined by default.

Furthermore, from the reporters' perspective, there is no particularly good way to deal with spin or to overcome the potentially duplicitous nature of politicians' efforts to frame debate. For example, simply presenting the Democratic and the Republican perspectives does not help the news consumer evaluate the relative validity of each position. Nor does it offer any other interpretations of events. The latter concern is important for both a Washington-based audience and the general public. The Washington audience, because it is more politically astute, is actually *more* susceptible to agenda-setting and alternative-selection influences from the media. Because they consume several news sources a day, media's influence on these actors will be *magnified*, not tempered.

AGENDA SETTING AND MEDIA ENTREPRENEURS: SURVEY ANALYSIS

Unquestionably, the case studies and the other interview data provide a number of valuable insights into the complexities of using the media in the agenda-setting process. Nonetheless, one may wonder to what degree these efforts are typical of the full Congress, or even of media entrepreneurs within Congress. By survey analysis, this section places these qualitative data into the larger context of the whole Congress.

As noted earlier, this chapter focuses on the second research question: When in the policy process do media entrepreneurs engage the media enterprise? The survey data strongly reinforce the argument that agenda setting and alternative selection are the key stages of the policy process. First of all, media entrepreneurs and nonentrepreneurs alike agree that agenda setting is the stage of the policy process in which members are most likely to use the media to influence public policy. The full set of respondents also ranked agenda setting's companion—framing the terms of debate—as the second most likely point in the policy process for members of Congress to go public. Each of these two options received mean scores over 3.7, indicating strong support across the board (see Table 4.1).

Second, the survey data provide more insight into the nature of media entrepreneurs. Here we find that even though there is consensus that agenda setting is the prime point in the policy process when members use the media to influence policy, media entrepreneurs are even more likely than their counterparts to consider agenda setting a purpose of the media enterprise. All three types of media entrepreneurs—the pool of media entrepreneurs, the likely media entrepreneurs, and the

Table 4.1. Perceived Importance of Media in Agenda Setting—All Respondents.

Question 7: The media may be used at various stages in the legislative process. When do you see members soliciting media attention for their policy proposals? (Please evaluate each item according to the following scale: 1 = very infrequently, 5 = very frequently.)

Variable Name	Mean Score	Median	N
Agenda setting	3.925	4	146
Framing the terms of debate	3.715	4	144
Respond to proposals from the White House	3.405	4	143
Influence interest groups	3.070	3	142
Respond to proposals from federal agencies	3.028	3	143
Generate floor support	3.021	3	141
Move bill in committee	2.599	2	142
Generate support in the other chamber	2.342	2	143

Source: Data compiled by author.

hard-core media entrepreneurs—are more likely than their comparison groups to rank agenda setting as a likely target for media entrepreneurs (see Table 4.2).

The same phenomenon is observed in alternative selection. All three groups of media entrepreneurs are more likely to see framing the terms of debate as a likely point in the process for members to use the media enterprise than their comparison groups. As in the case of agenda setting, the degree of statistical significance does not vary much between groups of media entrepreneurs (see Table 4.3).

Media entrepreneurs are also more likely to see the media as a useful tool to respond to proposals from the White House and to respond to federal agencies. In the case of responding to the White House, the difference is statistically significant for both the pool of media entrepreneurs and the likely media entrepreneurs. In terms of responding to federal agencies, the difference is statistically significant for the pool of media entrepreneurs, but the difference only approaches statistical significance for the likely media entrepreneurs. In both cases, the differences are not statistically significant for the hard-core media entrepreneurs. This result is probably due to the fact that some respondents classified as media entrepreneurs in one analysis move to the comparison group when narrower definitions of media entrepreneur were used. As a result, the differences between the groups gets smaller, and patterns observed become insignificant (see Table 4.4 and Table 4.5).

Regression analysis yields similar results. As respondents register a higher score on the media attitude variable, their perception of the importance of the media in agenda setting increases. The model, with no controlling variables, is reasonably predictive (R^2 = 0.24).[45] Similarly, a respondent's score on the "attitude" variable is a strong predictor of his

Table 4.2. Influence of Attitude on Perceptions of Media Effectiveness in Agenda Setting (t-test).

Variable: Agenda Setting

Respondent Group	Mean	Pearson's Correlation | r |	N
Comparison Group[a]	3.5522		67
Pool of Media Entrepreneurs	4.2405*****	0.3985*****	79
Likely Media Entrepreneurs	4.0408*****	0.3545*****	42
Hard-core Media Entrepreneurs	4.3636***	0.2148***	22

[a]The mean for the only narrowest definition of the comparison group is reported here. However, each t-test was conducted with the appropriate comparison group.

***$p \leq 0.01$

*****$p \leq 0.0001$

Source: Data compiled by author.

Table 4.3. Influence of Attitude on Perceptions of Media Effectiveness on Alternative Selection (t-test).

Variable: Frame the terms of debate

Respondent Group	Mean	Pearson's Correlation | r |	N
Comparison Group[a]	3.3881		67
Pool of Media Entrepreneurs	4.0000*****	0.3639*****	77
Likely Media Entrepreneurs	4.0488***	0.2508***	41
Hard-core Media Entrepreneurs	4.0952**	0.1872**	21

[a]The mean for the only narrowest definition of the comparison group is reported here. However, each t-test was conducted with the appropriate comparison group.

**$p \leq 0.05$

***$p \leq 0.01$

****$p \leq 0.001$

*****$p \leq 0.0001$

Source: Data compiled by author.

Table 4.4. Influence of Attitude on Perceptions of Media Effectiveness on Responding to White House (t-test).

Variable: Respond to proposals from the White House

Respondent Group	Mean	Pearson's Correlation $|r|$	N
Comparison Group[a]	3.1970		66
Pool of Media Entrepreneurs	3.5844**	0.2070***	77
Likely Media Entrepreneurs	3.7561**	0.2382**	41
Hard-core Media Entrepreneurs	3.5238	0.0526	21

[a]The mean for the only narrowest definition of the comparison group is reported here. However, each t-test was conducted with the appropriate comparison group.

** $p \leq 0.05$

*** $p \leq 0.01$

Source: Data compiled by author.

Table 4.5. Influence of Attitude on Perceptions of Media Effectiveness on Responding to Federal Agencies (t-test).

Variable: Respond to proposals from federal agencies

Respondent Group	Mean	Pearson's Correlation $|r|$	N
Comparison Group[a]	2.8209		67
Pool of Media Entrepreneurs	3.2105**	0.2025**	76
Likely Media Entrepreneurs	3.2439*	0.1426*	41
Hard-core Media Entrepreneurs	3.1428	0.0496	21

[a]The mean for the only narrowest definition of the comparison group is reported here. However, each t-test was conducted with the appropriate comparison group.

* $p \leq 0.10$

** $p \leq 0.05$

Source: Data compiled by author.

or her opinion of the media's role in framing the terms of debate ($R^2 = 0.14$). The relationship holds in terms of responding to the White House, responding to federal agencies, generating floor support, and generating support in the other chamber. These models were statistically significant, and the relationship was as expected. The predictive ability of these models, however, is quite small (See Table 4.6).[46]

Table 4.6. Regression Analysis of Attitude Toward Agenda Setting.

Variable Name	Parameter Estimate	Standard Error	p
Agenda setting			
Intercept	1.6636	0.3453	0.0001
Attitude	0.6002	0.0901	0.0001
$R^2 = 0.2355$			
Framing the terms of debate			
Intercept	2.0300	0.3580	0.0001
Attitude	0.4483	0.0936	0.0001
$R^2 = 0.1390$			
Respond to proposals from the White House			
Intercept	2.5400	0.4228	0.0001
Attitude	0.2302	0.1105	0.0390
$R^2 = 0.0299$			
Respond to proposals from agencies			
Intercept	2.1713	0.4357	0.0001
Attitude	0.2279	0.1139	0.0474
$R^2 = 0.0276$			
Generate floor support			
Intercept	1.3811	0.4936	0.0059
Attitude	0.4361	0.1290	0.0009
$R^2 = 0.0760$			
Generate support in the other house			
Intercept	0.8753	0.4136	0.0361
Attitude	0.3894	0.1079	0.0004
$R^2 = 0.0845$			

Source: Data compiled by author.

These phenomena help address the question: "Who are the media entrepreneurs?" Media entrepreneurs, like zebras, can be identified by their stripes. In this case, they are identifiable by their unmistakable faith in the effectiveness of using the media to set the agenda and to frame the content of the policy debate.

Although the differences between the media entrepreneurs and other members are interesting and theoretically important, the variations between definitions of media entrepreneurs are perhaps more fascinating. The pool of potential media entrepreneurs is slightly more likely to cite responding to the White House or federal agencies as potential reasons to use the media than would likely media entrepreneurs or hard-core media entrepreneurs. One reason for this difference may be experience in media enterprise. Old hands at the media enterprise game may have a more sophisticated understanding of exactly which situations are ripe for the media entrepreneur, and responding to the White House or federal agencies may be perceived as the domain of party leaders or subcommittee chairmen and ranking members. Publicly bucking the party leadership (or the administration) is difficult for any member. Technical areas, when agencies come into play, require credibility and specialization that an aspiring media entrepreneur may not carry.

The open-ended questions also add some insights into the reasons that media entrepreneurs try to influence the agenda. Most frequently, respondents replied that their members were likely to consider the media enterprise when they sponsored legislation of national importance. A second oft-mentioned reason is that members will use the media to establish themselves as "players" in an issue area. Agenda setting is an opportune time to establish credibility in order to be invited into the major policy negotiations in an issue area (see Table 4.7).

Furthermore, the responses to the open-ended questions also indicate that the media entrepreneurs understand that there are no guaranteed results from these efforts. When asked to evaluate the success of their national media campaigns, a preponderance of the respondents indicated that their efforts were moderately successful. Responses such as: "two in five," "B+/B-," or "fifty-fifty" were typical. Importantly, however, another 23 percent of the respondents felt that these efforts were very successful, especially in areas of their committee or subcommittee jurisdiction (see Table 4.8).

These results indicate that members have a sophisticated understanding of the complexities of the policy process and the uncertainty of

Table 4.7. Reasons Cited for Pursuing Media Strategies (Frequencies).

Question 17b: Under what circumstances does your office decide to use a media strategy [for the purpose of attracting support for specific legislation?

Response (volunteered)	Percentage	N
When bill is of national significance	28.2	20
Part of legislative strategy	16.9	12
Increase member's standing in area	9.9	7
Increase awareness of problem	5.6	4
Whenever possible	11.3	8
Varies	4.2	3

Source: Data compiled by author.

Table 4.8. Level of Success Achieved through Media Strategies (Frequencies).

Question 17d: In general, how successful were these efforts?

Response (volunteered)	Percentage	N
Moderately successful	55.8	29
Very successful	23.0	12
Success varies	19.2	10
Not very successful	3.8	2
Other response	11.5	6

Source: Data compiled by author.

using the media to influence the policy debate. However, even though they understand their chances for success are not overwhelming, the media entrepreneur remains interested in pursuing these strategies and opportunities. This willingness to approach the national media in an attempt to shape the policy debate is testament to the fact that the media are crucial to policy development, even in the close confines of the Washington community. Generating media attention raises the profile of the member and has a real chance to influence the eventual policy outcome.

CONCLUSIONS AND IMPLICATIONS

What do these disparate elements relate to us about the media enterprise and the process of agenda setting and alternative selection? First, in response to the research question dealing with when to go public, all of the survey data, case studies, and interviews clearly indicate that agenda setting is the most important part of the policy process for the media entrepreneur. All respondents see agenda setting as the most powerful opportunity for members of Congress to influence the policy process. The survey analysis lends another valuable insight into the media entrepreneur's personality. As a group, they are even more likely than their counterparts to see agenda setting and framing the terms of debate as fertile ground for the media enterprise.

Second, the case study and interview data from leadership press secretaries indicate that making laws goes hand in hand with making news. Even in the case of adult literacy, there was a lot of media attention during the Senate hearings on illiteracy. In the case of the Persian Gulf War debate, much of the coverage members received was unsolicited and sometimes inadvertent. Instead, it was a product of the newsworthiness of the developments themselves. Similarly, the press secretaries and the reporters both indicate that spin—attempts to define issues favorably—is part and parcel of the policy conversation.

Third, attempts to use the media enterprise to set the agenda or define the terms of debate encounter important limitations. This circumstance holds true regardless of whether an issue falls on the elite agenda or the mass agenda. For cases on the mass agenda, the demands of public opinion had to be accommodated in some way. In the case of AIDS, real concern about possible threats to the public from AIDS or HIV-infected health care workers influenced the actions of the Senate, the House, and the CDC. In the case of the Persian Gulf War, policy options were limited by historical events and general public support for the administration's policy in the region.

Campaign finance reform in one sense demonstrates both the power and the limitations of the media enterprise in terms of setting the elite agenda. The myriad reforms proposed in legislation illustrate the way members can use their positions to influence policy definition. However, Common Cause's continued attention to campaign finance issues and its successful media campaigns have transformed it into a veto force. They set out to define the problem and its solution, and their interest has lasted the longest. By comparison, many members look like "Johnny-Come-Latelys" to the policy debate.

Similarly, the literacy case study shows the success and frustrations that can be encountered when choosing alternatives without the spotlight of media attention. In this case, however, the force behind the legislation was the lobbyists. The SIPA worked hand in hand with the House staff to define a policy outcome that closely mirrored the SIPA's own policy recommendations. However, the lobbyists encountered intransigence on the Senate side. Without any media attention to focus the issue or to apply pressure on these politicians, the lobbyists were unable to persuade the Senate to adopt their recommendations.

Despite these caveats, agenda setting and framing the policy debate still offer the media entrepreneur the greatest potential to influence the policy process. An astute media entrepreneur will understand that this process is complex, and that many other factors will also shape the agenda. The astute media entrepreneur will take these circumstances into account and adapt the media enterprise accordingly. Furthermore, the astute media entrepreneur will also understand that success in these efforts is not guaranteed. Sometimes a media entrepreneur will receive favorable media attention and succeed in shifting the policy debate, and sometimes he or she will not.

ENDNOTES

1. Interview, March 9, 1992.
2. Interview, September 27, 1991.
3. Interview, March 9, 1992.
4. Interview, August 9, 1991.
5. Interview, March 23, 1992.
6. Interview, March 23, 1992.
7. Interview, April 30, 1992.
8. Interestingly, the *Wall Street Journal* carried no op-eds concerning the Persian Gulf crisis by members of Congress during this period.
9. The suit was eventually dropped by a federal judge, who declined to rule based on the fact that Congress itself had not addressed this issue. This particular issue in the Persian Gulf debate was diffused when the Bush administration called on Congress to vote on the authorization of force.
10. Interview, January 22, 1991.
11. Interview, February 12, 1991.
12. Stockmeyer Interview, November 3, 1991.
13. Fred Wertheimer had an interesting response to this situation. He asserted that public opposition to public financing is fueled by its experience with the presidential system. Wertheimer charged that trying to finance a campaign fund through a tax checkoff is a bad idea. Furthermore, the reason for the financial problems confronted by the fund is not a lack of public interest. Rather, it is because the size of the contributions have not increased since the fund was created, whereas the cost of campaigns has grown exponentially.
14. Other groups involved in this effort include the Public Interest Research Group, the Center for Responsive Politics, Public Citizen, and Congress Watch.
15. Wertheimer Interview, March 10, 1992.
16. Interview, November 3, 1991.
17. Interview, October 29, 1991.
18. Interview, February 22, 1991.
19. Their specific methods are discussed in a later chapter.
20. Interview, April 25, 1991.
21. Interview, June 23, 1992.
22. Interview, April 25, 1991.
23. Interview, March 5, 1991.
24. In the current media lexicon, a *pseudo event* is an event staged largely for the benefit of generating media attention. In a congressional context, hearings featuring Hollywood celebrities are a favorite tactic. On a campaign trail, it commonly includes favorable visuals to facilitate television coverage.
25. Interview, August 7, 1991.
26. Interview, May 13, 1991.
27. Interview, May 29, 1991.

28. Interview with Bob Franken, Congressional Correspondent for CNN, March 23, 1992.
29. Interview with Mike Freedman, Press Secretary for Representative David Bonior, Majority Whip, March 23, 1992.
30. In all cases, the term *spin* was used in the interviews with press secretaries and reporters. However, it was usually tempered with a phrase such as "without using it in a negative way, to what degree does 'spin' or attempts to frame issues become a part of your job?"
31. Interview, May 20, 1991.
32. Interview, June 11, 1991.
33. Interview, May 17, 1991.
34. Interview, May 17, 1991.
35. Interview, May 20, 1991.
36. Interview, July 11, 1991.
37. Interview, August 20, 1991.
38. Despite the professed local orientation, Simpson was the 36th most visible member of the 101st Congress (Foote 1991). In fact, this interview came shortly after Simpson was roundly criticized in the national media for his characterization of CNN reporter Peter Arnett as an "Iraqi sympathizer" for Arnett's coverage from Baghdad during the height of the Persian Gulf War.

    Simpson does have a reputation as a firebrand. Hess also noted (1988, 46) that Simpson has a unique way to avoid being quoted by reporters. He simply responds to questions in such ribald language that no journalist will dare quote him.
39. Interview, July 12, 1991.
40. Dole was first elected in 1968 (Duncan 1989, 552).
41. Interview, March 12, 1992.
42. Interview, April 21, 1992.
43. Interview, March 9, 1992.
44. Interview, March 9, 1992.
45. Regression analysis conducted with several control variables failed to improve the model's predictive ability. In fact, in all models but one, the "attitude" variable was the only significant independent variable in the model. The control variables included were: 1991 ADA score, age, party, house of Congress, gender, and race. In one case—generating floor support—the member's race was also statistically significant. However, this result could be an artifact of the small number of respondents working for members who are not white.
46. The low R^2 values in these regression results are probably due in part to the problems inherent in conducting regression analysis on ordinal-level data.

5

Building Legislative Coalitions with the Media Enterprise

The media entrepreneur has the greatest opportunity to influence the policy process at the agenda-setting and alternative-selection stages of the process. However, the media entrepreneur does not simply stop using the media enterprise as the legislative process churns along. Using the media to influence policy at later stages of the process is certainly more difficult. Nonetheless, it is important to recognize and analyze these efforts. This chapter analyzes how media entrepreneurs see more potential than their counterparts to use the media to influence floor votes, generate support in the other chamber, and move legislation through committees. This chapter also discusses the audience the media enterprise is intended to reach as well as important differences between media entrepreneurs and their colleagues who are less media oriented.

It is important to remember that media entrepreneurs are practical politicians acting within the legislative environment. As a result, they are keenly aware of the importance of more traditional approaches to building legislative coalitions. Personal contacts and support from the party leadership, the White House, and interest groups are also important ingredients to the media entrepreneur's successful efforts to build legislative coalitions. Nonetheless, media entrepreneurs still give more weight to various media strategies than do their counterparts who use the media less frequently.

USING THE MEDIA DURING THE LEGISLATIVE PROCESS

The full group of survey respondents agreed that agenda setting and issue framing are the main reasons members of Congress turn to media strategies. Yet the notion that the media might be used to influence other stages of the legislative process received remarkably less support from the respondents. For example, moving a bill in committee received an average response of 2.60[1] (*mdn* = 2), generating floor support received a mean response of 3.02 (*mdn* = 3), and generating support in the other House received a mean score of only 2.34 (*mdn* = 2). These responses are lukewarm at best, but they accurately reflect the political realities of Congress. The legislative process is extremely complex. Even after two decades of reform, committee chairmen and party leaders still exercise a great deal of personal autonomy when determining the legislative agenda. Therefore, personal contacts are considered the most effective means to capture the attention of these important members (see Table 5.1).

Table 5.1. Perceived Importance of Media in the Legislative Process (Frequencies).

Question 7: The media may be used at various stages in the legislative process. When do you see members soliciting media attention for their policy proposals? (Please evaluate each item according to the following scale: 1 = very infrequently, 5 = very frequently.)

Variable Name	Mean	Median	N
Agenda setting	3.925	4	146
Framing the terms of debate	3.715	4	144
Respond to proposals from the White House	3.405	4	143
Influence interest groups	3.070	3	142
Respond to proposals from federal agencies	3.028	3	143
Generate floor support	3.021	3	141
Move bill in committee	2.599	2	142
Generate support in the other chamber	2.342	2	143

Source: Data compiled by author.

Media Entrepreneurs and the Legislative Process

Media entrepreneurs, however, view the legislative process somewhat differently. Although they do not dispute the importance of individual contacts in the course of the legislative process, they do differ in their perceptions of how useful the media can be in terms of influencing the legislative process. First of all, the pool of media entrepreneurs are more likely than their comparison group to see the media as an effective tool to move bills in committee, to generate support before a floor vote, and to generate support in the other chamber of Congress.

Similar patterns, although somewhat weaker, also are exhibited in stricter definitions of media entrepreneurs. The likely media entrepreneurs are more apt to use the media to move bills in committee and to generate floor support. The hard-core media entrepreneurs demonstrate a tendency to use the media to generate floor support and to generate support in the other chamber (see Tables 5.2, 5.3, and 5.4).[2]

These results are not as mixed as they might appear. Instead, the tendency for the statistical relationship to weaken as the definition of media entrepreneurs narrows is a result of some respondents who were classified as media entrepreneurs being moved to the comparison group. Therefore, the differences between the control group and media entrepreneurs narrow. This general pattern makes the findings for generating support in the other chamber even more interesting. The difference between media entrepreneurs and the comparison group is significant for the pool of media entrepreneurs and the hard-core media entre-

Table 5.2. Media Entrepreneurs' Perceptions of Media Effectiveness in Legislative Process (t-test).

Variable Name: Move Bill in Committee			
Respondent Group	Mean	Pearson's Correlation |r|	N
Comparison Group[a]	2.3939		66
Pool of Media Entrepreneurs	2.7763**	0.1881**	76
Likely Media Entrepreneurs	2.8250*	0.1398*	40
Hard-core Media Entrepreneurs	2.7500	0.0604	20

[a]The mean for the only narrowest definition of the comparison group is reported here. However, each t-test was conducted with the appropriate comparison group.

* $p \leq 0.10$

** $p \leq 0.05$

Source: Data compiled by author.

preneurs (the narrowest and the widest definitions used here). But the relationship is not statistically significant for the intermediate group— the likely media entrepreneurs. More importantly, the pattern holds true for the likely media entrepreneurs, even though the difference is not statistically significant (see Table 5.4).

Table 5.3. Media Entrepreneurs' Perceptions of Media Effectiveness to Generate Floor Support (t-test).

Variable Name: Generate Floor Support

Respondent Group	Mean (t-test)	Pearson's Correlation |r|	N
Comparison Group[a]	3.2667		75
Pool of Media Entrepreneurs	2.7424***	0.2348***	76
Likely Media Entrepreneurs	3.3750**	0.1999**	40
Hard-core Media Entrepreneurs	3.4091*	0.1497*	22

[a]The mean for the only narrowest definition of the comparison group is reported here. However, each t-test was conducted with the appropriate comparison group.

*$p \leq 0.10$

**$p \leq 0.05$

***$p \leq 0.01$

Source: Data compiled by author.

Table 5.4. Media Entrepreneurs' Perceptions of Media Effectiveness to Generate Support in Other Chamber (t-test).

Variable Name: Generate Support in Other Chamber

Respondent Group	Mean (t-test)	Pearson's Correlation |r|	N
Comparison Group[a]	2.0923		65
Pool of Media Entrepreneurs	2.5513***	0.2433***	78
Likely Media Entrepreneurs	2.5122	0.1144	41
Hard-core Media Entrepreneurs	2.7727**	0.1952**	22

[a]The mean for the only narrowest definition of the comparison group is reported here. However, each t-test was conducted with the appropriate comparison group.

**$p \leq 0.05$

***$p \leq 0.01$

Source: Data compiled by author.

Senator Jesse Helms's efforts to influence policy regarding AIDS testing for health care workers described in the last chapter can also be applied in this context. Because AIDS is an ever present item on the health care agenda, this case also provides support for the idea that a member in one house of Congress can use the media to influence the actions of the *other* house. In this case, Helms was clearly successful in getting the House Subcommittee on Health and the Environment to consider his legislation.

Other case study data lend further evidence of this phenomenon. The unsuccessful overtures made by literacy activists to the editorial boards of two major papers was clearly an effort to put pressure on the Senate Democratic leadership to bring the literacy bill to a floor vote. Similarly, Common Cause regularly launches an aggressive media effort as campaign finance bills come to the floor of either chamber, move through conference, or approach other stages of the policy process.

These results coincide with the hypothesis that media entrepreneurs differ from their colleagues. In fact, media entrepreneurs differ in their views of other legislative strategies unrelated to the media, as well as their views of media strategies. For example, while remaining the single most important legislative strategy, personal contacts are found to be *less* important to the pool of media entrepreneurs than they are to the comparison group.[3] Similarly, hard-core media entrepreneurs consider federal agency contacts as a less important legislative strategy than do the rest of the respondents (see Table 5.6 and 5.7).

Despite these small differences, media entrepreneurs do function in the larger context of Congress. This work confirms other research that indicates that passing legislation is an intensely personal process. It frequently depends on personal contacts, endorsements from party leadership, and other inside strategies to convince other members to consider, cosponsor, and support legislation (Davidson and Oleszek 1981; Jewell and Patterson 1986).

THE IMPORTANCE OF THE MEDIA AS A LEGISLATIVE STRATEGY

We know that media entrepreneurs consider the media more important than their counterparts. However, an equally important question is: How do media entrepreneurs rank media strategies in comparison to other legislative strategies? In this regard, media entrepreneurs differ little from their counterparts who use the media less. They reinforce the existing political science literature that describes the importance of personal relationships and constituent relations in the modern Congress (see, for example, Davidson and Oleszek 1981; Hinkley 1988, 220-226).

First of all, the full group of respondents ranked personal contacts and contacts from constituents as the most important ways to generate support for legislation, receiving mean scores of 4.678 (*mdn*=5) and 4.094 (*mdn*=4),[4] respectively. Support from party leadership, interest groups, and the White House also were ranked fairly highly by the respondents (see Table 5.5).

All of these responses outranked the three media-related options. The strongest of the options was "op-ed articles" (m = 2.860; mdn = 3) followed by "television interviews" (m = 2.760; mdn = 3) and "news articles and press releases" (m = 2.820; mdn = 3). However, with mean scores below 3.0, these results indicate that most respondents considered them fairly ineffective legislative strategies, especially in comparison to the other strategies (see Table 5.5). The media responses taken as an aggregate are doubtlessly more important than any one single media option. The aggregate value of media exposure is probably comparable to getting support for any group outside Congress, such as the administration or interest groups, which enjoyed mean scores in the 3.0-3.5 range.

Regression analysis supports these findings. As respondents' scores on the attitude variable increased, so did their view of the effectiveness of television interviews, op-eds and news articles and press releases. The R^2 values of the television interviews and op-ed articles were above 0.10 (R^2 = 0.11 and R^2 = 0.13, respectively; see Table 5.8).

Table 5.5. Perceived Importance of Legislative Strategies—All Respondents.

Question 9: Comparatively speaking, how effective are the following approaches in generating support for policy proposals within Congress? (Please evaluate each item according to the following scale: 1 = not effective 5 = very effective.)

Variable Name	Mean	Median	N
Personal contacts	4.678	5	149
Contacts from constituents	4.094	4	149
Party leadership	3.893	4	150
Interest group support	3.613	4	150
Contacts from the White House	3.197	3	147
Op-ed articles	2.860	3	150
News articles and press releases	2.820	3	150
Television interviews	2.760	3	150
Contacts from political action committees	2.729	3	147
Contacts from federal agencies	2.725	3	149

Source: Data compiled by author.

Table 5.6. Personal Contacts as a Legislative Strategy: Differences Between Media Entrepreneurs and Other Members (t-test).

Variable Name: Personal Contacts

Respondent Group	Mean (t-test)	Pearson's Correlation |r|	N
Comparison Group[a]	4.7714		70
Pool of Media Entrepreneurs	4.5949*	0.1543*	79
Likely Media Entrepreneurs	4.6829	0.0055	41
Hard-core Media Entrepreneurs	4.7272	0.0360	22

[a]The mean for the only narrowest definition of the comparison group is reported here. However, each t-test was conducted with the appropriate comparison group.
*$p \leq 0.10$
Source: Data compiled by author.

Table 5.7. Federal Agency Contacts as a Legislative Strategy: Differences Between Media Entrepreneurs and Other Members (t-test).

Variable Name: Federal Agency Contacts

Respondent Group	Mean (t-test)	Pearson's Correlation |r|	N
Comparison Group[a]	2.6755		67
Pool of Media Entrepreneurs	2.7910	0.0671	80
Likely Media Entrepreneurs	2.7381	0.0075	42
Hard-core Media Entrepreneurs	2.3636*	0.1774*	22

[a]The mean for the only narrowest definition of the comparison group is reported here. However, each t-test was conducted with the appropriate comparison group.
*$p \leq 0.10$
Source: Data compiled by author.

Media Entrepreneurs and Media Strategies

Media entrepreneurs continue to distinguish themselves from the full set of respondents by their strong faith in the media's efficacy. Across the board, media entrepreneurs consider television interviews, op-eds, and news articles and press releases more powerful tools to build legislative coalitions than do their counterparts. This finding is consistent with the earlier finding reported in this chapter—just as media entrepreneurs find the media more useful in influencing the legislative process,

Table 5.8. Regression Analysis of Attitude Toward Media as a Legislative Tool.

Variable Name	Parameter Estimate	Standard Error	p
Television interviews			
Intercept	1.0634	0.3609	0.0037
Attitude	0.4528	0.0946	0.0001
$R^2 = 0.1340$			
Op-ed articles			
Intercept	1.3598	0.3537	0.0002
Attitude	0.4004	0.0928	0.0001
$R^2 = 0.1118$			
News articles and press releases			
Intercept	1.6812	0.4071	0.0001
Attitude	0.3040	0.1068	0.0050
$R^2 = 0.0519$			

Source: Data compiled by author.

here they see the media as a more effective means to gain the support of specific legislators.

For instance, the pool of media entrepreneurs consider television interviews, op-eds, and news articles and press releases more important than do their colleagues. The relationship is not only statistically significant, the differences are at times quite dramatic. For example, the comparison group gave television interviews a mean score of 2.471. By contrast, media entrepreneurs produced a mean score of 3.025—a difference of more than 0.5 on a 5-point scale (see Table 5.9, 5.10, and 5.11).

The same pattern remains consistent when applied to the stricter definitions of media entrepreneurs. Likely media entrepreneurs also find television interviews, op-eds, and news articles and press releases to be more important to build legislative coalitions than their comparison group. Likewise, hard-core media entrepreneurs also demonstrate statistically significant differences from their comparison group for television interviews. The direction of the relationship remains the same for op-ed and news articles; however, in the latter cases, the relationships cease to be statistically significant (see Tables 5.7, 5.8, and 5.9). The reason the relationships wane is that as the definition of media entrepreneurs narrows, more respondents shift from being classified as media entrepreneurs to the comparison group. Therefore, the differences between the two groups narrow. As the number of respondents classi-

Table 5.9. Media Entrepreneurs' Perceptions of Television Interviews' Effectiveness in Building Legislative Coalitions (t-test).

Variable Name: Television interviews

Respondent Group	Mean (t-test)	Pearson's Correlation | r |	N
Comparison Group[a]	2.4714		70
Pool of Media Entrepreneurs	3.0125*****	0.3078*****	80
Likely Media Entrepreneurs	3.0952***	0.2384***	42
Hard-core Media Entrepreneurs	3.0909*	0.1564*	22

[a]The mean for the only narrowest definition of the comparison group is reported here. However, each t-test was conducted with the appropriate comparison group.

*$p \leq 0.10$

***$p \leq 0.01$

*****$p \leq 0.0001$

Source: Data compiled by author.

Table 5.10. Media Entrepreneurs' Perceptions of Op-Eds' Effectiveness in Building Legislative Coalitions (t-test).

Variable Name: Op-ed articles

Respondent Group	Mean (t-test)	Pearson's Correlation | r |	N
Comparison Group[a]	2.5714		70
Pool of Media Entrepreneurs	3.1125*****	0.3180*****	80
Likely Media Entrepreneurs	3.1667***	0.2253***	42
Hard-core Media Entrepreneurs	3.0909	0.1128	21

[a]The mean for the only narrowest definition of the comparison group is reported here. However, each t-test was conducted with the appropriate comparison group.

***$p \leq 0.01$

*****$p \leq 0.0001$

Source: Data compiled by author.

fied as media entrepreneurs decreases, the differences between them and the comparison group must be more pronounced in order to be statistically significant.

These data are telling for several reasons. First, the statistically significant differences observed for television interviews and op-ed articles illustrate the importance of these options to the media entrepreneur. Media entrepreneurs and other respondents alike doubtlessly prefer op-

Table 5.11. Media Entrepreneurs' Perceptions of News Articles/Press Release Effectiveness in Building Legislative Coalitions (t-test).

Variable Name: News articles and press releases

Respondent Group	Mean (t-test)	Pearson's Correlation $|r|$	N
Comparison Group[a]	2.6000		70
Pool of Media Entrepreneurs	3.0125***	0.2176***	80
Likely Media Entrepreneurs	3.0476*	0.1501*	42
Hard-core Media Entrepreneurs	2.9545	0.0590	22

[a]The mean for the only narrowest definition of the comparison group is reported here. However, each t-test was conducted with the appropriate comparison group.

*$p \leq 0.10$

***$p \leq 0.01$

Source: Data compiled by author.

ed articles because they provide a unique opportunity for members to present longer, more thoughtful, and complex arguments regarding policy. Members have complete control over the subject matter. Their words are neither truncated nor distorted into a 30-second sound bite. Furthermore, op-eds enjoy a wide and interested readership, including many members of Congress. It is clear that the purpose of these articles is to influence policy (see also Hess 1991). For example, former Representative Dave McCurdy ran an op-ed article in the *Washington Post* on January 12, 1991—two days before the House vote to authorize the use of force in the Gulf. McCurdy described the purpose of that op-ed article this way:

> **Q: In the case of your *Post* article, who were you trying to reach?**
> McCurdy: Democrats in the House. . . . I felt it was important to speak out for the party. . . . I have had quite a few op-eds out over the years. I think they are an effective tool. It forces you to consolidate your arguments and to think carefully about what your arguments are. . . .
>
> In some instances, it makes all of the difference when you control the margin on an issue. And you can use the media to try to control the issue.[5]

Second, for all their potential drawbacks, television interviews are important for several reasons. Not only do they enhance a member's credibility, but they also serve to raise his or her profile with the general public. In Timothy Cook's survey of House press secretaries, he found that television was the preferred medium to sell a story (Cook 1989, 93). Furthermore, even though he found press secretaries are almost exclusively locally oriented, they did possess a deep appreciation for the power of television coverage. In the words of one press secretary, "Obviously, we salivate any time we can get on the networks" (Cook 1989, 85). One reason that television appearances are coveted is the paucity of broadcast media coverage of the Congress. Scarcity adds value.[6]

Yet coverage on the network news certainly can be problematic. As Cook stated, it can be difficult to articulate an effective argument in a few seconds. A 2-minute segment on the evening news may include a 30-second sound bite that does not represent the member's position accurately. However, a longer format, such as a public affairs talk show like "Larry King Live," can give the media entrepreneur a better opportunity to articulate complex ideas and to direct the interview. According to Cook, efforts to reach national media have little influence in the district. But, Cook added, they do influence the legislative process. As he stated:

> The national media can be especially important to members because they influence the legislative process . . . [and] influence the member's policy agenda. . . . Through the media, House members may introduce proposals for which they can act as authoritative sources. They seek reputations that can eventually be translated into influence within the institution. (Cook 1986, 86)

The contrast Stephen Hess (1991) drew between the "lordly op-ed" and the "lowly press release" is reflected here. News articles and press releases are considered the least useful media strategy. This perception is shared by media entrepreneurs and the full set of respondents alike. Press releases are the principal mechanism members use to claim credit in the local media (Cook 1986; Hess 1991). As a result, they are not commonly picked up by the national press. As Nancy Travor of *Time* magazine described her experience:

> The press on the Hill are constantly barraged with news releases and calls from aides. I send a weekly messenger to the galleries to get the stuff from my mailbox. I get a stack of press releases this thick [she holds her fingers about two inches apart] every week from both the House and the Senate about what members are doing. I have very little interest in that, so it takes very little of my time to go through them.[7]

News articles are probably less desirable because, unlike the op-ed format, the member relinquishes control of the eventual outcome of the article. For example, Timothy Cook related an anecdote about a junior member who avoided the national media after an interview became part of an unflattering article about the legislator's district (Cook 1986, 84). Nonetheless, coverage in the national media, especially print media, helps enhance a legislator's credibility on an issue. The comments generated on the survey are telling in this regard; over 10 percent of the survey respondents indicated (in an open-ended question) that print media allow more detail and thought or provide more space for in-depth discussion and substantive arguments. The best possible combination, then, would be to have a sympathetic reporter writing an article that complements an op-ed, which in turn leads to network television interviews and talk show appearances.

However, it is important to note that media entrepreneurs also understand the reality of the legislative process. Media strategies are less important to media entrepreneurs than are personal contacts, constituent contacts, support of the party leadership, interest group support, and White House contacts. Although media strategies remain more important to media entrepreneurs than to other respondents, media strategies remain less important in generating support for legislation than the traditional insider strategies (see Table 5.12).

The key then is to use media strategies in combination with more traditional approaches to building legislative coalitions. Based on the survey analysis, the most likely candidates would be personal contacts with other members and generating support from interest groups, the White House, and congressional leadership. The responses to the open-ended questions also add some important insights. In addition, respondents mentioned staff contacts, floor statements, and "Dear Colleague Letters" as important legislative strategies. Furthermore, of the 70 respondents who indicated circumstances under which their offices employed the media in the legislative process, typical responses included: "when we need the *votes*" (emphasis in original), "when we are dealing with recalcitrant chairmen or committee staff," or "combating administration policy" (see Table 5.13).

OTHER IMPORTANT DIFFERENCES IN USING THE MEDIA IN THE LEGISLATIVE PROCESS

Media entrepreneurs are not the only members of Congress who display interesting opinions about the nature of the media in the legislative process. Instead, there are important differences based on party affiliation, committee position, and chamber. These differences also shape the context in which media entrepreneurs operate.

Table 5.12. Relative Importance of Media Strategies and Other Legislative Strategies for Media Entrepreneurs.

Question 9: Comparatively speaking, how effective are the following approaches in generating support for policy proposals within Congress? (Please evaluate each item according to the following scale: 1 = not effective 5 = very effective.)

Variable Name	Pool of Media Entrepreneurs		Likely Media Entrepreneurs		Hard-core Media Entrepreneurs	
	Mean	N	Mean	N	Mean	N
Personal contacts	4.595	79	4.683	41	4.727	22
Contacts from constituents	4.075	80	4.119	42	4.045	22
Party leadership	3.938	80	3.952	42	3.901	22
Interest group support	3.675	80	3.810	42	3.682	22
Contacts from the White House	3.215	79	3.317	41	3.273	22
Op. ed. articles	3.113	80	3.167	42	3.091	22
Television interviews	3.013	80	3.095	42	3.091	22
News articles and press releases	3.013	80	3.048	42	2.955	22
Contacts from federal agencies	2.675	80	2.738	42	2.364	22
Contacts from political action committees	2.838	80	2.714	42	2.727	22

Source: Data compiled by author.

First, there is a clear partisan dimension to employing the media enterprise. Both Democrats and Republicans held low opinions of the media skills held by their own partisans and their own party leaders. However, they each gave the *other* party higher marks for media effectiveness than their own. Similarly, Republicans graded committee chairmen— all of whom were Democrats—more favorably than do Democrats. This phenomenon is echoed in the comments provided on the survey. Among those who saw differences in the way parties used the media, Democrats tended to assert that Republicans were more effective in dealing with the media. Democrats also considered Republicans more capable of produc-

Table 5.13. Reasons for Using Media Strategies in the Legislative Process (Open-Ended Question).

Response volunteered	N
Bill of national significance	20
Part of legislative strategy	12
Whenever possible	8
Political considerations	7
Bring outside pressure on Congress	6
Increase awareness of issue	4
Varies	3
Other	4

Source: Data compiled by author.

ing catchy sound bites than other Democrats. In addition, when this survey was conducted, Republicans were in control of the White House. As a result Democratic respondents cited the White House as a serious advantage for the Republicans. Once a Democrat entered the White House, congressional Republicans faced two major disadvantages to communicating their message: losing the White House bully pulpit, and minority status in Congress (Gugliotta 1994). With Republicans in control of both houses of Congress, Republicans will gain control of the policy machinery. They can use committees and subcommittees to get media attention, just as the Democrats did for decades. But they will have to compete with the White House news machine (see Table 5.14).

Conversely, Republicans perceived a number of Democratic advantages. Republicans saw two major Democratic advantages to attracting media coverage: their control of the legislative agenda, and their perceived strength on domestic issues. As one respondent put it: "D's [sic] are more "heart" than "head" generally, making their message appeal better via electronic media. R's [sic] are generally more capable in print, but with less impact on the emotion side." Or, in the words of a Republican colleague who found Republicans ineffective, "Republicans are stuck with the facts." Furthermore, Republicans frequently charged that Democrats had an advantage because the media itself carries a liberal bias. For example, one respondent wrote: "Democrats have easier access because they are akin to a majority of media personnel. All studies I have seen indicate at least 70 percent of the media self-identify as Democrats."

Second, subcommittee and full committee leaders also viewed the media in a slightly different way than do their rank-and-file counterparts. Respondents employed by full-committee chairmen and ranking members were less likely to see media strategies as an effective means to move a bill in committee. Similarly, respondents for subcommittee leaders considered media strategies less effective means to respond to White House proposals than do rank-and-file members (see Table 5.14).

Table 5.14. Other Differences in Perceived Importance Of Media Strategies.

Variable Name	Mean (t-test)	Pearson's Correlation |r|	N
Democrats' effectiveness			
Democrat	2.824****	0.4414*****	91
Republican	3.643		56
Republicans' effectiveness			
Democrat	3.527***	0.2556***	91
Republican	3.089		56
Your own party leadership's effectiveness			
Democrat	2.634*	0.1193	91
Republicans	2.860		57
Committee chairmen's effectiveness			
Democrat	2.693**	0.1892**	88
Republican	3.037		54
Move a bill in committee			
Committee chairman or ranking member	2.059**	0.1932**	17
Rank and file	2.659		123
Move a bill in committee			
House	2.975**	0.1991**	117
Senate	2.130		23
Respond to proposals from the White House			
Subcommittee chairman or ranking member	3.257**	0.1653**	67
Rank and file	3.567		74

*$p \leq 0.10$
**$p \leq 0.05$
***$p \leq 0.01$
****$p \leq 0.001$
*****$p \leq 0.0001$
Source: Data compiled by author.

These results are not surprising. In the first case, employees of committee chairmen are no doubt very attuned with their employers' habits and patterns. Their familiarity with the minute political developments related to particular legislation may have led them to underestimate the importance of media in the legislative process. Or they may also have had a more accurate picture of the real impact media pressure has on their employers. Similarly, the administration is likely to call subcommittee leaders directly when developing policy. Therefore, they (or their employees) are less likely to perceive the media as an important means to communicate to the administration. The telephone is their most important tool to reach the executive branch.

Next, respondents from the House of Representatives were more likely to see media strategies as important for moving a bill in committee than are respondents in the Senate (see Table 5.14). Once again, this result is not surprising for several reasons. First, the Senate is considered the smaller and more personally intimate of the two chambers; therefore, senators are better positioned to use insider strategies to move a bill in committee. Second, the decentralization of Congress and the proliferation of subcommittees mean that almost every senator in the majority party chairs a subcommittee; by the same token, minority party senators will serve as ranking members on at least one subcommittee (Hinkley 1988, 166). Thus, almost every senator (and certainly every majority party senator) is in a position to influence at least part of the legislative agenda; the opportunities for log rolling are almost limitless. Third, in the final analysis, failing to get committee consideration of a bill is simply not the legislative death knell it is in the House. Senate rules permit the introduction of nongermane amendments to legislation under consideration on the floor (Davidson and Oleszek 1981, 283). Therefore, seeing committee action is not as important in the Senate. As former Senator David Boren (D-Oklahoma) described in terms of his involvement on campaign finance reform:

> The issue will stay on the agenda as long as I am in Congress to reintroduce the bill. And I will make them vote on it, even if we can't get a bill out of committee. If that happens, I will introduce the bill on the floor as an amendment. That's what [retired Senator Barry] Goldwater [(R-Arizona)] and I did in the early 1980s when we couldn't get a hearing in committee.[8]

All of these findings describe the context in which the media entrepreneur operates. First and foremost, Congress is a partisan institution. The results of almost all roll-call votes can be predicted by party affiliation (Hinkley 1988, 210-222). Perks, power, and even parking spaces are all determined, at least in part, by partisan considerations. In this atmosphere, it stands to reason that partisanship will color interpretations of the media enterprise as well. The audience reading the op-ed pages or watching a public affairs talk show are likely to interpret what they see according to partisan considerations. By the same token, media entrepreneurs may—consciously or unconsciously—target their party colleagues or shape their message in other ways to accommodate partisan pressures.

Likewise, by virtue of their positions, subcommittee and committee leaders are bound to have a different perspective of the potential effectiveness media strategies will have on their operations. Certainly, committee chairmen probably consider themselves less influenced by media pressure than do the rank-and-file members who may be attempting to dislodge a bill from committee. Similarly, subcommittee chairmen are also less likely to see the media as an important means to generate White House support when they are apt to see the telephone as a more productive tool.

Finally, it is important to remember that there are distinctions between the two houses of Congress. Different rules and the huge difference in the size of the institutions are likely to influence the role of the media in terms of the legislative process. Therefore, what may be a very important and useful strategy in the House—using the media to move a bill through committee—will be unimportant and possibly ineffective in the Senate.

REACHING A CONGRESSIONAL AUDIENCE

What audiences are media entrepreneurs trying to reach through the media enterprise? I hypothesize that one important audience for these efforts are found right in Congress. It is comprised principally of fellow members of Congress who can form legislative coalitions with the media entrepreneur. However, committee and subcommittee chairmen, party leadership, and congressional staff can provide important cues to the ultimate objects of this exercise. Therefore, these groups are also important audiences for the media entrepreneur.

The primary audiences the media entrepreneur hopes to reach are extremely small. Whereas network television reaches an audience numbering in the tens of millions, the media entrepreneur wants to reach the issue network involved in an issue. Even with the decentralized population of modern-day Washington, the media entrepreneur's target audience is likely to number only in the hundreds, even dozens.

The idea that the media are used to move a bill in committee or to generate floor support or support in the other chamber exemplifies the very idea of sending a focused message to a minute audience. A good hypothetical example would be a media entrepreneur writing an op-ed article in an attempt to dislodge a piece of legislation from a recalcitrant committee chairman—a circumstance that this research clearly indicates could happen. The audience, in its narrowest definition, is the committee chairman. Other possible targets of the op-ed are other committee members, committee staff, and interest groups—audiences who could, in turn, influence the chairman. However, even in its broadest definition, the audience is still very small. But if media entrepreneurs did not think these efforts could be fruitful, they would not engage in them. The data indicate that, indeed, media entrepreneurs do engage in these efforts. The same holds true for generating floor support or generating support in the other house of Congress, although in these cases the target audience will number into the hundreds rather than scores.

The survey analysis indicates that media entrepreneurs see the media as a more important mechanism to reach Congress itself. The most important audience in Congress that the media entrepreneurs are trying to reach is their party leadership. They are also more likely than their counterparts to employ media strategies as a means to communicate with these half-dozen people. In this case, the relationship is strongly significant for both the pool of media entrepreneurs and likely media entrepreneurs, and the observed pattern is consistent with hard-core media entrepreneurs, even though the relationship is no longer statistically significant (see Table 5.15).

Table 5.15. Media Entrepreneurs and Target Audiences: Party Leadership (t-tests).

Variable Name: Party leadership			
Respondent Group	Mean (t-test)	Pearson's Correlation |r|	N
Comparison Group[a]	2.7000		70
Pool of Media Entrepreneurs	3.2821****	0.3021***	78
Likely Media Entrepreneurs	3.2439*	0.1526*	41
Hard-core Media Entrepreneurs	3.1905	0.0777	22

[a]The mean for the only narrowest definition of the comparison group is reported here. However, each t-test was conducted with the appropriate comparison group.

*$p \leq 0.10$

***$p \leq 0.01$

****$p \leq 0.001$

Source: Data compiled by author.

Second, media entrepreneurs are more likely than their counterparts to use the media to reach their party colleagues. This relationship is statistically significant for the pool of media entrepreneurs and approaches significance for likely media entrepreneurs; the differences observed in hard-core media entrepreneurs are not statistically significant. Finally, the pool of media entrepreneurs and likely media entrepreneurs perceive congressional staff as an important potential audience for their media efforts. Once again, although the relationship is not statistically significant for hard-core media entrepreneurs, the pattern continues to hold (see Tables 5.16 and 5.17).[9]

These data do provide some evidence that media entrepreneurs use the media enterprise to convey a message to a congressional audience. They are relatively more likely to use the media to reach their party colleagues, their party leadership, and congressional staff than their comparison groups. Even added together, these audiences number only in the few thousand—certainly a microscopic number of people in comparison to even the smallest cable television audience or the circulation of most daily newspapers.

It is important to remember the context of these activities. In comparison to other potential audiences that are identified in the next two chapters, reaching a congressional audience is small potatoes. Across types of media entrepreneurs, party leadership, which is the most important congressional audience media entrepreneurs try to reach, falls behind audiences as varied as constituents, interest groups, and other

Table 5.16. Media Entrepreneurs and Target Audiences: Party Colleagues (t-tests).

Variable Name: Party colleagues

Respondent Group	Mean (t-test)	Pearson's Correlation |r|	N
Comparison Group[a]	2.7794		68
Pool of Media Entrepreneurs	3.2532***	0.2332***	79
Likely Media Entrepreneurs	3.2143	0.1126	42
Hard-core Media Entrepreneurs	2.9546	0.0329	22

[a]The mean for the only narrowest definition of the comparison group is reported here. However, each t-test was conducted with the appropriate comparison group.

***$p \leq 0.01$

Source: Data compiled by author.

Table 5.17. Media Entrepreneurs and Target Audiences: Congressional
Staff (t-tests).

Variable Name: Congressional staff			
Respondent Group	Mean (t-test)	Pearson's Correlation $|r|$	N
Comparison Group[a]	2.0000		69
Pool of Media Entrepreneurs	2.3125*	0.1439*	80
Likely Media Entrepreneurs	2.4419*	0.1612**	43
Hard-core Media Entrepreneurs	2.5000	0.1277	22

[a]The mean for the only narrowest definition of the comparison group is reported here.
However, each t-test was conducted with the appropriate comparison group.
*$p \leq 0.10$
**$p \leq 0.05$
Source: Data compiled by author.

media. These findings provide further evidence that media entrepreneurs understand the complexities of the legislative process and the realities of the institution in which they operate. Therefore, media strategies
are likely to be used to augment personal contacts and other traditional
insider strategies to build legislative coalitions (see Table 5.18).

OTHER VARIATIONS IN CONGRESSIONAL COALITION BUILDING

Once again, it is important to remember that media entrepreneurs do
not operate in a vacuum. Instead, coalition building in Congress is a
complex process that includes partisan, ideological, regional, and constitutional ramifications. There are several interesting differences between
groups in Congress and the way they use the media to build legislative
coalitions. The first difference is seen between the houses of Congress.
Senate respondents considered congressional staff a more important
audience for media efforts than did respondents from the House. This
result reflects that staff play a larger role in the Senate, where senators
are confronted with broader legislative agendas. As a result, professional staff members specialize to a greater degree than they do in the
House, and take on more importance to any individual senator.
Therefore, they are a more important means to reach senators when
building coalitions (see Table 5.19).

Table 5.18. Importance of Intended Audiences for Media Entrepreneurs.

Variable Name	Pool of Media Entrepreneurs		Likely Media Entrepreneurs		Hard-core Media Entrepreneurs	
	Mean	N	Mean	N	Mean	N
Constituents	4.0506	79	4.0238	42	4.0000	22
Other media	3.5844	77	3.8049	41	4.0909	22
Public outside constituents	3.5823	79	3.6190	42	3.8181	22
Interest groups	3.4684	79	3.4651	43	3.2727	22
White House	3.3750	80	3.3721	43	3.1818	22
Party leadership	3.2821	78	3.2439	41	3.1905	21
Party colleagues	3.2532	79	3.2143	42	2.9545	22
Federal agency executives	2.9625	80	2.9535	43	2.7727	22
Colleagues in other party	2.7000	80	2.7442	43	2.6818	22
Think tanks	2.6795	78	2.5854	41	2.5000	22
Congressional staff	2.3125	80	2.4419	43	2.3333	21

Source: Data compiled by author.

The next observed difference is partisanship. Democrats were more likely to use the media to reach their party colleagues than are Republicans. There are several possible reasons for this difference. First, party colleagues are most likely to be ideologically receptive to any ideas promoted by members of similar thinking. It makes sense to start building a coalition first with those most likely to support one's initiatives. Second, Democrats were the majority party in Congress at the time of this writing. As such, they have a decided advantage in terms of constructing winning coalitions. Finally, Republicans lived in the shadow of the administration. Taking a high profile to promote issues or ideas is likely to be seen as a break from the administration. Fellow Republicans were not likely to look kindly on this kind of disloyalty to a Republican president.

Subcommittee and full committee positions remain salient variables. Subcommittee leaders were much less likely to see the media enterprise as an effective way to reach their party colleagues, the White House, or federal agency executives than their rank-and-file counterparts. Similarly, full committee chairmen and ranking members were less likely than the rank and file to see the media as a useful tool to reach the White House. These differences reflect the modern reality of Congress. Subcommittee and full committee chairmen control much of the legisla-

Table 5.19. Differences in the Intended Audience for Media Coverage.

Variable Name	Mean	Pearson's Correlation |r|	N
Congressional staff			
House	2.0488**	0.1992**	123
Senate	2.6250		24
Colleagues in their own party			
Subcommittee chairman or ranking member	2.8684*	0.1577*	76
Rank and file	3.1884		69
Colleagues in their own party			
Democrats	3.1724**	0.1834**	87
Republicans	2.7931		58

*$p \leq 0.10$
**$p \leq 0.05$
Source: Data compiled by author.

tive agenda and work hand in hand with federal agencies and the administration to develop public policy. It is no small wonder, then, that they do not see the media as an important tool to reach these audiences.

However, as we saw earlier, leading a full committee or a subcommittee provides an important platform from which to launch the media enterprise. Sam Nunn, Les Aspin, William Dannemeyer, and Paul Simon are all notable examples of this effort. Furthermore, these positions provide these members with the necessary credibility to make the media enterprise work on their behalf. Subcommittee and full committee leaders are considered experts in their respective policy jurisdictions, and they have the power to act on their beliefs. Nonetheless, these same actors were less likely to use the media to build coalitions in Congress. Thus, these findings provide further evidence that media entrepreneurs are more likely to engage the media enterprise at the agenda-setting stage of the process rather than later.

CONCLUSIONS AND IMPLICATIONS

Although the media entrepreneur is most likely to engage the media enterprise during the agenda-setting stage of the policy process, this chapter demonstrates that there are still other opportunities to use the media to influence the legislative process. Specifically, media entrepreneurs consider moving a bill through committee, generating floor support, and generating support in the other chamber opportune times to use the media. Furthermore, media entrepreneurs consider television interviews, op-ed articles, and press releases more valuable tools to generate legislative support than do their non-media-oriented colleagues.

Second, media entrepreneurs do indeed use the media enterprise in an effort to influence several congressional audiences. Party leadership, partisan colleagues, and congressional staff are all more important potential audiences for the media entrepreneur than they are for other members of Congress.

Third, all of these findings paint an interesting picture of media entrepreneurs. Consistently, these members more strongly value using the media to influence the policy process. They also envision a more diverse audience for their media efforts. Many members of this audience can function as cue givers to members of Congress who are the ultimate object of these activities.

However, it is important to remember that these findings occur in the context of legislative reality. As a result, other approaches to building legislative coalitions are also important. In fact, they may even be more important than media strategies, even to the media entrepreneur. For example, no matter how a member may covet a television interview, there is simply no substitute for the importance of personal contacts. Likewise, support from the leadership will smooth a bill's legislative path. The importance of these findings is that media entrepreneurs see media strategies as more important *relative to traditional insider strategies* than their colleagues who are not as media-oriented. Media strategies augment, but do not replace, traditional approaches to the legislative process.

Finally, media entrepreneurs operate in a complex world. Much of what transpires on Capitol Hill can be traced to other considerations: partisan squabbling, differences in the operations of the House and Senate, or the quirkiness of a particular subcommittee or committee chairman. All of these circumstances will color the way a media entrepreneur approaches the media enterprise and makes decisions regarding when or how to engage it.

ENDNOTES

1. Based on a 5-point Likert scale, where 5 is the highest possible value.
2. Regression analysis demonstrates the same relationship in the expected direction for these variables—moving bills in committee, generating support before a floor vote, and generating support in the other chamber. However, the predictive power of the model is very low, with $R^2 \leq 0.10$. These results are probably due to the problems inherent in conducting regression analysis on ordinal-level data.
3. This relationship disappears for likely and hard-core media entrepreneurs.
4. Based on a 5-point Likert scale, where 5 is the highest possible value.
5. Interview, July 25, 1991.
6. The dearth of congressional coverage on television is well documented (see Green 1974; Kaid and Foote 1985; Ornstein 1989; Ornstein and Robinson 1986).
7. Interview, March 16, 1992
8. Interview, June 23, 1992.
9. Regression analysis demonstrates the same relationship for these variables—media entrepreneurs are more likely to consider congressional staff, party leaders, and party colleagues as potential audiences for media strategies. However, the R^2 values generated by these models are very low, $R^2 \leq 0.10$. These results are probably due to the problems inherent in conducting regression analysis on ordinal-level data.

6

Coalition Building in the Washington Community

Thus far, we have seen how media entrepreneurs consider the media a more effective tool to influence the legislative process than their counterparts who are less media-oriented. However, Congress is only one of the media entrepreneurs' potential audiences. In addition, these members may be trying to reach audiences outside Congress, but inside Washington. Reaching these actors can serve several purposes. For example, the media entrepreneur may want to influence federal agency officials who are drafting regulations that affect his or her district. Or perhaps a media entrepreneur wants to reach other Washington actors who function as cue givers to other members of Congress. These audiences provide yet another means to reach fellow policymakers on Capitol Hill. This chapter examines the context of the media enterprise by examining the nature of the modern-day Washington community. Second, it continues to address the third major research question motivating this research by identifying additional audiences for the media enterprise within the Washington community. Third, this chapter compares the perceived effectiveness of the media enterprise vis-à-vis other coalition-building strategies employed in the Washington community.

Finally, it investigates the fourth major research question of this project by identifying which media sources are best used to communicate in Washington.

THE CONTEXT: THE WASHINGTON COMMUNITY

The sense that Washington is somehow distinct and removed from the rest of the United States is a concept that has been popular for decades. In his 1964 presidential campaign, Barry Goldwater railed against "pointy headed bureaucrats" located in Washington. In 1976, President Carter ran for office as an outsider, willing to bring fresh ideas into the rarified atmosphere of official Washington. In his 1988 attempt, Representative Richard Gephardt (D-Missouri) tried to portray himself as a Washington outsider, even though he was on the leadership track in the House of Representatives (Barone and Ujifusa 1991, 711). Even in 1992, all of the major presidential candidates were trying to paint themselves as agents of change, far removed from business as usual in Washington.

But what is "business as usual" in Washington? It is doubtful that the Washington community is out of touch with the general public. Nonetheless, conventional wisdom is correct insofar as Washington is distinct in a number of ways. First, Washington is the seat of national government. In this way, the city resembles many other "one-industry" towns, except in this case, the industry is the federal government (Polsby 1981). But Washington is distinct from other one-industry government towns, like state capitols, because in Washington, the stakes are higher. Even a state budget the size of California's is small potatoes compared to the scope of the federal government. Similarly, stories that are classified as "national news" elsewhere in the country are actually local news in Washington. For both of these reasons, bureaucrats, congressional staff, elected officials and political appointees, journalists, and lobbyists inside the beltway have a much greater appetite for news.

Second, Washington is distinct because of the growth it has experienced in the last half-century. This growth has come about for several reasons. The first is the expanding influence of government. Beginning with the New Deal and followed by the Great Society programs, the level of legitimate federal government involvement in the economy and social fabric of the country has expanded. With it, the population of administrators and other interested parties has grown. For example, Hugh Heclo (1981) argues that the federal bureaucracy dispersed the administration of many new programs to the state and local level. Therefore, whereas the size of the federal bureaucracy—both inside and outside of Washington—did not grow, the size of state and local governments did. As a result, many state and city governments, along with umbrella organizations such as the National Governors' Association and the U.S. Conference of Mayors, saw a need to establish Washington offices for the purpose of coordinating with and lobbying the federal government.

This growth in intergovernmental lobbying mirrors the growth in the number of lobbies more generally within the Washington community. Interest groups of all kinds have made their way inside the beltway. Previous investigations of lobbying registries show that some 25 percent of all lobbies were first registered after 1970. Some 40 percent have been founded since 1960 (Berry 1989). Interest groups are diverse, including everything from foreign governments and insurgents to children's issues, corporations, and trade and professional associations (Berry 1989; Carlson 1990). Interest groups, including law and public relations firms who engage in lobbying for their clients, number into the thousands.

Although the number of federal bureaucrats nationwide remained stable between 1950 and 1980 (Heclo 1981), the 20th century has seen a growth in the number of presidential employees. As King and Ragsdale (1988) discovered in their statistical analyses, there has been steady growth in the size of presidential staff, even after allowing for large increases attributable to wars and other military actions. This growth parallels the growth in the president's executive responsibilities in administration and budget authority and the president's increased autonomy in foreign policy and rule making.

Simultaneously, changes in Congress have led to a burgeoning number of congressional staff (Fox and Hammond 1977; Hinkley 1988). In the three and a half decades prior to 1977, the number of congressional staff on Capitol Hill increased dramatically. For example, the number of personal staff members increased from under 900 in 1935 to about 7,000 in 1977. In 1987, the number was 7,584 (Hinkley 1988, 88-89; Ornstein, Mann, and Malbin 1990, 130, 133). Granted, about 2,500 of the staff are located in the districts. However, that leaves almost 4,600 personal staff based in Washington, many of whom are legislative professionals. These so-called "legislative assistants" and "legislative directors" are responsible for monitoring legislation, the calendar, and other legislative developments on behalf of their members. At the same time, the size of committee staffs also increased. Aside from a few support personnel, committee staffs are completely comprised of professional legislative staff, working on behalf of the majority or minority members on the committees. These staff members draft legislation, collect cosponsors, and conduct congressional investigations—all as part of the legislative responsibilities of the committee.

At the same time, Congress established or expanded a number of its research organizations. An alphabet soup of in-house think tanks are available to members, including the Congressional Research Service (CRS), the Congressional Budget Office (CBO), the General Accounting Office (GAO), and the Office of Technology Assessment (OTA). These offices provide research and policy analysis services to Congress, and they further expand the number of congressional staff. All of these organizations boast sizeable payrolls. The GAO has some 5,000 employees alone; CRS carries another 700. The smallest is OTA, with approximately 100 employees (Fox and Hammond 1977, 130-135; Ornstein, Mann and Malbin 1990, 130). As a result of these expansions, the total number of congressional staff now numbers over 30,000. As the number of congressional staff has grown, they have become more important to the process of developing legislation, as they too are approached by other members of the burgeoning issue networks.

The number of reporters based in Washington has also grown dramatically over the last several decades. The precise size of the Washington press corps is difficult to establish; however, in 1982, over 4,000 journalists held a congressional press pass, considered the basic Washington press corps' credential. This figure does not include free-lance writers and others who may not be congressionally accredited, last estimated at approximately 4,000 writers (Bonafede 1982). The journalists who comprise the press corps represent all forms of media: television, radio, newspapers, wires, news services, periodicals, and trade publications. They report for both local and national outlets. Once considered an elite group who hail from eastern states and Ivy League schools (Hess 1981), over time, Washington journalists have become more representative of the nation as a whole (Hess 1991, 110-130).

A third distinct characteristic of the Washington community is a sense of impermanence. Polsby (1981) and Heclo (1977) described an official Washington in which almost everyone is from somewhere else. Members of Congress hail from their districts and states; their staffs are drawn overwhelmingly from the same areas. As administrations change, so do the top layers of the federal bureaucracies and the entire population of the White House and the Old Executive Office Building. Reporters from all over the country are assigned to cover Washington. They frequently cover several beats during their time in Washington and are sometimes reassigned back to their home states. Every state has its own "state society," and many major universities have active local chapters of their alumni associations.

Not only is everyone from somewhere else, most are on their way to somewhere else. Washington is a city of high turnover. The average tenure of a member of the House of Representatives is only 12 years;

the median length of service is 5 terms. Senators in the 101st Congress averaged only 9.8 years in the institution (Ornstein, Malbin and Mann 1990, 18-19). Similarly, Michael Malbin (1980), in his study of congressional staffs, depicted the typical congressional staffer as a young professional whose Capitol Hill experience is a stepping stone to other careers in Washington (see also Bisnow 1990). In fact, turnover is high in the ranks of congressional staff and political appointees alike. The average tenure of political appointees and congressional staff members is about two years (Heclo 1977; Twenhafel 1991). In fact, the tenure for even the most senior congressional staff members, such as press secretaries or administrative assistants, is not only under two years, but appears to be falling (Twenhafel 1991).

These data provide a valuable composite of the Washington community. However, they cannot document the revolving-door phenomenon prevalent in the Washington community. For example, a policy activist might, at one time or another in his or her career, hold any number of positions. One might start a career in the legislative branch, then jump to a "Schedule C" position in the administration after a presidential election. After a few years there, one might move to a lobbying organization or to a think tank for a few years before shifting back to government service. Another hitch in the public sector might then lead to a move to a public relations firm or to the media. Former White House Chief of Staff John Sununu is a good example of part of this process. After he left his post with the Bush administration, he signed on part time with CNN. Similarly, former Chairman of the Joint Chiefs of Staff William Crowe works part time as a commentator for ABC News. The staff director to former Speaker Thomas "Tip" O'Neill now works for the public relations firm, Hill and Knowlton.

All of these circumstances make policymaking more difficult and the media enterprise more important. The expanding size of the executive, legislative, and interest group communities simply means that there are more stakeholders to reach. Furthermore, one important dynamic of these "issue networks" (Heclo 1981) is that they change constantly. It is difficult to predict precisely which groups and other actors may be involved in a particular policy issue. Similarly, the sheer number of relevant actors may also preclude intimate, one-on-one contacts.

Furthermore, the transient nature of political appointees and congressional staff makes establishing long-term relationships more difficult. Although many of these actors simply move through a "revolving door" and surface in another part of the issue network later, coalition building depends on reaching the person occupying a particular *position*, not necessarily a particular person. For example, the media entrepreneur wants to reach the health legislative assistant for Senator Smith—not

Susan Jones who happens to hold that position. Therefore, maintaining personal relationships becomes more difficult and time-consuming given the transient nature of the professional staff. Certainly, telephone calls and personal meetings are the fundamental basis of many of the coalition-building efforts in Washington. However, press coverage eases these efforts by establishing the media entrepreneur as a player in the process.

Among all of these centrifugal forces, one centripetal force in the Washington community (aside from the Washington Redskins) is the local media. It is the one common source of news and gossip about local events and notables. Although the local media play the same role in many communities outside Washington, the impermanent, transient nature of the Washington community means that the media take on an elevated importance.

The media become more important, too, because of the level of interest in public affairs and public policy the Washington audience carries. As one press secretary related: "The Washington audience [tends] to be in tune with these things. They are more politically and geographically proximate, so they will tend to be aligned with one side or another, more so than the general public."[1] Other research reinforces this perception. For example, the Sunday morning television talk shows have notoriously low ratings. Even "This Week With David Brinkley," which enjoys the highest viewership of the genre, has an audience only one-sixth the size of the audience for a top-rated, prime-time sitcom. Yet the Washington audience tuned into these programs is proportionately larger than elsewhere in the country. Although these shows score Nielsen ratings points between 1.9-3.4 nationally, the ratings in the Washington media market is 3.0 to 4.0 (Matlack 1990). These facts provide further evidence of the importance of news outlets as a unifying force in the Washington community.

The media's exaggerated importance as a means to communicate in Washington heightens the importance of getting media coverage. As former Representative Mike Synar (D-Oklahoma) commented, "[Media coverage] is absolutely vital. Without it you don't have focus and you can't get anything done. Period."[2] As a result, there is a great deal of competition for media coverage. The prevalence of public relations firms are indicative of the importance of getting media attention in this city of policymakers. One of the common services they provide to their clientele is to manufacture media events—complete with eye-catching visuals that will not only draw the attention of passers-by, but more importantly, guarantee a few seconds on the evening news. Frequently, these organizations even arrange "exclusives" with news programs such as "60 Minutes" in order to move an issue onto the agenda. Less extravagant measures simply mean that Teddy Bears lobby Congress on textile legislation, and various Hollywood celebrities testify before Congress on issues ranging from the environment to breast cancer or nutrition (Carlson, 1990).

It is within this context that the media entrepreneur engages the media enterprise in order to build coalitions within Congress and in the Washington community. There *is* a beltway mentality to the degree that a large proportion of Washington residents makes its living in politics. Combined with the primacy of television as the medium to reach the American public outside the beltway, the result is a heavily charged, media-conscious, chaotic atmosphere in which getting and sustaining media coverage is essential to establish credibility and to influence public policy.

REACHING THE WASHINGTON COMMUNITY

This chapter, like the previous, seeks to identify what audiences media entrepreneurs are trying to reach. The previous chapter concluded that media entrepreneurs do target their message through the media enterprise in an effort to reach specific audiences in Congress. Yet, in comparison with other potential audiences of the media enterprise, reaching various members of Congress is not important. It stands to reason that media entrepreneurs have an audience in mind that is found elsewhere than in the corridors of the Capitol complex. Instead, the target audience may include a number of people associated with issue networks, think tanks, and the media.

The survey data yield more valuable insights. Potential audiences found in the Washington community receive higher scores than do the congressional audiences identified in the previous chapter. For instance, the full set of respondents indicted that, in terms of reaching a Washington audience, media strategies were designed to reach interest groups first and foremost ($m = 3.439$; $mdn = 3$). The second most important Washington audience is other media ($m = 3.374$; $mdn = 4$). Third, respondents thought members used the media to reach the White House ($m = 3.126$; $mdn = 3$; see Table 6.1). These results indicate that using the media is considered more valuable in terms of building coalitions *outside* Congress rather than *inside* Congress.

These results support the notion that the media enterprise is a valuable tool for communicating inside the Washington community. If the old "iron triangles" still existed, then the media would not be as important to communicate with interest groups, the administration, or any other audience in Washington. Yet, it is important to note that of all

Table 6.1. Intended Audience—All Respondents.

Question 6: Many members of Congress use strategies such as writing op-ed articles and conducting interviews with reporters from the national media to publicize their ideas and policy positions. According to your experience, who are legislators trying to reach through these efforts? (1 = very infrequently; 5 = very frequently)

Potential Audience	Mean Score	Median	N
Constituents	3.906	4	149
The public outside the constituency	3.439	4	148
Interest groups	3.439	3	148
Other media	3.374	4	148
White House officials	3.126	3	148
Colleagues in their own party	3.030	3	147
Party leadership	3.006	3	148
Colleagues in the other party	2.970	3	150
Executives in federal agencies	2.832	3	149
Think tanks	2.612	3	147
Congressional staff	2.168	2	149

Source: Data compiled by author.

the Washington audiences listed, the single most important were still interest groups. This result underscores the important role interest groups play in terms of securing support for policy initiatives. Securing the support of interest groups no doubt helps gain credibility inside Congress and elsewhere in the Washington community.

Identifying interest groups and the White House as important audiences reaffirms Heclo's assertion regarding issue networks. The policymaking network must be diffuse enough so that simply depending on personal contacts or other strategies is not sufficient to communicate to all interested parties. If issue networks did not exist, then the media would be no more useful to reach a Washington audience than it would be to reach a congressional audience.

Reaching the White House serves other purposes as well. Principally, the media are a means to communicate one's position to the White House in a public way. This finding is supported by the interview data. In addition to reaching his fellow Democrats in the House, former Representative Dave McCurdy related that his op-ed article that immediately preceded the vote to authorize force in the Persian Gulf was also aimed toward the administration. In his analysis:

You are clearly trying to reach the administration. You do anything to bolster your own position. Remember, two-thirds of politics is a good bluff. In some instances, it makes all of the difference when you control the margin on an issue. And you can use the media to try to control the issue. And the administration uses it every day—both through official means and through leaks.[3]

One important finding that the media itself is an intended audience of the media enterprise is also not entirely surprising. Even the full set of respondents seemed to understand the importance of reaching the media, because reporters consume news. Using the media to capture the attention of other members of the press corps is a good way to ensure additional coverage. The more coverage a member receives, the more likely he or she will be considered "a player" in a policy area and be able to influence public policy.

One crucial part of the typical Washington reporter's job is *watching* the news as well as reporting it. For instance, much of the influence of Sunday morning talk shows stems from the fact that they are watched by reporters. If a guest on the program says something newsworthy, it is likely to be reported on the Sunday evening newscasts and in the Monday editions of the newspapers. Because Sunday is typically a slow news day, these shows take on even more importance (Matlack 1990). Similarly, part of the importance of the *Washington Post* and the *New York Times* is that other journalists read these sources and take their cues from them. It is widely accepted that whatever appears on the front page of the *New York Times* will be the lead story on the evening news. One press secretary to a House Democratic leader put it this way:

The first [audience] is the press filter, though which communications go to the public. . . . The elite press, like the big daily newspapers, matter for two reasons, one big and one small.

The big reason is that there is a mutual reinforcement between the evening newscasts and the major newspapers regarding story selection. The television people read the *Washington Post* and the *New York Times*, and those editors watch evening news shows. That leads them to reinforce ideas about what is important.[4]

Another important finding is which Washington audiences were not considered important. Among these are federal agency executives (m = 2.832; mdn = 3) and think tanks (m = 2.612; mdn = 3). These results perhaps reflect how both think tanks and federal agencies can be removed from the immediacy of coalition building, yet remain important during other stages of the policy process. Many think tanks perceive their role as one of studying issues and commenting on policy. Their proposals will become a part of the cacophony of competing ideas; with luck their ideas will become part of law as it is developed. By contrast, agency officials are rarely involved in developing policy approaches—that is the role of the White House. The bureaucrats are technicians set to the task of writing regulations and enforcing rules. Therefore, they become part of the policy process long after Congress has taken action (see Table 6.1).

Despite the growing diffusion in the Washington community, it is important to remember that the media entrepreneurs' combined target audiences on the Hill and elsewhere in the beltway are still very small—in other words, their message is cast to just a few thousand policy activists. The growth in Congress, the executive branch, interest groups, and journalists represents a target audience of at best several hundred thousand. Most media entrepreneurs try to reach an even more specialized audience: 100 Senators, 435 House members, 5 party leaders, 200 interest groups, 10 agency executives, or 1 president.

Media Entrepreneurs and the Intended Audience

Not surprisingly, media entrepreneurs differ from their colleagues when it comes to defining their audience in the Washington community. The most interesting difference is the relative importance of reaching the media itself. The full set of respondents considered interest groups the second most important audience for media efforts—and the most important Washington audience. By comparison, the media occupied the same status for media entrepreneurs. The difference of means tests shows that all media entrepreneurs consider other media a more important target audience of the media enterprise than do their colleagues. Unlike most of the other findings reported here, this relationship does not weaken as the definition of media entrepreneurs narrows. Instead, the mean response actually *increases*. This finding provides evidence that the hard-core media entrepreneurs are, at least in one very important instance, more sophisticated about the media enterprise than their counterparts who have a more modest sense of the media's efficacy (see Table 6.2).

Second, media entrepreneurs see the White House as a more important audience than the full set of respondents. The relationship is statistically significant for the pool of media entrepreneurs and the likely media entrepreneurs. The pattern remains consistent for the hard-core media entrepreneurs, but it fails to be statistically significant (see Table 6.3). Using the media to reach the White House—to bolster one's position in McCurdy's words—is a likely purpose for the media enterprise. As liberal Democrats, many media entrepreneurs are likely to have had more to gain from posturing against the Republican White House than would the Republicans. Furthermore, it is the media entrepreneur who

Table 6.2. Media Entrepreneurs and Target Audiences: Other Media (t-tests).

Variable Name: Other media

Respondent Group	Mean (t-test)	Pearson's Correlation |r|	N
Comparison Group[a]	3.1428		70
Pool of Media Entrepreneurs	3.5844**	0.2036**	77
Likely Media Entrepreneurs	3.8049***	0.2474***	41
Hard-core Media Entrepreneurs	4.0909****	0.2777****	22

[a]The mean for the only narrowest definition of the comparison group is reported here. However, each t-test was conducted with the appropriate comparison group.

**$p \leq 0.05$

***$p \leq 0.01$

****$p \leq 0.001$

Source: Data compiled by author.

Table 6.3. Media Entrepreneurs and Target Audiences: The White House (t-tests).

Variable Name: The White House

Respondent Group	Mean (t-test)	Pearson's Correlation |r|	N
Comparison Group[a]	2.8428		70
Pool of Media Entrepreneurs	3.3750***	0.2504***	80
Likely Media Entrepreneurs	3.3721*	0.1466*	43
Hard-core Media Entrepreneurs	3.1818	0.0216	22

[a]The mean for the only narrowest definition of the comparison group is reported here. However, each t-test was conducted with the appropriate comparison group.

*$p \leq 0.10$

***$p \leq 0.01$

Source: Data compiled by author.

has the motivation to distinguish him- or herself from the rest of the pack in a public forum.

THE MEDIA ENTERPRISE AND COALITION BUILDING

How important are media strategies in comparison to other coalition-building strategies used in the Washington community? Just as in the case of pushing legislation in the halls of Congress, the full set of respondents found that personal contacts are the single most important tool to building coalitions in the Washington community. Support from party leadership and the White House were also listed as crucial elements. Nonetheless, the full respondent group did see the media as more useful to build coalitions within the larger Washington community than inside Congress itself. Television interviews, op-eds, and news articles and press releases all received higher mean response scores in the context of reaching a Washington audience than they did in the context of reaching other members of Congress (see Table 6.4).

These findings underscore two facts. First, coalition building in Washington is still predicated on personal relationships and support from political leaders in Congress and the administration. The revolving door and the high rates of turnover indicate that policy actors are apt to hold several positions during their careers, but they are likely to remain within the issue network. Second, the media are relatively more important in this context than on Capitol Hill. This result reflects the obvious fact that Washington is bigger than Congress. Therefore, using the media is a more effective tool to reach this wider audience.

Table 6.4. Building Coalitions in the Washington Community—All Respondents.

Question 10: Comparatively speaking, how effective are the following approaches in generating support for policy proposals among political elites *inside Washington,* but *outside Congress*? (1 = very infrequently; 5 = very frequently)

Strategy	Mean Score	Median	N
Personal contacts	4.328	5	140
Party leadership	3.577	4	137
Grass-roots pressure	3.486	4	138
White House contacts	3.474	4	137
Op-ed articles	3.389	4	139
Television interviews	3.324	3	139
News articles and press releases	2.949	3	138
Interest group/PAC endorsements	2.763	3	139
Federal agency contacts	2.729	3	133

Source: Data compiled by author.

Media Entrepreneurs and Media Strategies

As discussed earlier, when reaching a congressional audience, media entrepreneurs have more faith in the efficacy of using media strategies—specifically television interviews and op-ed articles—to reach a Washington audience than their counterparts. The strongest difference is in the attitude toward television interviews. The difference between media entrepreneurs and their comparison groups remains statistically significant across all three definitions of media entrepreneurs (see Table 6.5). By contrast, op-ed articles are statistically significant only for the pool of media entrepreneurs and the likely media entrepreneurs, although the direction of the relationship holds true for the hard-core media entrepreneurs (see Table 6.6). News articles and press releases have the weakest relationship. Only the broadest definition of media entrepreneurs—the pool of media entrepreneurs—consider news articles and press releases as more important coalition-building tools than their comparison group. Even here, the relationship only approaches significance at the 0.05 level (see Table 6.7).[5]

Just as was discussed in the context of reaching a congressional audience, media entrepreneurs consider television the most influential medium to reach the Washington community, closely followed by op-ed articles. News articles and press releases remain the least-coveted media strategies. The reasons are doubtlessly the same. Because television reaches the widest audience both inside and outside the beltway, it carries the most prestige—even within the insular community of official

Table 6.5. Television Interviews and Coalition Building in the Washington Community (t-tests).

Variable Name: Television interviews			
Respondent Group	Mean (t-test)	Pearson's Correlation |r|	N
Comparison Group[a]	3.1290		62
Pool of Media Entrepreneurs	3.4805**	0.2076**	77
Likely Media Entrepreneurs	3.6585***	0.2573***	41
Hard-core Media Entrepreneurs	3.7143**	0.1958**	21

[a]The mean for the only narrowest definition of the comparison group is reported here. However, each t-test was conducted with the appropriate comparison group.

*$p \leq 0.10$

**$p \leq 0.05$

***$p \leq 0.01$

Source: Data compiled by author.

Table 6.6. Op-ed Articles and Coalition Building in the Washington Community (t-tests).

Variable Name: Op-ed articles

Respondent Group	Mean (t-test)	Pearson's Correlation |r|	N
Comparison Group[a]	3.2258		62
Pool of Media Entrepreneurs	3.5195*	0.1633*	77
Likely Media Entrepreneurs	3.6097*	0.1601*	41
Hard-core Media Entrepreneurs	3.6667	0.1313	21

[a]The mean for the only narrowest definition of the comparison group is reported here. However, each t-test was conducted with the appropriate comparison group.
*$p \leq 0.10$
Source: Data compiled by author.

Table 6.7. News Articles/Press Releases and Coalition Building in the Washington Community (t-tests).

Variable Name: News articles and press releases

Respondent Group	Mean (t-test)	Pearson's Correlation |r|	N
Comparison Group[a]	2.7869		61
Pool of Media Entrepreneurs	3.0779*	0.1533*	77
Likely Media Entrepreneurs	3.0488	0.0686	41
Hard-core Media Entrepreneurs	3.0476	0.0442	21

[a]The mean for the only narrowest definition of the comparison group is reported here. However, each t-test was conducted with the appropriate comparison group.
*$p \leq 0.10$
Source: Data compiled by author.

Washington. Op-ed articles are widely read by politicos and reporters alike and offer an unfettered forum for a member to expound his or her ideas. News articles offer the media entrepreneur the fewest opportunities to control the message, and press releases are rarely picked up by the national media.

There is one important way in which media entrepreneurs mirror the full group of respondents. Both groups consider the three media strategies as a more effective means to build coalitions in Washington than to build coalitions in Congress. In terms of reaching a Washington audience, the only response that consistently carries more weight than the media options is personal contacts, which are universally considered the most important tool for coalition building in Washington—just as they were in Congress. This result lends further credence to the notion that the Washington community is far more decentralized and permeable than the federal city of a few decades ago. Therefore, media entrepreneurs and the full set of respondents alike are more likely to see the value of receiving press attention in Washington (see Tables 6.2 and 6.8).

Table 6.8. Relative Importance of Various Coalition Building Strategies for Media Entrepreneurs.

Question 10: Comparatively speaking, how effective are the following approaches in generating support for policy proposals among political elites *inside Washington* but *outside Congress?* (1 = not effective; 5 = very effective.)

Variable Name	Pool of Media Entrepreneurs Mean Score	N	Likely Media Entrepreneurs Mean Score	N	Hard-core Media Entrepreneurs Mean Score	N
Personal contacts	4.3247	77	4.3415	41	4.3333	21
Grassroots pressure	3.6364	77	3.7073	41	3.4286	21
Support from party leadership	3.5600	75	3.5750	41	3.3500	20
White House contacts	3.5263	76	3.6000	40	3.6000	20
Op-ed articles	3.5195	77	3.6097	40	3.6667	21
Television interviews	3.4805	77	3.6585	41	3.7143	21
News articles and press releases	3.0779	77	3.0488	41	3.0476	21
Interest group/PAC endorsements	2.8701	77	2.9268	41	2.8051	21
Federal agency contacts	2.6533	75	2.6750	40	2.4000	20

Source: Data compiled by author.

CHOOSING THE MESSENGER: WHAT IS READ
AND WATCHED IN CONGRESS?

The fourth major research question posed in this analysis is: How can media entrepreneurs best reach their target audience? Aside from one early effort by Robinson and Clancy (1983) that identified the *Washington Post* as the hegemonic news source on Capitol Hill, little has been done to identify the important sources of news to reach a Capitol Hill audience. This section analyzes survey data designed to discern which sources of news are most widely consulted on Capitol Hill and thus are the wisest choices for the media entrepreneur.

Although these data reveal the media consumption patterns of only one potential audience targeted by the media entrepreneurs—congressional staff—these findings are more generalizable than one might think at first blush. First of all, the semistructured interviews did not uncover any systematic differences in media consumption by subjects on or off the Hill. Many of the potential audiences in the Washington community are employed to monitor the activities of Congress. Therefore, their sources of information about the legislative branch of government are likely to be the same as those used by Hill people. The sources listed on the survey instrument were all national media sources or widely read specialized publications like *Congressional Quarterly Weekly Report*.

The survey analysis revealed that the major sources of news break down easily into three tiers, based on the degree that members of the full-response set regularly consult the source. Each tier is comprised of a mix of broadcast, print, and electronic media. The first tier of media sources—the most important sources of information for Congress—are *Congressional Quarterly Weekly Report*, the *Washington Post*, and Cable News Network (CNN). In every case, the average Likert scale responses were over 4.0 on a 5-point scale. The importance of *Congressional Quarterly* and the *Washington Post* is difficult to overstate. Their average Likert-scale scores were over 4.5 on a 5-point scale. The written comments and the interview data underscore these findings. As one respondent penciled in the margin of his or her survey, "the *Post* is essential to us all." Others agreed. As an aide to Representative Ron Dellums (D-California) related regarding the lawsuit Dellums led against the President over Persian Gulf policy, "the Washington media was an important way to reach Washington. Certainly everyone reads the *Post*, and access was fairly facile"[6] (see Table 6.9).

Reporters for the *Washington Post* and *Congressional Quarterly* are aware of the unique roles they play in official Washington. As one congressional correspondent to the *Post* said when asked to characterize the role of her paper:

Table 6.9. Reported Use of Various Media Sources—All Respondents.

Question 8: If you are seeking information regarding legislation, White House proposals, and current issues being discussed on Capitol Hill, which media sources do you consult most frequently? (1 = never consulted; 5 = consulted frequently)

News Source	Mean Score	Median	N
TIER ONE:			
Congressional Quarterly Weekly Report	4.544	5	149
Washington Post	4.527	5	148
CNN	4.034	4	148
TIER TWO:			
C-SPAN	3.850	4	147
Wall Street Journal	3.753	4	1150
New York Times	3.520	4	150
National Journal	3.493	4	150
National network news	3.428	3	147
Roll Call	3.154	3	149
"MacNeil-Lehrer New Hour" (PBS)	3.095	3	147
TIER THREE:			
National Public Radio	2.993	3	147
Specialized Trade Publications	2.944	3	144
"Nightline"	2.709	3	148
"This Week with David Brinkley"	2.689	3	148
Time	2.671	3	149
Newsweek	2.631	3	149
U.S. News and World Report	2.621	3	149
"Meet the Press"	2.601	3	148
"Washington Week in Review"	2.479	2	148
"Faxed" news, such as The White House Bulletin	2.036	2	149
Washington Times	2.027	2	150
Christian Science Monitor	1.852	2	149
"The Hotline"	1.801	2	149
Los Angeles Times	1.798	1	149

Table 6.9. Reported Use of Various Media Sources—All Respondents. (cont.).

News Source	Mean Score	Median	N
OVERALL USE:			
Overall use of national newspapers and newsmagazines	3.858	4	127
Overall use of Washington-based Publications	3.841	4	126
Overall use of broadcast news sources	3.504	4	123
OTHER:			
District media	4.232	4	138

Source: Data compiled by author.

> [W]e [the *Post*] are the memo pad for government. And we have that role by virtue of being at the doorstep every morning. In fact, for a long time, we were a memo pad from Senator [George] Mitchell [(D-Maine), Majority Leader] to the White House. It was a way for the Congress to get the attention of the White House, in a way that is effective when you can't get telephone calls answered, because you know the *Post* will be on the doorstep in the morning.[7]

Mary Hager, Press Secretary to then-Majority Whip William Gray (D-Pennsylvania), made a similar observation about the role of the *Post*: "I depend a lot on the Post to find out how the administration feels. Of course, I don't take their statements in the paper as the gospel truth, buy they are largely accurate."[8]

For its part, *Congressional Quarterly Weekly Report* carries a solid reputation for two reasons. First, its beat is Congress, and it provides an important product for a specialized audience of congressional staff and Congress watchers, both inside and outside the beltway. Second, they have an impeccable reputation for timely, fair, balanced, and impartial reporting of all congressional activities. Although most congressional correspondents are forced to pick and choose between hundreds of potential stories, *Congressional Quarterly* ("CQ" in the Hill lexicon) specializes in the activities of Congress, allowing it the luxury to cover events that other correspondents could not hope to get space or time for. As Chuck Alston, a reporter for *Congressional Quarterly*, characterized his publication:

> We provide a threefold service. First, we sort through the various proposals and summarize them for the people on the Hill. Second,

we provide a framework for thinking on the issue. We like to step back and ask "how to think about [an issue]." Third, we want to do a decent analysis of what is likely to happen on the issue in the coming Congress.[9]

As a result, one committee staffer commented, "CQ is just outstanding at providing information about what goes on in Congress. For the average staffer, it is the Bible."[10] As a further testament to the importance of *Congressional Quarterly*, two separate interviewees, after a lengthy and scathing criticism of media coverage of campaign finance reform, made a point to say that nothing they said applied in any way to the coverage by *Congressional Quarterly*.

Because *Congressional Quarterly* rarely editorializes and is considered a publication "of record," there is little interpretation that appears in its pages. As a result, it is rarely used by press secretaries and members to frame debate. However, because it is, in the words of one Republican press secretary, "based more on facts"[11] than interpretation, it plays an important role in establishing members' credibility as "players" in an issue area.

CNN's role is truly unique, and its popularity among Hill staffers is testimony to the growing importance of immediate information about political events around the world. It was a rare occasion when I visited an office and did not see CNN or C-SPAN on the television. Senator Bob Kerrey's press office, in which I worked, had CNN on all day. One of our duties was to watch for breaking news, especially as it related to the Persian Gulf crisis, so that Kerrey could make a response, as appropriate. Several interviewees related similar experiences to my own. For example, "on the Gulf crisis, CNN was critically important. . . . They were covering the war in real time. And many members felt that the Pentagon briefings being held for them were not as useful as watching CNN."[12] Another agreed: "Members started to complain that their briefings were less informative and comprehensive than the latest news report on CNN."[13]

Furthermore, CNN is an important news source because of its 24-hour format. News junkies, busy members, and staff can tune in at any time of the day or night. Even though the network newscasts, "Nightline," and the "MacNeil-Lehrer Newshour" are rebroadcast daily to every congressional office through the Library of Congress's internal cable system, few congressional staff and members have time to watch the network news then or when they are originally broadcast. Even more important, however, the interviewees tended to consider network news coverage far too superficial to be useful to monitor the Washington conversation. As one staffer to a northeastern Democrat put it, "We don't watch Brokaw in order to get information about what's happening on the

Hill. The only time a Hill staffer will watch the nightly news will be when the boss is on or to get a handle on what is happening worldwide."[14]

Reporters and media commentators are certainly aware of CNN's unique role. As their congressional correspondent, Bob Franken, said:

> CNN has become the character of the message. We help shape the agenda and the reason is we're watched by opinion makers. For example, last Thursday, I did a live shot at noon. I showed a Democrat criticizing Foley for his handling of the House Bank. As a result of *Democratic* criticism, Foley held a media availability to say that he was going to crack down on perks. We don't have power, but in the battle for public perception, the media is the means to shape that. CNN is unique because we are the principal vehicle for the coverage.[15]

One Republican leader's press secretary saw CNN as another way to influence the message as events are happening:

> It [CNN] is extremely useful when you have fast-breaking events. You can get in to influence the news spin much more quickly. You can also get to influence the way people are interpreting the events as they happen. By contrast, the networks are much later in the debate. They frame events, but they don't influence the course of events.[16]

The second-tier media sources also enjoy enviable readership and viewership on Capitol Hill. The second tier includes the *Post*'s companions in the troika commonly called the *elite press*: the *New York Times* and the *Wall Street Journal*. They are joined by several other national news sources, including the network news and PBS's "MacNeil-Lehrer News Hour." The second tier also includes several Washington-based news sources: the weekly news magazine *National Journal*; *Roll Call*, the biweekly newspaper featuring Congress; and the Cable Satellite Public Affairs Network (C-SPAN).

Interview data indicate that these sources remain quite important to Hill staff operations. The importance of the nightly news doubtlessly reflects the prestige a member feels when he or she appears on one of these programs, despite the fact that Hill staff and members rarely watch these programs. Similarly, the *New York Times* and the *Wall Street Journal* are commonly lumped together with the *Washington Post* as critical partners of the "major papers." A typical response to a question regarding the most important sources of information on the Hill runs like this: "The best sources of information on the Hill are the *Post*, the *New York Times*, the *Wall Street Journal*, *Congressional Quarterly*, and the *National Journal* ."[17] A Republican staffer put it this way: "The definition of what it means to 'be informed' in this town means reading the *Wall Street Journal*, the *Post*, and the *New York Times* every day"[18] (see Table 6.9).

The major difference between the *Post* or *Congressional Quarterly* versus the *National Journal*, the *Wall Street Journal*, and the *New York Times* is probably the level of each publication's congressional coverage. The *Post* and *Congressional Quarterly* clearly offer the most comprehensive coverage of Congress, whereas these other publications see their mandates as more broad. As Chuck Alston of *Congressional Quarterly* characterized the *National Journal*: "CQ and *National Journal* are not at all competing publications, even though we share the same readership. *National Journal* engages more in that kind of journalism, the what's on somebody's mind journalism."[19]

In many ways, C-SPAN is the broadcast version of *Congressional Quarterly*. C-SPAN principally broadcasts House and Senate floor debates. Absent a floor debate, C-SPAN will cover a committee hearing. As such, C-SPAN is understandably a vital resource to congressional staff and media alike. It provides a way to monitor floor debate while staying in the office or to watch committee proceedings taking place in rooms filled to capacity with other journalists, lobbyists, and staff. As such, it is an important information resource for both members and staff who religiously monitor its programming.

For members, however, C-SPAN provides another important service. It is a ready source of clips of floor speeches for television and radio clips for other newscasts. In this way, C-SPAN, especially through floor debates and the use of Special Orders, provides another way for members to shape the policy debate and advertise their pet legislative initiatives. C-SPAN's coverage is often used for footage by CNN and the commercial networks, thus increasing the potential audience both inside and outside Washington. As Representative James Traficant (D-Ohio) related regarding his daily "1-minute" speeches that are his trademark, which are broadcast nationwide over C-SPAN:

> As a side effect, I get a lot of national press, especially electronic. It overshadows the amount of press I get locally, and my colleagues don't know it because they don't watch TV. . . . At one time I appeared on a major network newscast for 14 straight weeks. And several of those were "consensus" or "universal" appearances, where I was on all three networks, "MacNeil-Lehrer," and CNN making a statement.[20]

C-SPAN also has regular viewer call-in shows, in which members of Congress are regular guests. This feature provides another opportunity for members of Congress to send out their message to a congressional audience.

Roll Call received the lowest mean score of the second-tier publications. Nonetheless, evidence suggests that it too is an important source in the Capitol Hill world. *Roll Call*'s lower score (m = 3.154; mdn = 3) no doubt reflects the nature of the publication. *Roll Call* spends little time covering the specifics of legislation and world affairs. Instead, *Roll Call* promotes itself, quite accurately, as the "newspaper of Capitol Hill." According to then-Editor James Glassman, the newspaper's founder saw Capitol Hill and Congress as a distinct community, with its own culture, language, and geographic boundaries.[21] Its success over three decades lends credence to this view.

Several interviewed staff and members indicated that *Roll Call* has become an increasingly important source in recent years because its focus has shifted away from, as one staffer put it, "births and weddings and stuff like that," to harder news about Congress and issues concerning it. In particular, several interview subjects cited *Roll Call* as an important source on campaign finance reform, in which they take an editorial position distinct from that of the elite press. Glassman, like the representatives of the *Post* and *Congressional Quarterly*, has a very specific vision of his paper's role on Capitol Hill:

> We . . . cover legislation when it deals with the Congress. For example, we don't cover 12 of the 13 Appropriations subcommittees. We are only interested in one—the one that deals with Legislative Appropriations. And we cover the House Administration Committee extensively. We have to cover them.
>
> We cover legislative activity when it is interesting from an institutional or informational point of view. For example, we broke the story on the House Intelligence Committee hearings on the Senate Appropriations provision moving the CIA. We were not interested in the move per se. But the interest was in the jurisdictional battles between the House and Senate, and McCurdy and Byrd.[22]

Several of the congressional staff and members agreed. As a staffer to then Representative Barbara Boxer expressed: "For gossip, I turn to *Roll Call*. It's a good little paper with good articles. It was good on the coverage of the Keating Five and it's irreverent, which is something we need around here."[23] In terms of relating how her boss came to write an op-ed in *Roll Call* on his campaign finance proposal, Sharon Gang, an aide to former Representative Don Pease (D-Ohio), recalled:

> *Roll Call* is widely read on Capitol Hill and by the lobbyists downtown. We wanted to get some different ideas discussed as a way to get involved in the debate. So, it was a way to get ideas out there. . . .

It was another way to get attention. You know "Dear Colleague" letters often don't get attention. *Roll Call* is read by a lot of staffers, not
just those who focus on an issue, and it is read by the Senate as well.
So, it's another way to reach an audience. *Roll Call* is also very much
respected. It has come into its own in the last five years or so, and
it's "Guest Observer" column is a well-respected forum.[24]

Former Representative Dave McCurdy (D-Oklahoma), then-
Chairman of the House Intelligence Committee, shared this perception
of the Intelligence Committee coverage:

Roll Call has become a real player. It has become a real source of gossip on Capitol Hill, and that's because members read it. It's
Thursday. I don't think there's a member here who hasn't read it.
There was a piece in today's edition on the public hearings we're
having about moving the CIA to West Virginia. And all day, I've
had members coming up to me and commenting on it—saying "go
for it!" And that's probably the only public hearing we're going to
have, given the nature of our topic.[25]

There is a third tier of news sources widely available on Capitol
Hill, but these sources do not approach either the first or second tiers in
terms of readership or viewership on Capitol Hill. As a result, they are no
doubt less important to media entrepreneurs and others when devising a
media strategy. First, although Washington is awash with journalists who
write for specialized trade publications and newsletters (Hess 1981), these
publications, taken together or individually, do not enjoy a broad readership on Capitol Hill. The newest kids on the block are the electronic news
sources, such as the *National Journal's Congress Daily* or the *Congressional
Quarterly's Congressional Monitor*, which are distributed via facsimile
machines or the Campaign Hotline (now known as simply *The Hotline*),
an online computer news source. None of these sources are widely read.
In an interview, one press secretary hailed these inventions as "the wave
of the future." Although this prediction may be true, this research indicates that they are not the wave of the present. Other national publications, such as the weekly newsmagazines and other well-respected newspapers such as the *Los Angeles Times* and the *Christian Science Monitor* also
are infrequently read by the respondents (see Table 6.9).

In aggregate, respondents indicated that their overall use of
Washington-based publications national publications, and broadcast
media sources are roughly equal. Their reported means were 3.84, 3.86,
and 3.50, respectively. These results reflect a high appetite for news about
political events that one can expect from this population (see Table 6.9).

TARGETING MEDIA COVERAGE: VARIATIONS IN NEWS CONSUMPTION

The previous discussion analyzed and identified the media sources most commonly consulted by Capitol Hill operatives, providing a solid, overall picture. However, there are some news sources that are even more important as a tool for reaching a particular audience. The astute media entrepreneur will understand the value of getting coverage in these sources as a means to reach a particular subpopulation of the Washington community. This section analyzes some of the demographic differences in the way news is consumed on Capitol Hill.

First, there is one statistically significant difference between the House and the Senate. Respondents from the House of Representatives ranked *Congressional Quarterly Weekly Report* more highly than did Senate respondents. However, we know that *Congressional Quarterly* is almost universally read. This difference is like saying that *Congressional Quarterly* is vital to the House, but only essential to the Senate. A similar finding can be observed regarding committee chairs and ranking members, who are less likely to read the *National Journal* than their rank-and-file counterparts. Despite this difference, the publication is still quite popular among the offices of committee leaders (see Table 6.10).

The real story lies in the partisan differences. Democrats are more slightly more likely to read the *National Journal* or the *New York Times* and to listen to National Public Radio (NPR). This finding regarding NPR is interesting given the conservatives' charges of liberal bias in public broadcasting. Despite their reputations for being either very conservative or very liberal, no partisan difference was found in the readership of the *Wall Street Journal* or the *Washington Post*. In the latter case, this result simply means that absolutely everyone in the Washington community has to read the *Washington Post*, no matter how they might view the paper's partisan bent (see Table 6.10).

The most remarkable difference is in the case of the *Washington Times* (see Table 6.10). Although Democrats registered a mean score of only 1.867 when queried about reading the *Washington Times*, Republicans reported a mean score of 3.034. In short, Republicans commonly read both Washington papers, whereas the Democrats read the *Post* exclusively. One press secretary who did not want to be quoted on the record called the *Washington Times* the "Republicans' newsletter." Both Democratic and Republican interviewees talked about the importance of using the *Washington Times* to reach a Republican audience in Washington. Former Representative Dave McCurdy (D-Oklahoma) remarked that he has on occasion run op-ed articles in the *Washington Times* in order to stimulate Republican support for his policy ideas.[26]

Table 6.10. Differences in Media Consumption by Demographic
Groups.

News Source	Mean	Pearson's Correlation |r|	N
Congressional Quarterly			
House	4.6504**	0.2010**	123
Senate	4.0417		24
National Journal			
Republicans	3.0517***	0.2690****	58
Democrats	3.7777		90
New York Times			
Republicans	3.0862****	0.2915****	58
Democrats	3.7888		90
Washington Times			
Republicans	3.0345*****	0.4511*****	58
Democrats	1.8667		90
National Public Radio			
Republicans	2.5263***	0.2724****	58
Democrats	3.3068		90

**$p \le 0.05$
***$p \le 0.01$
****$p \le 0.001$
*****$p \le 0.0001$
Source: Data compiled by author.

Similarly, Tony Blankley, press secretary then Minority Leader Newt
Gingrich, said of the *Washington Times*:

> One important component to getting into the media is to communi-
> cate within Washington. It's hard to reach over 100 members of the
> Republican Conference. But I don't think there is a Republican on
> the Hill who doesn't read the *Washington Times* every day. So, it's
> easy to get a message out to House Republicans that way.[27]

News Consumption and Media Entrepreneurs

There are some remarkable differences between media entrepreneurs and their comparison groups and how they each consume the media. These differences have some applications in terms of coalition building. Because the pool of media entrepreneurs comprises approximately half of all respondents, there is strong evidence that using the media enterprise will reach a substantial audience of other media entrepreneurs. These data also provide more evidence that media entrepreneurs are quite different from their counterparts. In this sense, media entrepreneurs are greater news *consumers* than their counterparts. Furthermore, the narrowest definition of media entrepreneurs, the hard-core media entrepreneurs, have the biggest appetite for news and consult the most sources. As a result, it is not surprising that media entrepreneurs are more likely to see the media as an effective tool to influence policy—they are also more likely to be influenced by the same media efforts themselves.

The pool of media entrepreneurs, the most inclusive definition of media entrepreneurs used here, demonstrates a clear tendency to use more broadcast media sources than their counterparts. The pool of media entrepreneurs is more likely to listen to National Public Radio (NPR) and to watch CNN, C-SPAN, and "This Week with David Brinkley," the most popular of the Sunday morning talk shows. They did not differ in their reported use of any print news sources (see Table 6.11).

The likely media entrepreneurs show even fewer differences from their comparison group. The only statistically significant difference in broadcast media remains for CNN. The likely media entrepreneurs are not more likely than their comparison group to watch or listen to any other broadcast news sources. Interestingly enough, there is a statistically significant difference in the readership of the *Washington Times*. The likely media entrepreneurs are more likely to read the *Washington Times* than their comparison group (see Table 6.11).

The hard-core media entrepreneurs show the most dramatic differences of all. Not only are they more likely than their comparison group to watch both CNN and "This Week with David Brinkley," but they are also more likely to read the *Washington Times*, the *New York Times*, and the *Wall Street Journal* than their comparison group. To place these results in context, remember that in addition to reading or watching the previous news sources, the hard-core media entrepreneurs are most likely doing their regular "required reading" of the *Washington Post* and *Congressional Quarterly*. Hard-core media entrepreneurs have a remarkably heavy appetite for news, and they consult a wide variety of different sources to satiate this appetite. These results are even more dramatic when one considers the relatively small number ($n = 22$) of hard-core media entrepreneurs. The differences must be stark to overcome the "small N" problem (see Table 6.11).[28]

Table 6.11. Differences in News Consumption by Media Entrepreneurs.

Respondent Group	Mean (t-test)	Pearson's Correlation |r|	N
Variable Name: "This Week with David Brinkley"			
Comparison Group[a]	2.4783		69
Pool of Media Entrepreneurs	2.8734**	0.1732**	79
Hard-core Media Entrepreneurs	3.1429***	0.1621**	21
C-SPAN			
Comparison Group[a]	3.6764		69
Pool of Media Entrepreneurs	4.0000*	0.1563*	79
NPR			
Comparison Group[a]	2.7794		68
Pool of Media Entrepreneurs	3.1772*	0.1415*	79
CNN			
Comparison Group[a]	3.8406		68
Pool of Media Entrepreneurs	4.2025**	0.1864**	79
Likely Media Entrepreneurs	4.3415**	0.1907**	41
Hard-core Media Entrepreneurs	4.4286*	0.1658**	21
Washington Times			
Comparison Group[b]	2.1111		108
Likely Media Entrepreneurs	2.8571***	0.2656****	42
Hard-core Media Entrepreneurs	3.0455***	0.2385**	22
New York Times			
Comparison Group[c]	3.4297		128
Hard-core Media Entrepreneurs	4.0455**	0.1861**	22
Wall Street Journal			
Comparison Group[c]	3.6641		128
Hard-core Media Entrepreneurs	4.2727***	0.2099***	22

[a]The mean for the only narrowest definition of the comparison group is reported here. However, each t-test was conducted with the appropriate comparison group.

[b]Data reported here are for the comparison group for likely media entrepreneurs.

[c]Data reported here are for the comparison group for hard-core media entrepreneurs.

*$p \leq 0.10$

**$p \leq 0.05$

***$p \leq 0.01$

****$p \leq 0.001$

Source: Data compiled by author.

CONCLUSIONS AND IMPLICATIONS

The purpose of this chapter has been to understand how media entrepreneurs use the media to reach the Washington community. Media entrepreneurs have a small target audience for their media efforts. In terms of reaching a Washington audience, they want to reach the media, interest groups, the administration, and to a lesser extent federal agencies. However, reaching out to the issue networks is another way to ensure that the ultimate audience—members of Congress or other policymakers—hears the media entrepreneur's message. Media coverage also raises the media entrepreneur's profile and enhances his or her credibility. As a result, other players in a policy area may turn to the media entrepreneur for input in the future.

Reaching other media is key to this process for several reasons. The media are consumers as well as reporters of news. Networks and the elite press frequently follow each other's leads when selecting stories. The more media coverage that a media entrepreneur receives, the more credibility he or she will have. Simultaneously, media coverage enhances the chances that the media entrepreneur's message will reach its intended audience—both members of Congress and various cue givers within the Washington community.

This activity is important and effective in large part because of the nature of the Washington community. The growth of congressional and presidential staff, the press corps, and lobbyists have made maintaining personal contacts more difficult, although certainly not impossible. The short average tenure of many members of official Washington further exaggerates the impermanent and transient nature of the Washington community. As a result, media coverage takes on an important role when reaching all of the important members of an issue network.

First, the astute media entrepreneur knows that a targeted media effort can be an effective way to reach appropriate audiences—like other members of Congress. Of primary importance is getting coverage in the *Washington Post*, CNN, and *Congressional Quarterly*. Second, attention from the elite press, the network news, C-SPAN, *Roll Call*, or the *National Journal* will also carry one far. Third, coverage on any of the Sunday talk shows or weekly news magazines will raise the stakes of the debate. The influence of the coverage also can be enhanced by targeting members of one party or another. The *Washington Times* will reach Republicans more than Democrats, whereas National Public Radio, the *National Journal*, or the *New York Times* will reach more Democrats than Republicans.

Finally, this analysis provides further evidence that media entrepreneurs are quite distinct from their counterparts. The media entrepreneurs consider the media and the White House important audiences for the media enterprise. Media entrepreneurs also consider television interviews and op-ed articles more important vehicles to communicate in Washington than do their non-media-oriented counterparts. Furthermore, media entrepreneurs are remarkably different in the way they use the media themselves. Media entrepreneurs consult more sources of news, and the stronger they feel about the effectiveness of the media, the more sources they are likely to consult. It is obvious that media entrepreneurs' sense of efficacy regarding the media cuts both ways. Not only do they see the media as a more effective means to reach a Washington audience, to set the agenda, and to influence the legislative process, but they also have a greater appetite for news and are willing to consult a panoply of sources for their information. Furthermore, there are a lot of media entrepreneurs in Congress. They themselves are a potent audience for the media enterprise.

ENDNOTES

1. Interview, September 18, 1991.
2. Interview, July 29, 1991.
3. Interview, July 25, 1991.
4. Interview, June 11, 1991.
5. Regression analysis demonstrates the same relationship—media strategies are considered more valuable for those who have higher scores on the attitude scale. However, the R^2 values generated by these models are very low, with $R^2 \leq 0.10$. These results are probably due to the problems inherent in conducting regression analysis on ordinal-level data.
6. Interview, March 22, 1991.
7. Interview, May 7, 1991.
8. Interview, May 10, 1991.
9. Interview, March 5, 1991.
10. Interview, March 7, 1991.
11. Interview, May 20, 1991.
12. Interview, March 1, 1991.
13. Interview, February 12, 1991.
14. Interview, February 12, 1991.
15. Interview, March 23, 1992, emphasis is Franken's.
16. Interview, May 20, 1991.
17. Interview, January 15, 1991.
18. Interview, May 20, 1991.
19. Interview, March 5, 1991.
20. Interview, October 1, 1991.
21. Interview, August 8, 1991.

22. Interview, August 8, 1991.
23. Interview, March 1, 1991.
24. Interview, November 2, 1991.
25. Interview, July 25, 1991.
26. Lunch with Sunbelt Caucus Staff, May 1992.
27. Interview, May 20, 1991.
28. Regression analysis with the "Attitude" variable yielded statistically significant models in the cases of the *New York Times* and CNN. However, these models were not strongly predictive, probably due at least in part to the problems associated with conducting regression analysis on ordinal-level data.

7

Reaching Out Beyond the Beltway

Media entrepreneurs clearly use the media enterprise to reach audiences in the halls of Congress and in downtown Washington, DC. However, this process does not happen in isolation. The media outlets commonly used to reach issue networks, congressional audiences, and the Washington press corps enjoy a wide audience outside Washington as well. At the same time, the messages will be amplified as reporters take their cues from other news sources and report the media entrepreneurs' messages themselves. As a result, the policy debate is "overheard," so to speak, by a noticeable portion of the voting public. Media entrepreneurs are also interested in reaching the general public. Like the audiences in Congress and the Washington community, the public is an important cue giver to policymakers.

Reaching constituents and the general public serves several purposes. First, constituents are important sources of voting cues for other members of Congress, and public opinion polls frequently function as general guideposts for policy decisions. Therefore, reaching the public is a powerful tool to garner the support of other members of Congress and the administration. Second, the media enterprise can serve double duty for the creative media entrepreneur. Not only might media entrepreneurs try to influence policy, but the message could be recast for local media consumption. In this way the media enterprise can reinforce members' other constituent communication efforts. Third, becoming a "player" in Washington and getting favorable coverage in the national media can result in favorable media coverage in the local press, as local reporters pick up favorable cues from the national press corps. This is a goal of members who are always looking to the next election, or who have ambitions for higher office.

This chapter first shows through survey analysis that media entrepreneurs place even greater stock in constituent contacts and public pressure as a means to influence the legislative process than their counterparts. In fact, there is some evidence that media entrepreneurs make an even greater effort than their counterparts to keep in touch with the district.

Second, the special role of congressional leadership is examined. During a long period of divided government and the rise of television as a medium to communicate with the public, the Democratic congressional leadership moved into the media spotlight. They had to answer, in a very public forum, partisan charges leveled against them by their partisan adversaries in the White House. The Republican party leadership was placed in a high profile position as the President's lieutenants. Republicans today play a similar role as counterpoint to the efforts of the Democratic White House.

Third, the case studies provide some interesting examples of how the media enterprise—as employed by members of Congress and by other organizations or individuals—can be used to influence the public debate and simultaneously communicate with constituents in the district. The case studies show that communicating with constituents is different from communicating in Washington. However, the same event can provide material for both efforts. The case studies also show that the media enterprise is not the exclusive domain of members of Congress. Rather, its techniques may be adopted by interest groups as well as members of Congress.

THE PUBLIC CONNECTION TO THE MEDIA ENTERPRISE

Efforts in Washington and on the Hill notwithstanding, the single most important audience for the media enterprise is constituents. The full set of respondents indicated overwhelmingly that their primary audience was constituents ($M = 3.906$; $Mdn = 4$). Similarly, there was consensus among the full set of respondents that the public outside the constituency are also an important audience for these media efforts (M = 3.439; Mdn = 4) (see Table 6.1).

The public connection is important in terms of coalition building. According to the full set of respondents, constituent contacts (M = 4.094; Mdn = 4) are the second most important tool for building a legislative coalition in Congress (see Table 5.5). The only legislative strategy to register a higher score was personal contacts. The pattern remained consistent in terms of coalition-building strategies in the Washington community. The full set of respondents ranked grass-roots pressure (M = 3.486; Mdn = 4) as the third most important strategy to build coalitions in Washington—ranked after party leadership and personal contacts (see Table 6.4).

Likewise, we learned earlier that congressional offices share at least two items of required reading: the *Washington Post* and *Congressional Quarterly Weekly Report*. Major district newspapers should be added to this list. The full group of respondents indicated that consulting the district media is a daily ritual in congressional offices (M = 4.232). Relatively speaking, district media outranked even CNN. All of these facts argue that maintaining close ties with the world outside the beltway is an important part of the congressional world (see Table 6.9).[1]

Media Entrepreneurs and the Public Connection

The survey analysis shows consistently that media entrepreneurs are distinct from their congressional counterparts in the way they use the media to communicate inside Washington and inside Congress. Yet we see here that media entrepreneurs also differ from their colleagues in terms of using the media to reach the public *outside* the beltway. This trend is demonstrated in several different ways. First, hard-core media entrepreneurs consider the public (not just their own constituents) a more likely audience for media strategies than do their comparison group. The same pattern is seen in likely media entrepreneurs, but the difference is not statistically significant. The pool of media entrepreneurs—the most inclusive definition of media entrepreneurs—is also more likely to see constituents and the general public as a potential audience for members' media initiatives (see Tables 7.1 and 7.2).

Second, there is some evidence that media entrepreneurs hold an even stronger opinion of the influence the public can exert on policymakers in Washington. For example, all definitions of media entrepreneurs ranked constituent contacts very highly on the list of legislative strategies; the average Likert-scale score was over 4.0[2] in every case. Similarly, grass-roots pressure performed very well when building a coalition outside Congress. In fact, there is weak statistical evidence that the pool of

Table 7.1. Media Entrepreneurs' Intended Audience: Constituents (t-test).

Variable Name: Constituents

Respondent Group	Mean (t-test)	Pearson's Correlation |r|	N
Comparison Group[a]	3.7429		70
Pool of Media Entrepreneurs	4.0506*	0.1444*	77
Likely Media Entrepreneurs	4.0238	0.0694	42
Hard-core Media Entrepreneurs	4.0000	0.0368	22

[a]The mean for only the narrowest definition of the comparison group is reported here. However, each t-test was conducted with the appropriate comparison group.
*$p \leq 0.10$
Source: Data compiled by author.

Table 7.2. Media Entrepreneurs' Intended Audience: The General Public (t-test).

Variable Name: Public outside constituents

Respondent Group	Mean (t-test)	Pearson's Correlation |r|	N
Comparison Group[a]	3.2754		69
Pool of Media Entrepreneurs	3.5823*	0.1435*	79
Likely Media Entrepreneurs	3.6190	0.1061	42
Hard-core Media Entrepreneurs	3.8181*	0.1484*	22

[a]The mean for only the narrowest definition of the comparison group is reported here. However, each t-test was conducted with the appropriate comparison group.
*$p \leq 0.10$
Source: Data compiled by author.

media entrepreneurs see grass-roots pressure as a *more important* coalition-building strategy than their comparison group (see Table 7.3).

Third, we know that the district media are a vital source for information for all members of Congress. The data also show that media entrepreneurs, especially the hard-core media entrepreneurs, have a voracious appetite for political news. This appetite extends beyond simply reading several sources from the national press. Hard-core media entrepreneurs—the strictest definition used in this analysis—are even more likely to consult district news sources. Therefore, media entrepre-

Table 7.3. Media Entrepreneurs and Perceived Importance of Grass-roots Pressure (t-test).

Variable Name: Grass-roots pressure
  (building coalitions in Washington)

Respondent Group	Mean (t-test)	Pearson's Correlation $|r|$	N
Comparison Group[a]	3.2951		61
Pool of Media Entrepreneurs	3.6364*	0.1482*	77
Likely Media Entrepreneurs	3.7073	0.1261	41
Hard-core Media Entrepreneurs	3.4286	0.0211	21

[a]The mean for only the narrowest definition of the comparison group is reported here. However, each t-test was conducted with the appropriate comparison group.
*$p \leq 0.10$
Source: Data compiled by author.

neurs not only have a heavy appetite for national news, but they monitor local news more closely than their counterparts (see Table 7.4).

These findings are critical. They indicate that media entrepreneurs have a strong belief that communication with the public is an effective way to influence policy in Washington. Therefore, in addition to reaching out to congressional audiences and the Washington community, media entrepreneurs try to generate local support for their ideas in

Table 7.4. Media Entrepreneurs' Use of District Media (t-test).

Variable Name: District media (Read as news source)

Respondent Group	Mean (t-test)	Pearson's Correlation $|r|$	N
Comparison Group[a]	4.2121		66
Pool of Media Entrepreneurs	4.2500	0.0211	72
Likely Media Entrepreneurs	4.2821	0.0352	39
Hard-core Media Entrepreneurs	4.5714*	0.1607*	21

[a]The mean for only the narrowest definition of the comparison group is reported here. However, each t-test was conducted with the appropriate comparison group.
*$p \leq 0.10$
Source: Data compiled by author.

order to influence fellow policymakers. This perception underscores how many policymakers approach their jobs as delegates rather than trustees in the Burkean sense. They are very willing to support policy initiatives that have broad appeal. Thus, proving that one's ideas have broad appeal is an important component of the media enterprise.

Furthermore, these findings dispute the often implicit assumption that being a "national" legislator somehow precludes spending time with the local media. Perhaps there is a sense that media entrepreneurs are likely to lose touch with their districts by trying to become players in Washington. In fact, some of the survey data support this contention; several respondents whose members' did not aggressively pursue national media attention frequently cited their local orientation as the reason they avoided the national stage. Similarly, some of the political science literature also hints at this conclusion—that national media attention somehow detracts from local press relations (Cook 1989, 82-86). Yet media entrepreneurs, for all their interest in the national media, seem to be more concerned with their constituents and the general public than the rest of Congress. All media entrepreneurs have strong faith in the importance of public pressure on Congress and Washington. Furthermore, the strongest media entrepreneurs are actually more likely to pursue the local media than their counterparts.

CONGRESSIONAL LEADERS AS ENTREPRENEURS

One of the most notable developments in the modern Congress is the elevation of congressional leadership in the media spotlight. The last speaker who was trained exclusively in the traditional insider strategies of the old Congress and elected using those methods was Carl Albert, who ascended to the speakership in the 1960s. Albert's opponent in his first race, Richard Bolling of Missouri, is remembered for using a public strategy in his campaign for speaker that failed (Cook 1989, 149-150). Albert's tenure covered the period in the history of the House that initiated the reforms that are the hallmark of the class of 1974.

There are several reasons why relations between the congressional leadership and the media are more important now than they were in Albert's era. One reason for the heightened profile of the speaker and other leaders stems from the institutional changes in Congress itself. The class of 1974 hailed a new generation of legislators who put greater stock in media coverage. They demanded leaders who would take a high public profile. Similarly, the press came to recognize that the presidency can be used (or misused) as a partisan "bully pulpit." After years of divided government, the media began looking for spokespersons to provide some balance. The Democrats in Congress were a natural place to go. "Democratic responses" provided by Democratic congressional leaders became part of the normal routine following presidential addresses, a role Republican leaders play vis-à-vis the Democratic president today.

Albert's successor, Thomas P. "Tip" O'Neill, was the first speaker who really adopted the role of media entrepreneur. O'Neill was thrust into the national spotlight after the election of 1980. During the period when Republicans controlled the White House and the Senate, O'Neill moved into the national spotlight as the single major spokesperson of the Democratic party—operating in a sense like the opposition party leader in a parliamentary system. Furthermore, O'Neill began to act much like a media entrepreneur. He accepted talk show appearances, gave interviews more frequently, and institutionalized a regular press conference. Aside from O'Neill, there was no other obvious choice to articulate the Democratic party positions before the American public. As one scholar of the speakership stated: "O'Neill realized that the war with Reagan was a battle to win public opinion" (Peters 1990, 239). The audience that had to be won over by O'Neill's media enterprise was not Congress or the administration, or even interest groups or other attentive publics. Rather, it was the American public residing outside the Washington community.

As the presidency remained in Republican hands and Congress continued to be controlled by the Democrats, electing media savvy and telegenic leaders had become a top priority for the congressional Democrats. After Speakers O'Neill and Wright, both of whom were easily caricatured by cartoonists and not terribly telegenic, one advantage Speaker Tom Foley enjoyed on his election was the sense among congressional Democrats that he would come across well on television (Hook 1989). Democrat Richard Gephardt, the current Minority Leader, is not only telegenic, but he is very comfortable with television as a medium (Cook 1989, 6). Apparently, Gephardt's television skills were a factor in winning his current post as Minority Leader, despite a challenge from Representative Charlie Rose (D- North Carolina) (Monk, 1994).

Media skills clearly are now a consideration in the selection of party leaders. It is no longer sufficient to have solid political skills to guide legislation through the political maze. Party leaders must also be able to articulate programmatic ideas to the American public. This function is arguably more important in terms of the party that does not control the White House. But the party that also holds the presidency takes on many of the same functions. The minority leaders in the current Congress may play cheerleader for the Clinton administration, just as the Republicans did under Reagan and Bush. Sometimes congressional leaders may take a position that is more extreme than the White House in order to facilitate the compromise. Or, in rare instances, such as the case of the 1990 budget agreement, then Minority Whip Newt Gingrich (R-Georgia) publicly repudiated the deal negotiated by the Bush administration and the congressional Democrats. Gingrich justified his opposition by asserting that he represented the House Republicans, not the Republican administration.

Interviews with leadership press secretaries clearly reflect the mandate to communicate a coherent message to the American public. The following are some typical responses to a query regarding the intended audience for the leadership's press efforts:

> The American public. We want a Democratic response to a White House spin.[3]

> The secondary audience is the national audience. The public is the audience eventually.[4]

> There are really two audiences. One that he is trying to reach is the press. . . . Second, we're trying to reach the people who are watching—the public.[5]

> We have two principal audiences. The first is the press filter through which communications go to the public. The second is the middle class, broadly defined.[6]

In the cases of both the majority and minority leadership, there was a clear sense of responsibility to communicate a specific message to the American public. In the words of Stan Cannon, press secretary to then Senate Minority Whip Alan Simpson (R-Wyoming), "We . . . try to represent the White House position on things. In the minority party, it's all that much more important to hold solidarity together."[7] Similarly, as Missy Tessier, Press Secretary to Bob Michel (R-Illinois) then House Minority Leader: "We are the voice of the White House on Capitol Hill."[8]

The effort to make a clear counterargument against the White House is best exemplified by comparing the responses of the press secretaries to then Majority Leader Gephardt and former Speaker Foley. Their reflections mirror the different approaches these two leaders took toward the media enterprise. As David Dreyer, Gephardt's press secretary, saw it:

> We want to draw a distinction between Bush's view and the Democratic view of the world. The current occupant of the Majority Leader's office, Gephardt, has an easier time of it. He is a national figure, since he ran for President. Therefore, he is a more visible person. . . .

The President demands a commanding podium. No single Democratic leader can command the same level of attention. There is no way that you can get the press to follow you to your vacation home anywhere! We can only generally hope to break even in the news coverage.[9]

By contrast, Jeff Biggs, Foley's spokesperson, characterized the speaker's approach in this way:

Foley wants to set up the speakership as an arbiter of House rules. Foley is not good at one-liners and sound bites, like some people around here.

Even as titular head of the party, Foley has to share the spotlight with a wider number of people than before, even a wider circle than Gephardt or Grey. It's also committee chairmen and the like. So, the leadership is more collaborative than in the past. That was not something that was faced even by Speaker O'Neill.[10]

Finally, then Minority Leader Gingrich still sees his role in terms of articulating a message that is occasionally distinct from the administration. As Tony Blankley characterized Gingrich's approach:

Gingrich may have a different emphasis or idea, which means that we will pull out in front of the White House on something. In which case, we will be looking for ways to pull the White House along. The White House, for other reasons, maybe wants to pull back or be cautious. For example, on domestic policy, we are usually trying to pull them along.[11]

Two distinct patterns arise from this analysis. First, it is clear that the congressional leadership positions in both Houses and in both parties have evolved into very public positions. While their predecessors like Albert shunned the spotlight, the current generation of congressional leaders seek it out. Simultaneously, the leaders are called on by the press and their colleagues in Congress to articulate a coherent message to the American public. The public, rather than other members of Congress or the administration, is clearly the audience of the leaders' media enterprise. Important differences remain within the leadership ranks. Media-oriented leaders, such as Dole, Gephardt, or Gingrich, display a more sophisticated understanding than their counterparts of how the media interpret and shape the content of their message. The media-oriented leaders all demonstrate a clearer understanding of reaching the media audience in order to eventually reach the public.

THE PUBLIC CONNECTION IN THE MEDIA ENTERPRISE: CASE STUDY DATA

As we saw earlier, media entrepreneurs are very aware of the importance of reaching the greater American public in order to set the agenda and build legislative coalitions. Furthermore, using the media enterprise to stimulate conversation in the Washington community does not preclude using the same event to generate publicity in the local press. This section describes two ways in which the media can be used to reach the public and constituents in order to affect policy in Washington. The first way is to "prime the pump"—to raise enough general awareness of a public problem to make legislators receptive to passing legislation. The second is to apply pressure on legislators through news reports and editorials in the local media in order to influence their vote in Washington. In addition, the media enterprise also can overlap into more traditional means of constituent communication.

Priming the Pump: Adult Literacy

The role of the media in adult literacy was principally to raise public awareness of the issue. In so doing, the media primed the policy pump enough to pave the way for reform. Public interest was piqued in several ways. Beginning in the mid-1980s, there was increasing public awareness of the existence of widespread adult illiteracy. Literacy became something of a fashionable social issue. At the same time, many major corporations started to experience difficulty recruiting applicants with sufficient literacy and numerical skills to be trained for employment. Corporate executives began to realize that the problem was endemic.

Since the mid-1980s, a number of efforts were undertaken to raise public awareness of the issue. The most notable is the Project Literacy U.S. (PLUS) Campaign that is jointly sponsored by ABC and PBS. PLUS consists of a series of public-service announcements, documentaries, and episodes in prime-time television series designed to discuss illiteracy in one way or another. In addition, newspapers offer an annual spate of publicity in response to a commemorative literacy day that usually falls in September. The effort to raise general public awareness of illiteracy was aided by several public figures, including Wally "Famous" Amos, the cookie promoter who is also the spokesperson for Literacy Volunteers of America (LVA); Barbara Bush; and several governors, including Buddy Roemer (R-Louisiana) and John Ashcroft (R-Missouri).

Media attention to illiteracy followed a predictable pattern. These stories tended to be human interest pieces that focused on the personal ramifications of the problem rather than on the public policy surrounding the issue or the potential impact of an underskilled work force on the American economy. Literacy media coverage was parodied this way by one activist:

> [The] "typical literacy story" . . . is always a human interest story about Mrs. Jones. Mrs. Jones is always either an older white woman from Kentucky who always wanted to read the Bible, or she is a single, black mother on public assistance. They always go to The Literacy Center, which is always sponsored by The Reporter's Newspaper, and in some amazingly short amount of time, Mrs. Jones learns how to read. She is taught by a tutor who is always female and from a higher SES than Mrs. Jones. And then, she can either read the Bible and die a happy woman or she can get a job and support her family. This story is a fiction in every respect. It is not critical or in-depth.[12]

The literacy activists interviewed for this project universally condemned the media. They charged that the media completely failed to discuss the nature of federal policy in adult education or to analyze critically the proposed legislation or its ramifications. The only member of the elite press to receive any kudos was the *New York Times*, which ran a series of articles on literacy policy in September 1989. Similarly, the *Washington Times* received credit for their coverage of the legislation.

Interestingly enough, the coverage in the *New York Times* resulted from special contacts activists in the literacy community enjoyed. The editor of the *New York Times*, Arthur Sulzberger, was a former member of the board of the Business Coalition for Effective Literacy (BCEL) and was a signatory of the letters generated by BCEL's ad-hoc "business lobby for literacy." Another literacy activist had some contacts at the *New York Times*, which helped stimulate that paper's coverage.

The media's role in keeping the pump primed has not evaporated. The PLUS campaign is ongoing. ABC continues to incorporate stories about illiterate adults into its programming. Public service announcements are still being produced and broadcast in a continuing attempt to recruit students into adult literacy programs. However, the emphasis seems to be shifting to "family literacy" or "intergenerational literacy." Literacy, in terms of its importance to economic growth, job training, and competitiveness, is not a part of these public awareness campaigns; however, these issues remain part of the public policy debate within the issue network in Washington.

However, aside from the spate of public attention that resulted from the Senate hearings featuring Dexter Manley, there was little coverage of the literacy bill as it moved through Congress. Rather, the

National Literacy Act exemplifies the traditional, insider approach to policymaking. The media were crucial, however, in awakening public and elite awareness of the adult illiteracy problem in the United States. Without this effort, finding any member to sponsor legislation would have been impossible. After all, what would motivate a member to solve a problem that did not seem to exist?

Nonetheless, when the literacy bill was bogged down in the Senate at the close of the 101st Congress, the initial media coverage Simon received was not sufficient to pry the bill loose from its "hold" in the Senate. The same holds true today. Even though ABC and others continue their public information campaigns, literacy remains a low-profile issue.

Activating the Local Media: Campaign Finance Reform

Campaign finance reform is an interesting case because of the primacy of local media as a legislative cue giver. Their role becomes even more important because of the confused and poorly informed nature of public opinion on the subject.

My interview subjects widely acknowledged that most members of Congress have little genuine interest in pursuing campaign finance reform. They credit media attention as the key reason that campaign finance reform remains on the congressional agenda. The media play two important roles in this process. First, editorial boards in newspapers across the country are pivotal because they pressure Congress to consider campaign finance reform legislation regularly. Second, the pressure from editorial boards is reinforced by a regular stream of investigative news articles on campaign finance. Although investigative reporting usually occurs in the major newspapers, which have the resources to conduct exhaustive research and statistical analyses, there is a remarkable "trickle-down" effect as reporters for smaller news organizations pick up local angles on the stories. Without this attention, campaign finance reform would be dead on arrival.

The most ambitious media entrepreneurs involved with campaign finance reform, however, are not members of Congress. Rather, the effort is made by several interest groups, principally Common Cause. This fact demonstrates that the media enterprise is not unique to members of Congress. Rather, it can be employed by any organization interested in influencing the policy process. Through its continued involvement and attention to this issue, Common Cause, just like any media entrepreneur in Congress, has established itself as a player inside Washington, and it has credibility among reporters on this issue. The following section analyzes Common Cause's role in generating press attention on the campaign finance issue, and the impact this attention has on members of Congress.

Editorial Boards: The Media as Commentators

> When 98 percent of House incumbents are returned to office, when a candidate for the House must spend nearly $400,000 and for the Senate nearly $4 million, when special interest political action committees provide the lion's share of campaign funding, then something is seriously wrong. Our system of choosing our representatives is badly off track.[13]

Common Cause has, over the last two decades, cultivated strong relationships with editorial boards across the country. The centerpiece of these efforts is their editorial memoranda (also known as *edit memos*). These documents produced by Common Cause are typically about 10 pages in length, with, as one activist put it, "a minimum of rhetoric."[14] Instead, the memoranda include finance data generated from FEC reports that the editorial writers can readily repackage for a local audience.

The striking similarity of many of these editorials, like the example at the beginning of this section, is frequently cited as evidence of Common Cause's influence with the media. Other analyses confirm this perception. In the 100th Congress, some 300 newspapers nationwide wrote editorials in favor of the campaign finance bill supported by Common Cause (Alston 1989). Similarly, in the 101st Congress, over 200 editorials favoring campaign finance reform appeared in local newspapers across the country. Approximately 75 cited Common Cause or quoted the organization's president, Fred Wertheimer; another two dozen were virtually identical.[15] And, like the local press, the elite press was equally susceptible to the influence of Common Cause.

Common Cause's unusual success has not gone unnoticed by commentators and political scientists. One study of the *New York Times*, the *Los Angeles Times*, and the *Washington Post* found that because Common Cause was regularly the first to comment on any campaign finance development, its interpretation or data analyses commonly were adopted without question for further analysis (Sorauf 1987). In a case study of the *New York Times*, David Paletz and Robert Entman (1981, 138-146) discovered that Common Cause received extremely favorable press coverage on a wide variety of issues over 90 percent of the time. Both studies reached the same conclusion: Common Cause is very effective in generating favorable press attention because its leaders understand the structural biases of the media. In terms of campaign finance reform, Common Cause activists play into reporters' professional skepticism, who are inclined to think that politicians are corrupt—or at the very least corruptible. Providing reports with solid statistical analyses and a shared point of view enhance Common Cause's chances of getting favorable press coverage.

My interview data support these conclusions. Both friends and foes alike of Common Cause agree that the group's success in the media stems from its reputation for solid research. Furthermore, Common Cause and other good government groups are politically astute. They know that the most effective way to get to a member of Congress is through his or her district. According to a staff person working with the House Task Force on Campaign Finance Reform:

> Common Cause has the editorial boards in their pocket. They don't trust members, but whenever they thought they had problems, they would have the editorial boards gin up—it happened on PAC limits, tax audits, not enough money on PACs. We may have had a great bill, but they would oppose it because of the PAC limits. . . .
>
> About a week [before the bill was brought to the floor], Fred Wertheimer came in and said, "In the last 36 hours we have contacted 332 editorial boards across the country, and we will have 325 editorials appearing in the next 72 hours."[16]

Another activist agreed: "Our goal is to get coverage in papers around the country, and to get them more savvy on the issue. The *Washington Post* is largely discarded by members of Congress because it is not read in their districts."[17]

The widely shared perception is that although the *Washington Post* and the *New York Times* consistently run editorials in favor of campaign finance reform, the most important editorials are those in the local papers. As one former Senate staffer analyzed it:

> The relationship is fairly tense. I sensed in meetings with Members that when we were discussing strategies of what can be done, the question, "how will this sell to the media?" always came up. Before it was, "how can we sell this to Common Cause?" Because Common Cause has influence at the *Washington Post*, and the *Washington Post* has influence over the *St. Louis Post-Dispatch*, which in turn has influence over the *Joplin News* and I'm weak in Joplin.[18]

Another staffer was more blunt: "Members don't give a shit about what's in the *Washington Post* or the *New York Times*. They only care about their district."[19]

Fred Wertheimer, President of Common Cause, had a somewhat different view. He asserted that any success Common Cause has achieved is solely a result of its high-quality research. He did not admit to any unique relationships with editorial boards in the country. Instead, he said:

> Since [1971] we have analyzed and distributed information. The information has always demonstrated problems in the campaign finance system. We have always communicated to editorial boards, through our national and our state and local offices. . . . It wasn't too long ago that I could have met with the editorial boards of all the major newspapers in the country. . . .
>
> This is important: I didn't *get* editorial support. We put out our case, and let it stand on its merits. We have to deal with the media and make our case like everyone else.[20]

Former Representative Mike Synar (D-Oklahoma), considered a liberal on campaign finance, agreed. Although he acknowledged Common Cause's extraordinary relationship with local and regional editorial boards, he concluded with this assessment, "Editorial boards have resisted some of the Common Cause program. Common Cause advocates public financing, and editorial boards have resisted advocating public financing thus far."[21]

Because of their success with the media enterprise, Common Cause clearly has affected legislation. They had a healthy relationship with the Senate leader on this issue, former Senator David Boren (D-Oklahoma), whose bills included many of their suggestions. They also worked with several House offices as the Task Force developed a bill in the 102nd Congress, in part because the House Democrats wanted to avoid the experience of the 101st Congress, when Common Cause instituted an editorial campaign against the House bill, claiming it was weak and failed to constitute real reform. In the words of one person involved with developing the House bill in the 102nd Congress:

> When the proposal was out there, people started making suggestions for improving it. But we argued that we had press support for the bill as designed, and we didn't want to jeopardize the press support we had. And if we started changing the bill, we might lose support.[22]

The editorial board strategy worked. The final legislation passed by the 102nd Congress included a voluntary public financing provision that met constitutional requirements and satisfied Common Cause and the editorial writers. The strategy was very effective.

Common Cause and its leaders clearly understand many of the dynamics of the media. Editorial writers and reporters need solid, easily digestible information, and Common Cause's research efforts and edit memos provide this kind of data. Second, the media need complex arguments distilled into simple, clear-cut issues. Common Cause, once again, is able to provide this service. Furthermore, Common Cause is successful because it has credibility with the media. Its research is considered first rate. Therefore, it becomes a simple step for the editorial writers to promote Common Cause's position.

Because of these and other tactics adopted by Common Cause, like placing full-page ads in district newspapers accusing members of obstructing campaign finance reform, or being "on the take" from special interest groups, Common Cause is not terribly popular on Capitol Hill. Not only is Common Cause "the dog that barks at its friends" (Alston 1989), but the amount of grass-roots support it actually carries is considered minimal. As one congressional staffer put it: "the numbers aren't there. I bet that Fred [Wertheimer] couldn't mobilize 1 percent of the vote. I mean, they're not the NRA [National Rifle Association]. But they are effective because of their focus on public policy."[23]

The editorial board strategy is an effective means to reach members of Congress for two reasons. First, editorial writers represent the opinion leaders in the district. If these people criticize their member of Congress, relations with other community leaders in the district may be adversely affected. Second, the district press reaches the voting public as well. Negative editorials may stimulate angry letters from constituents or find voter ire registered in public opinion polls or the ballot box. Conversely, supporting campaign finance reform can benefit members for the same reasons.

The Media as Investigators

The pressure exerted by editorial boards is augmented by a constant stream of investigative reports on campaign finance. Once again, the investigative activity occurs principally in the elite press. These news organizations have sufficient resources to conduct the extensive research and statistical analyses necessary to find patterns in thousands of campaign disclosure forms. These stories are frequently adopted by district press, who look for a local angle on the larger story. Their findings on PAC donations, campaign war chests, and expenditure patterns may augment the editorial board policies of many of these same newspapers.

Because the Federal Election Commission (FEC) is widely considered a weak bureaucratic agency, investigative reporters who specialize in campaign finance consider themselves a vital part of the oversight process. Headed by a board of six commissioners (three Democrats and three Republicans), the FEC has few staff and few enforcement mechanisms. The FEC does some data analysis of campaign finance information; however, its principal function is to make information available to those who wish to see it. As one staff member put it:

> The entire organization is designed for disclosure. All of our reports are on microfilm and available to the public within 24 hours. Anyone can come and look at them. You don't have to identify yourself or indicate why you want the information. . . . We know that our records are reviewed by political parties, special interest groups, academics, political opponents, etc.[24]

Enforcement of campaign finance laws, however, rarely occurs at the initiative of the FEC staff or its commissioners. Rather, disclosure and the threat of embarrassment from what may be found in the FEC records are the principal deterrents. According to this same staffer:

> Even enforcement responsibility is placed on the public. They [the Congress] didn't want a big investigation [effort]. In order to launch an investigation we have to have a majority of the Board, which is made of three Democrats and three Republicans. But any complaint that is brought up by the public must be investigated. That puts a lot of responsibility on the media and the public. . . .
>
> We disclose spending. It is up to the public to decide if that's OK.[25]

This view is shared by a small cadre of investigative reporters who have spent considerable time and effort tracing the flow of campaign money. Sara Fritz of the *Los Angeles Times* put it this way:

> The system was designed to restrain behavior through public disclosure. The penalties and enforcement procedures are weak. The disclosure has to come through the media. I once asked an official at the FEC why they weren't more aggressive in dealing with people who exceeded the legal limits of donating. And their response was that they enforced through disclosures. The media are the primary force in that case, and it was intended to be that way.[26]

Chuck Babcock of the *Washington Post* agreed:

> My job is to disclose. The FEC is a joke as far as enforcement. But they are not a joke in disclosure of disbursement and expenditures. So that is the reporters' role. . . . My job is to tell how the world works. I write

two kinds of articles. One is the "gotcha" exposé. The other one is simply more descriptive. I think this is important because Washington is a political town. Campaign finance is a local story here in this town, and I need to tell my audience how it works.[27]

The dean of the delegation is Brooks Jackson of the Cable News Network. His book, *Honest Graft* (1988), documents former Representative Tony Coehlo's (D-California) campaign fundraising efforts while head of the Democratic Congressional Campaign Committee (DCCC). Jackson made his reputation as an investigative reporter for the *Wall Street Journal*, who focused on campaign finance. He argues that the media have kept the spotlight on the campaign finance reform issue. As he stated:

If the press paid no attention to campaign money, then there would be even more abuse. These is a fear of being tagged as turning a campaign contribution into a favor, even if that fear is subconscious.

Money has become more and more important as of late, and more and more extensive. We have entered a period of capital extensive politics, rather than labor extensive politics. Without reporters shining a light, then politicians would have no compunction against voting for special interest money.[28]

The news organizations employing these reporters are willing to commit large sums of time and money to poring over FEC documents and generating sophisticated statistical analyses of them. For example, in the 1990 election cycle, the *Washington Post* purchased data tapes from the FEC and did independent analyses of congressional campaign fundraising. The *Post* learned that the Republicans are right when they charge that campaign funds are raised primarily from outside the members' congressional districts. Babcock also described other kinds of stories he had covered, including an investigation of a fundraiser held by former Senator Tim Wirth (D-Colorado), hosted by cable television operators. Apparently the event raised $80,000, and even the cost of the food and hotel became "in-kind" contributions that did not appear on the FEC reports.

The most ambitious recent project of this ilk was conducted by the *Los Angeles Times*. Sara Fritz and Dwight Morris published a series of articles that traced campaign expenditures in the 1990 election cycle rather than sources of campaign funds. The series disclosed some startling findings. The most surprising was that the largest expenditures in congressional campaigns were for salaries and fundraising expenses. Media buys, especially television and radio, constituted only a small portion of the candidates' budgets. Their analysis disclosed that only one-third of the money spent in Senate races was used to pay for advertising, whereas less than a quarter of expenditures in House race was dedicated to media buys (see, for example, Fritz and Morris 1990).

This finding runs contrary to the conventional wisdom that argues that successful Senate candidates have to spend upwards of 60 percent of their campaign chests on television advertising. The importance of these results were not lost on the staff of the *Los Angeles Times*. When asked about their strategy for disseminating this information, Sara Fritz recalled:

> We didn't set out to reach the people in DC. Our paper typically isn't read in this area. But once the articles were published, we distributed copies of the articles around Washington. They were sent to members and to other reporters. We felt strongly that the things we found were pertinent to the debate, and that the people involved in writing the laws ought to know what's going on. . . . We wanted to be sure that people read our stuff, and that doesn't happen routinely.[29]

The *Los Angeles Times*, then, made an attempt to influence the parameters of the debate surrounding campaign finance reform, and there is some evidence that they succeeded. First, in several of my interviews, these findings were cited time and again as particularly startling developments in the campaign reform debate. Other reporters, in particular, wished that their news organizations would commit the same level of resources to investigating campaign finance issues. Second, hearings held by the Committee on House Administration's Task Force on Campaign Finance Reform included testimony that focused on Fritz and Morris's findings—and the relevant news article was reprinted in the proceedings. In response to the *Los Angeles Times* article, Representative William Thomas (R-California) asserted:

> We have been bombarded by various self-styled civic action groups describing the fact that the very foundation of Democracy is under siege because so much money is being spent on television. . . . That is why I want to place in the record this *Los Angeles Times* article which is very enlightening. (U.S. House of Representatives, Committee on House Administration Task Force on Campaign Finance Reform 1991a, 2)

The final bill developed by the Task Force Majority included a provision that dealt with the rates television and radio station owners may charge political candidates for their campaign advertisements (Committee on House Administration 1991b). This provision represents a modest change in the existing laws governing the way broadcasters must deal with candidates for political office. More ambitious proposals, such as providing free air time to political candidates for advertisements, or federal subsidies for media advertising for candidates do not appear in the final version of the bill, nor does the bill include any variable spending limits that attempt to account for differences in the cost of advertising between television markets.

It would be going too far to state that the *Los Angeles Times* pieces are directly accountable for the final shape of the bill. However, as the bill was developed in committee, the Task Force kept two things in mind. According to a committee staff member, the Task Force based its bill "on the numbers." The data from the 1990 election cycle were the basis of the bill's final provisions; these data would reflect the same findings as the *Los Angeles Times* study.

The Regional Angle

In addition to this group of reporters from major newspapers, there are regional reporters who look for a local or regional angle to campaign finance stories. Although the evaluations of the reporters for the "elite" press were generally favorable, the evaluations of the local and regional press were much more varied. In general, commentators complained that few reporters understand, or are willing to master, the complexities of the issue, which leads to shoddy journalism. As one observer remarked,

> Sadly, not many newspapers have used the information [from the FEC] well. They have focused on PACs to the exclusion of other things. I think it is sad that PACs are getting blamed. But that is the most easily obtainable information, and it's not the primary problem.[30]

An official at the FEC expressed this frustration:

> We have new reporters and those who don't think they need to consult the FEC for anything other than the number. They may get erroneous information from another source about the law, and they call me to figure out how they got the erroneous information from the other source. Well, I don't know, but I wish they called me before they got into trouble.[31]

A Republican Senate staff member remarked, "Outside of Washington, papers are pretty ignorant. The regional newspapers tend to follow the big three or four."[32] A Democratic House staffer agreed. In his assessment:

The media have not been good about finding out about the law. They don't understand the interests or the finance parts. They only know the most egregious examples of abuse.

For example, I talk to reporters, and they will say, "Incumbents can hold over $600,000. Isn't that a lot?" And I will respond, "But currently the average member holds over close to a million on average." Then the reporter says, "Oh." Or the reporter will ask, "$200,000 in PAC money, isn't that a lot?" And then I tell them that the average member received $320,000 in PAC money in 1990, so we are asking the average member to take a cut of $120,000. And I get another, "Oh." And so it goes on.[33]

Many of the same commentators indicated that they understood the pressures facing reporters from smaller news organizations: They are assigned a number of issues to cover; they suffer from a lack of resources to do extensive investigative reporting; and the issue itself is difficult to master. In fact, in order to stimulate further examination of this issue, the *Los Angeles Times* made its data available to local and regional news organizations. As a result of all of these factors, news organizations around the country are extremely receptive to information that has been processed on their behalf.

One public interest group recognized these problems and sought to increase understanding of the campaign finance issue among local and regional reporters. The Center for Responsive Politics conducted a series of conferences for the print media to educate these reporters on campaign finance as an issue. In the words of Ellen Miller, the Executive Director of the Center:

We have to sell the media on the idea that this is a good story. We then discuss the tools and resources open to them. We will have a reporter or official of prominence talk to them, too, so the reporter will have someone to connect with. We have been very successful in these efforts. We have had over 150 newspapers represented during these weekend seminars.[34]

Clearly, stories on campaign finance and expenditures have become more important to smaller publications. And the level of frustration expressed by people in Congress over the quality of these stories indicates that members are worried about the content of the coverage they receive back home.

The activities of Common Cause and the case of campaign finance reform clearly indicates that the media are an important means to generate congressional support for legislation. Common Cause has aggressively pursued local opinion leaders to weigh in on an issue that is not important to the great mass of potential voters. Working hand in hand with Common Cause's efforts to reach editorial boards are the independent investigative reporters who have followed the money trail. Spinoffs of their work, coupled with the encouragement of other good government groups, have led local newspapers to run their own campaign finance stories. As a result, members have been forced to act on an issue they would just as soon ignore.

Media Enterprise and Constituent Communications

Timothy Cook noted that media attention is crucial to the reelection efforts of members of Congress; the sole exception to this rule is getting national media coverage. He asserted that members commonly believe that constituents are not interested in the national media; therefore, it is not worth their time and effort to seek coverage (Cook 1989, 105). Cook may be right insofar as a short 20-second spot on one network newscast may not reach enough voters to be worth the effort. However, the media enterprise and constituent communications do overlap in some important ways. Often, the subject matter that leads a member to get involved in the Washington debate can be reshaped into a story of interest to the local news.

The public exchange between then Republican National Committee Chairman Clayton Yeutter and Senator Bob Kerrey (D-Nebraska) is an interesting example of how the media enterprise may be reformulated for constituent communications. As described in the Introduction, the Kerrey press office aggressively pursued national media attention in order to rebut Yeutter's assertions that Democrats would suffer political damage because of their opposition to the use of force in the Persian Gulf. Kerrey first made an angry floor speech. Then the staff transcribed Yeutter's comments and sent them to various national media sources. The national media were then contacted in an effort to get the story covered in the elite press. This incident received national media attention for about a week.

Although characterized by at least one pundit as something of a Washington community "tempest in a teapot," the Kerrey office also used the story as the basis for an aggressive *local* media campaign. Copies of the floor statement were prepared and immediately faxed to the Nebraska press. A portion of Kerrey's floor statement was edited into a "video press release." Satellite time was purchased to broadcast the release to all the Nebraska television stations. The staff also prepared a "radio actuality" that was sent out over the telephone lines to all interested Nebraska radio stations to generate additional broadcast coverage.

The story was not billed in the same way for the local press as it was for the Washington corps. The story was interesting to the Nebraska audience because both Yeutter and Kerrey were Nebraska natives, between whom there was no small amount of animosity. Kerrey wanted to diffuse any potential political damage his rival could inflict at home, and the local press could play the story as "two local boys who go off to Washington and get involved in important foreign policy debates." Certainly the events did not change. However, the arguments used by the press secretary to sell the importance of the story varied depending on the reporter. A Nebraska reporter got the local angle while the national press was sold on the interparty warfare. As a result, the fact that both Kerrey and Yeutter hailed from Nebraska was never mentioned to any national reporters. If it had been, the reporters may have considered the story only of parochial interest and killed it.

Certainly, Kerrey is not unique in the way he framed his Washington efforts to get both local and national media attention. As Mary Hager, press secretary to then House Majority Whip William Gray, said:

> As a press secretary, I have to be very careful to write things in a different way when I am gearing a release to a local paper. It has to be in simpler language. The release can't be confusing at all, or the papers won't pick it up and people won't read it if it is.[35]

Richard Fenno's (1991) case study of Senator Pete Domenici's (R-New Mexico) tenure as Senate Budget Committee chairman provides additional evidence of how national press attention can affect local press attention. Fenno wrote that prior to his ascent to the chairmanship of this committee, Pete Domenici was a low-key, Republican Senator from a small state. In the two years prior to January 1981 when he took the reigns of the Budget Committee, Domenici had been mentioned on the national news only five times (1991, 3). By 1983, however, Domenici was ranked among the 10 Senators who received the most national media coverage (1991, 163).

Furthermore, the national "media scorekeepers" (as Fenno calls them) who evaluate the performance of highly visible legislators gave Domenici high praise. He was consistently characterized as effective, thoughtful, and not afraid to take on the Reagan administration as necessary in order to pass sound budgets. These judgments, although valuable in and of themselves, take on exaggerated importance as the local media, who pay less attention to events in Washington than do the pundits, take their cues from the national press. Fenno noted in his study that local and state columnists and editorial writers took on a praiseworthy tone when writing about Domenici. They were proud that a New

Mexico Senator was a major power broker in Washington—one who enjoyed the accolades of the national media. The only exception to this rule was the *Albuquerque Journal*, which took a decidedly skeptical tone in its coverage of Domenici's exploits. The *Journal*'s coverage was credited with dampening, but certainly not exorcising, the impact of Domenici's national media attention (Fenno 1991, 163-169).

Due at least in part to the overwhelmingly favorable national and local media coverage he had received, Domenici was in an enviable position when he embarked on his 1984 reelection campaign. Domenici enjoyed an 87 percent job approval rating, a 99 percent name-recognition rate, and a 77 percent name-recall rate. Furthermore, a full 20 percent of poll respondents spontaneously mentioned Domenici's chairmanship of the Budget Committee as a reason for giving him high marks (1991, 162-163). Fenno's account of Domenici's reelection campaign is replete with descriptions of glowing introductions from unlikely sources of support, remarkably good press, and a record-breaking margin of victory in November. Fenno concluded that Domenici's national reputation played no small part in his reelection victory.

What was successful for Domenici was not successful for another one of Fenno's cases. In his study of Dan Quayle's Senate career, Fenno noted that Quayle's most important achievement, his stewardship of the Job Training Partnership Act (JTPA), did not receive a lot of press attention initially. However, during his 1986 reelection campaign, JTPA figured prominently in Quayle's credit claiming efforts. He mentioned it in debates, television commercials, and campaign literature. Polls taken at the time recorded that some 20 percent of the business community in Indiana was aware of Quayle's work on JTPA (Fenno 1989, 149-170).

But when Quayle was nominated as George Bush's running mate in 1988, the national media were simply not interested in Quayle's efforts with JTPA. When they did mention the job training bill, the reporters simply credited Quayle with working with Senator Edward Kennedy (D- Massachusetts). There was no mention of the fact that Quayle was chairman of the subcommittee that developed the bill or that Quayle approached Kennedy for support, not vice versa.

Fenno (1989) argued that the national media were simply not going to pick up the JTPA story for two reasons. First, a scenario of effectiveness and success did not square with their judgment of Quayle as a lightweight. Second, the way JTPA was structured, with its emphasis on involving local Private Industry Councils (PICs), did not endear Quayle with organized labor or the other interest groups typically involved in job training issues. Therefore, issue network activists were not inclined to either call attention to Quayle's work on JTPA or to praise Quayle for its enactment.

There are two other reasons for Quayle's inability to benefit from favorable press on this issue. First, job training is much like adult literacy insofar as it holds little appeal to the national media. The policy debate is technical and centered within a tiny issue network. It is generally not a big-ticket item, and it does not rank high on public opinion polls. As a result, national reporters are completely unfamiliar with the history of or the issues behind the policy. As a result, the story on Quayle has never been rewritten to accommodate his success with this legislation.

Second, Quayle was able to generate positive local press coverage on JTPA at home only through the aggressive efforts of his office and campaign staff. However, the national media do not take cues from local press coverage like the local media take cues from the national media. Because of all of these factors in combination, it was simply impossible for Quayle to receive any credit for his achievements on the Job Training Partnership Act.

In addition, members' efforts to get successful local press coverage are not always successful—just as their efforts to get national press attention through the media enterprise are not always successful. One good example of this is Domenici's lukewarm relationship with the *Albuquerque Journal*, which dated from Domenici's days on the city council (Fenno 1991).

CONCLUSIONS AND IMPLICATIONS

Although media entrepreneurs clearly aim their message at a wide variety of actors within Congress and the Washington community, the connection to constituents and the general public simply cannot be overlooked.

Tip O'Neill's oft-quoted statement, "all politics is local," comes to mind in this context. Survey data show that constituents are the single most important audience for members' national media efforts; reaching the general public is almost as important. The data also indicate that using constituent contacts and grass-roots pressure are critical to building coalitions in Congress and in Washington. Furthermore, reading the press clips from the local newspapers is a daily ritual in congressional offices. These results all underscore how members work to maintain close touch with their constituents and to understand the importance of constituent support as a means to achieve legislative support.

Media entrepreneurs also take these messages to heart. They put even more stock in the efficacy of constituent contacts and grass-roots pressure in order to build coalitions. Furthermore, the most ardent media entrepreneurs are the same people who monitor the district media most religiously.

This chapter explored how the media enterprise reaches the general public. First, the congressional leadership of both parties are critical to this process. They all see the purpose of their media relations to reach the American public with a coherent message. This exercise is incredibly vital to leaders of the party that does not hold the White House. Nonetheless, all congressional leaders, regardless of party, have in common a duty to reach the public. In the modern Congress, no speaker or other major party leader has the option of maintaining a low profile. They must be proficient in designing legislative strategy, run a tight whip organization, *and* aggressively embrace the media.

The case study data show two ways that the media enterprise can be used to influence legislation by reaching to a public audience in addition to a Washington audience and one example of converting the constituent relations. The case of adult literacy shows how a public relations campaign geared to raising general public awareness of illiteracy as a problem primed the pump for the National Literacy Act. It piqued enough interest in the issue area to get the legislative ball rolling. This public relations campaign continues today, with the same emphasis on educating the general public that illiteracy actually exists, recruiting students, and encouraging reading in families. Still, the media coverage failed to place enough pressure on the Senate to overcome partisan battles.

Campaign finance reform demonstrates how the media enterprise can be used to mobilize local media for the purpose of building a legislative agenda in Congress. A steady stream of news articles and editorials put members under constant pressure to support campaign finance reform legislation supported by Common Cause. These pieces are generated in part by Common Cause and other public interest groups and in part by investigative reporters writing for major newspapers. In either case, the tedious, consuming work of poring through FEC reports is done by organizations who have credibility among reporters for accurate analyses and an acute understanding of the issues. Because of its long involvement in this issue, Common Cause carries a credibility and a sensitivity to the dynamics of the media. As a result, it is consistently able to generate dramatic local newspaper support for their program. The astounding and sustained success Common Cause continues to enjoy is evidence that the media enterprise is not the sole domain of members of Congress. Rather, it is a set of strategies that any individual or group with sufficient resources can employ.

The Bob Kerrey-Clayton Yeutter exchange regarding the political ramifications of the Persian Gulf War vote exemplifies how a member of Congress can use the same event to court both the national and the local media. The story, which was newsworthy in Washington because of its political ramifications, was newsworthy in Nebraska in part because both Yeutter and Kerrey hailed from that state. Two local politicians were engaged in an important policy debate. Importantly, however, the events were repackaged to appeal to the local audience.

The lesson here is that policy actors in Washington understand that the political system is a representative democracy. As such, the public cannot be ignored in the process of conducting policy debate. In fact, media entrepreneurs understand that courting the public is an important tool to influence policy inside the Washington community.

ENDNOTES

1. Regression analysis yielded similar results. However, the R-squared statistics are low, below $R^2 = 0.05$, probably due to the problems associated with conducting regression analysis on ordinal-level data.
2. Based on a 5-point Likert scale, in which 5 is the highest possible value.
3. Mary Hager, Press Secretary to Representative William Gray, Majority Whip, Interview May 10, 1991. These interviews were conducted while President Bush was in office. Not surprisingly, the comments often reflect this dynamic.
4. Mike Freedman, Press Secretary to Representative David Bonior, Majority Whip. Interview, March 23, 1991.
5. Walt Riker, Press Secretary to Senator Bob Dole, Minority Leader. Interview, July 11, 1991.
6. David Dreyer, Communications Director to Representative Richard Gephardt, Majority Leader. Interview, June 11, 1991.
7. Interview, July 12, 1991.
8. Interview, May 20, 1991.
9. Interview, June 11, 1991.
10. Interview, May 17, 1991.
11. Interview, May 20, 1991.
12. Interview, May 29, 1991.
13. This quotation is the opening paragraph in the following editorials, all of which were identical:
"Bush Campaign Reform Proposal Good for Starters." *Cadillac News*. Cadillac, Michigan. July 12, 1989.
"Campaign Spending Laws Need Reform." *The Daily Herald*. Provo, Utah. July 12, 1989.
"Cutting PACs Is Only a Start." *Vallejo Times-Herald*. Vallejo, California. July 10, 1989.
"Ending the PAC Addiction." *Marlboro Enterprise/Hudson Daily Sun*. Marlboro, Massachusetts. July 24, 1989.

"Hitting PACs Only a Start." *Robertson County Times.* Springfield, Tennessee. July 20, 1989.

"Limiting PACs Is Start." *Green Valley News and Sun.* Green Valley, Arizona. July 14, 1989.

"Need Public Financing Plan." *The Daily Sentinel.* Rome, New York. July 12, 1989.

"A Needed Reform." *Noticias del Mundo.* Los Angeles, California. July 12, 1989.

"On the Right Track." *The News and Courier.* Charleston, South Carolina. July 28, 1989.

"PACs Only a Start." *Yakima Herald-Republic.* Yakima, Washington. July 17, 1989.

"Political Funding by PACS Is Magnifying Small Voices." *Aiken Standard.* Aiken, South Carolina. July 9, 1989.

"Pricking PACs." *The Clover Herald.* Clover, South Carolina. July 26, 1989.

"Pricking PACs." *The Daily Press.* St. Mary's, Pennsylvania. August 8, 1989.

"Pricking PACs." *Yorkville Enquirer.* York, South Carolina. July 27, 1989.

"Pricking PACs Is Just the Start." *Big Spring Herald.* Big Spring, Texas. July 13, 1989.

"Pricking PACs Is Only a Start." *The Daily Bulletin.* Brooklyn, New York. July 25, 1989.

"Pricking PACs Is Only a Start." *Daily News.* Red Bluff, California. July 18, 1989.

"Pricking PACs Is Only a Start." *Lincoln Times-News.* Lincolnton, North Carolina. July 21, 1989.

"Pricking PACs Is Only a Start." *The Tribune.* San Diego, California. July 6, 1989.

"Pricking PACs: Only a Start." *Sioux City Journal.* Sioux City, Iowa. July 14, 1989.

"Pricking PACs Should Only Be Start of Reform." *Watertown Public Opinion.* Watertown, South Dakota. July 15, 1989.

"The Real Scandal: PAC Funds." *Amarillo Globe Times.* Amarillo, Texas. July 14, 1989.

"Trim Campaign Costs." *Lincoln Courier.* Lincoln, Nebraska. July 10, 1989.

14. Interview, March 29, 1991.
15. Compiled by author. Editorials were collected by Common Cause.
16. Interview, December 5, 1991.
17. Karen Hobart, Public Citizen. Interview, February 22, 1991.
18. Interview, April 25, 1991.
19. Interview, December 5, 1991.
20. Interview, March 10, 1992.
21. Interview, July 29, 1991.
22. Interview, December 5, 1991.

23. Interview, October 29, 1991.
24. Interview, December 6, 1991.
25. Interview, December 6, 1991.
26. Interview, November 4, 1991.
27. Interview, December 6, 1991.
28. Interview, April 24, 1991.
29. Interview, November 4, 1991.
30. Interview, November 4, 1991.
31. Interview, December 6, 1991.
32. This pattern was widely noted by my interview subjects. In fact, in a sample of some 160 newspaper editorials dating from the 101st Congress provided to the author, a number of newspapers adopted the *New York Times*'s phrase "sewer money" when referring to soft money donations.
33. Interview, December 6, 1991.
34. Interview on March 21, 1991
35. Interview, May 10, 1991.

8

Conclusions and Implications

The purpose of this book is to analyze how members of Congress use the media to influence public policy. The underlying assumption behind this research is that these activities are distinct from members' efforts to use to the media to communicate with constituents or to campaign for reelection. The findings from this research verify this assumption. However, a distinct group of members of Congress actively solicits media attention to influence policy: the "media entrepreneurs." They engage the media enterprise by soliciting national media coverage through interviews, op-eds, or committee hearings. The purpose of these activities is to influence the outcome of policy. Media entrepreneurs differ from other members in other ways as well. They consistently perceive the media as a more important tool to reach a variety of audiences for the purpose of influencing policy. This chapter summarizes the principal findings of this research, discusses their implications, and justifies their importance.

MAJOR RESEARCH FINDINGS

This research used a survey of congressional offices and case studies to investigate four major research questions: First, who uses the media to influence the development of policy? In other words, who are the media entrepreneurs? Second, when are members most likely to use the media with this goal in mind? Third, who are members trying to reach with these efforts? And fourth, what sources of news are most important in terms of reaching a congressional audience?

Who are the Media Entrepreneurs?

Media entrepreneurs are those members who believe the media are an effective tool to influence policy. Media entrepreneurs tend to be non-Southern, young, liberal Democrats. There are several possible reasons for these demographic characteristics. At the time of the survey, Democrats were the majority party in Congress. The Democrats controlled the agenda in large part and could create a numerical majority simply by reaching their party colleagues. They rarely had to make the effort to reach many of their Republican colleagues who would be less likely to support their efforts.

Interestingly, media entrepreneurs are not more likely to be Senators than House members. Certainly the Senate enjoys a distinct advantage receiving media coverage, and it always boasts a few "originals" (Hess 1986), who lead Congress in sheer numbers of television appearances and quotations. Yet, for all these advantages, Senators are not more likely to actively engage the media enterprise than are their counterparts in the House.

Liberals are slightly more likely to become media entrepreneurs than are conservatives. Because Southern Democrats are more conservative than their counterparts in the rest of the country, this fact accounts in part for the regional difference. Also, all of the major national news outlets, save CNN, are headquartered outside the "old South." As a result, Southern members may see less political benefit to using these outlets to influence policy. Furthermore, they may well believe that the "elite press," commonly based in New York or other northern cities, is hostile to Southern moderates and conservatives.

Media entrepreneurs are more likely to be young members. This result is in part due to a generational shift in Congress. Another important variable is having access to a bully pulpit, such as a subcommittee or a full committee chairmanship. The ability to conduct hearings and the credibility that comes from holding a position of political power mean that these members are well situated to launch the media enterprise. The media enterprise is not only an option employed by members who lack access to any other levels of power, it is also most easily used by members who have status within the institution, such as Les Aspin, former Chairman of the House Armed Services Committee.

This situation also helps explain why Democratic media entrepreneurs outnumber Republican media entrepreneurs. At the time the survey was conducted, there was not one committee or subcommittee chaired by a Republican member of the House or Senate. Any leverage Republican members had over committee proceedings, selection of witnesses, or in consideration of legislation was completely at the discretion of the Democratic chairman. Therefore, Republicans had fewer opportunities to influence policy later in the process. Their best bet was to try to shape the agenda. I predict that more Republicans will join the ranks of media entrepreneurs now that Republicans chair all the subcommittees and committees in both the House and the Senate.

There are, of course, exceptions to every one of these cases. There are conservative and Republican media entrepreneurs; Newt Gingrich and Jack Kemp rose to prominence through their willingness to go public. There are older members who are very proficient at the media enterprise; Robert Dole, for example, is in his 70s. Many young members such as Tom Sawyer do not solicit media attention at all. Southern members are not absent from this process; Dave McCurdy and Sam Nunn both hail from the South, and neither one can be considered a part of the liberal faction of their party. Yet, for every exception, there are several Les Aspins, Maxine Waterses, Patricia Schroeders, and Bob Kerreys who fit the profile more exactly.

It is important to remember that we are really dealing with a continuum of media activity. At one extreme is a member like Gingrich or Schroeder, who have ambitious national media operations and appear frequently in the national press. On the other end falls former Representative Jamie Whitten (D- Mississippi), former chairman of the House Appropriations Committee and indisputably one of the most powerful members of Congress, who shunned the spotlight. Most members fall between these two extremes. By and large they understand that the news media are the principal way in which we as a society communicate. Even Whitten has a press operation, even if it was only to communicate with his district. Media entrepreneurs are a product of a generational shift in Congress. They will become more and more common as the younger generation continues to replace the old.

Demographically speaking, media entrepreneurs differ little from their counterparts, which makes them harder to identify. They do, however, differ dramatically from their colleagues in their attitude toward the media enterprise. Across the board, media entrepreneurs consider the media an effective policy tool. They see it reaching more audiences. They consider the policy process and legislative machinery more permeable to the media's influences than their counterparts, and they themselves consume more news than their colleagues.

The crucial difference between media entrepreneurs and their counterparts is that media entrepreneurs have made a conscious decision to court the media. Media attention rarely "just happens." Instead, it must be solicited. Chairmen call hearings and invite witnesses who will capture the media's attention. Leaders accept talk show invitations and hold regular press conferences. Rank-and-file members make floor statements or use "1-minute" speeches and special orders to send a message. And still others choose to do nothing, preferring a low-profile approach to legislation.

Credibility

The key to being a successful media entrepreneur is establishing oneself as a credible spokesperson in a policy arena. Clearly, chairing a committee or subcommittee is helpful in this regard. Likewise, party leaders also carry legitimacy as spokespersons for their partisans. However, some media entrepreneurs successfully establish credibility in an issue area without these institutional benefits. Bob Kerrey, for example, was able to use his status as a veteran and Congressional Medal of Honor recipient as a means to discuss American policy in the Persian Gulf. Maxine Waters's credibility as an expert on urban problems was predicated on her position as the House member representing a district decimated by the unrest following the Rodney King verdicts.

It is important to remember that press coverage itself is not the object of the media enterprise; influencing policy is. It is possible to receive a lot of press coverage, but fail to influence the policy process. Paul Wellstone is a good example; he received a lot of attention for his attempts to keep the United States out of the Persian Gulf War, but he was a stunning failure in terms of leading any opposition to the authorization of the war. Therefore, credibility is a necessary but not a sufficient condition to achieve success in the media enterprise. Without establishing him- or herself as a legitimate authority to comment on public policy, the media entrepreneur may succeed in achieving notoriety, but he or she will not successfully influence the policy debate.

WHEN IS THE MEDIA ENTERPRISE IMPORTANT?

The Primacy of Agenda Setting and Framing an Issue

The hypothesis behind the second research question is that the agenda-setting and alternative-selection stages are the best points in the policy process for members of Congress to engage the media enterprise. At this stage, the potential to influence policy outcome is greatest. Successfully defining an issue will establish a media entrepreneur as a major player in an issue area and will enhance his or her efforts to influence the shape of policy as it develops. There is broad consensus among all survey respondents that, indeed, members are most likely to pursue media attention in order to place an issue on the national agenda or to frame an issue once it is on the agenda. Media entrepreneurs share these perceptions. Setting the agenda and defining alternatives allow media entrepreneurs to be proactive; they can work to define policy solutions. At later stages in the legislative process, media entrepreneurs can only react to proposals developed by others. Their ability to shape debate is hindered.

Certainly, influencing the agenda is easier for some members than for others. Committee and subcommittee chairmen are best able to shape the policy debate by conducting hearings. These hearings can be comprised of witnesses who agree with policies favored by the chairman. The discussion can be structured so that the only feasible outcome is legislation that addresses the problems as defined in the hearings. In any case, hearings can be a powerful tool to influence the debate, even if their proceedings cannot be rigidly controlled. The hearings held by the Senate and House Armed Services committees before the Persian Gulf War vote clearly served to raise issues critical to the debate's progress on Capitol Hill.

Likewise, the major purposes of the leadership's media enterprise are agenda setting and framing issues as part of their party's message to the country. Leadership press secretaries perceive themselves as foot soldiers in a partisan war to determine and interpret the agenda. Leadership, regardless of party, understands the importance of convincing the American public and the Washington community to accept its interpretation of events and problems as the fundamental basis of winning legislative battles on Capitol Hill.

Another reason for the importance of using the media to set the agenda and frame debate is related to the political realities on Capitol Hill. The minority party does not control the legislative process. Therefore, agenda setting and alternative selection are even more important to them. If minority members waited until a problem is defined through the normal process of drafting and debating legislation, then they are relegated to deciding which majority party proposal they can support most. On the other hand, if they can successfully change the way the debate is framed, then the majority must develop or support legislation that addresses the concerns of members in the minority party.

The case of the unrest in Los Angeles is a good example. The Democrats (the majority party at the time) completely controlled the policy definition process, successfully packaging the events as a result of deep-seated urban economic problems. Republicans were completely unsuccessful in their efforts to characterize the events as a series of individual wanton acts of violence. The Republicans' definition of the problem would have called for a heavy police crackdown on the demonstrators and stiff punishments for those found guilty. Instead, Congress passed an urban aid package that treated Los Angeles less like a riot zone and more like the victim of a natural disaster. In neither case did the debate examine whether the unrest stemmed from a breakdown in the criminal justice system.

When their party controlled the White House, however, congressional Republicans, as the minority party, had a better chance to influence the final outcome of public policy by defining issues early in the process and forcing the Democrats (the majority) into a reactive position. The Civil Rights bill is a fine example. The Republican minority in Congress, starting with Jesse Helms's 1990 reelection campaign, successfully connected civil rights legislation with reverse discrimination and "quotas" that hurt white employees. Even though President Bush eventually signed a civil rights bill that differed little from the one he initially vetoed, Republicans successfully forced Democrats into defending their civil rights bill in terms the Republicans controlled.

The Media Enterprise at Later Stages in the Policy Process

Media entrepreneurs, however, do see more potential to influence policy at later stages than do their counterparts. Media entrepreneurs are more likely to see the media as a helpful tool to move legislation through committee, to generate floor support, and to generate support in the other chamber. When this research was conducted, Democrats had numerical majorities in both houses, thus a Democratic media entrepreneur stood a better chance of constructing a majority coalition of co-partisans. Likewise, all committees and subcommittees were chaired by Democrats, who were likely to be more receptive to overtures from fellow party members than from Republicans.

SUMMARIZING THE PROCESS

The third research question asked who are the media entrepreneurs trying to reach? The process of using the media enterprise—and its complex structure of audiences—is depicted in Figure 8.1. First and foremost, the media entrepreneur wants to get the media's attention. The media are important for two reasons: They reach out to the other audiences a media entrepreneur wants to eventually reach, and they also talk to each other. In the latter case, the media will take their cues from each other. By covering the same stories as their colleagues, journalists will help amplify the media entrepreneur's message. His or her standing as a "player" will be enhanced, and the probability of reaching the potential audience will also be increased.

THE MEDIA ENTREPRENEUR

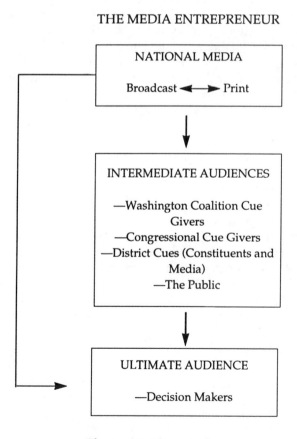

Figure 8.1. The enterprise process

In this case, choosing the media to contact first is the key. The fourth research question sought to identify the important media sources to reach Capitol Hill. This research found that the single most important medium to reach a Washington audience is the *Washington Post*. Media also take their cues from the Sunday morning talk shows, network news, and the *New York Times* and *Wall Street Journal*. In terms of directly reaching a Capitol Hill audience, the *Washington Post*, CNN, and *Congressional Quarterly Weekly Report* are the single most important sources. The rest of the elite press and national television news are also widely consumed on Capitol Hill. In addition, coverage in *Roll Call*, *National Journal*, and C-SPAN enhance the media entrepreneurs' chances of reaching a Capitol Hill audience.

A media entrepreneur can use the media enterprise to target a partisan audience. Although the *Washington Times* is not widely read in the aggregate, it is a crucial source for Republicans on Capitol Hill. A less remarkable but still important difference is in the audiences of the *New York Times* and National Public Radio, which are preferred by Democrats. An astute media entrepreneur will know that the an op-ed in the "Republican's newsletter"—the *Washington Times*—is well placed to reach that specific audience, and an interview on "All Things Considered" is not a bad way to reach Democrats.

If they could design an ideal strategy to reach other members of Congress, media entrepreneurs would opt for op-ed articles and television interviews over news articles and press releases. Op-ed articles provide members with an unfiltered opportunity to present their arguments to a policy-oriented audience. Television interviews also offer an opportunity to put out a message. In fact, the scarcity of congressional coverage in general enhances the networks' prestige on the Hill. However, by consenting to an interview, members do sacrifice some control over the content. Even more control is sacrificed when members stand to get only a 30-second sound bite on a newscast. As a result, some members shy away from national media attention. Yet television interviews and op-ed pages enjoy a wide audience in Washington and outside the beltway. Op-ed pages are read more frequently than the front page of a newspaper, and television coverage reaches a wide audience nationally and in Washington.

The media in turn reach several intermediary audiences, both inside and outside the beltway. First, media entrepreneurs target Washington issue networks. These are comprised of interest groups and the administration. They are important because these actors provide voting cues to other members of Congress. Interest groups provide factual information and solid data to members of Congress. Administration support can help congressional leaders to forge bipartisan coalitions.

Second, media entrepreneurs try to reach a congressional audience. Depending on the purpose of the particular media enterprise, members of Congress may be either the media entrepreneur's ultimate target or they may be an intermediate audience who provide cues to or lobby other members of Congress to support the media entrepreneur's goals. For example, media entrepreneurs may target party leaders. Leadership support is crucial in terms of building legislative coalitions. Leaders not only provide voting cues, but exercise some party discipline through the whip organizations. Therefore, reaching the party leadership is important in terms of being an intermediary audience to other members and in terms of receiving the support of the leaders themselves. Similarly, rank-and-file members can put pressure on recalcitrant committee chairmen to move a piece of legislation. The only exception to this rule is congressional staff, who for obvious reasons can only provide cues to their members.

The third audience is outside the beltway: constituents, district media, and the general public. Political reality indicates that grass-roots pressure and contacts from constituents are possibly the single most important cues that members can receive when making policy decisions, and influencing public opinion and generating letters to members of Congress are the best ways to get other members' support. Because much of the media enterprise takes place in the national media that penetrates outside the Washington area, constituents and the public are apt to overhear the policy conversation in Washington. The most politically efficacious of them will act on this information and contact their members of Congress.

The ultimate audience of the media entrepreneur is other policymakers, most often members of Congress. Depending on the purpose of the media enterprise, the size of the target audience may be as large as one entire chamber—either the House or the Senate—or as small as one committee chairman or a few party leaders. Because most of these efforts are concentrated in agenda setting, the ultimate audience are the members of Congress involved in developing specific legislation in a policy area. However, if there is any administrative law making underway, as in the case of the Centers of Disease Control guidelines regarding health care workers with AIDS, other policy actors may on occasion become the target of the media enterprise.

Because the object of the media enterprise is to influence the outcome of public policy, success may take many forms. Success may not necessarily come in the form of a hard-fought victory on the House floor. In fact, floor debates in both the House and the Senate are usually foregone conclusions. More importantly, the media entrepreneur wants to be considered an important legislator who should be consulted during back-room policy negotiations.

IMPLICATIONS OF THE MEDIA ENTERPRISE

Media entrepreneurs do not see the media enterprise as a way to replace other, traditional ways of influencing policy. They still engage in insider strategies to influence policy. Personal contacts and getting administration and party leader support for legislative ideas are important to media entrepreneurs just as they are important to their counterparts. The difference lies in the fact that media entrepreneurs see their efforts to attain coverage in the national press as more important relative to these traditional strategies than do their colleagues.

Furthermore, the media entrepreneurs consider using media as a perfectly legitimate means to influence policy. The media enterprise is not pursued only by members who lack any other institutional mechanism to influence policy. Rather, committee and subcommittee chairmen are as likely to solicit national attention as any younger member who lacks any sort of institutional platform. Media entrepreneurs are likely to become more common in Congress as younger members who are comfortable with these efforts move into the institution and gain seniority within it. The principal difference between committee and subcommittee chairmen and other media entrepreneurs is that committee leaders put less stock in the media effectiveness of the media enterprise at later stages of the legislative process.

The importance of using the media has increased in recent years for several reasons. In the last several decades, the Washington community has become larger. Issue networks have replaced the cozy relationships once enjoyed by agency executives, committee chairmen, and interest groups. Now coalitions shift depending on the politics of the policy debate. The numbers of interest groups and PACs, congressional staff, and think tanks have expanded. Using the media to reach this audience has become more and more important and will not wane in the near future.

Similarly, the expanding importance of television and the growing realization of the president's power to use it as a political tool have pushed the Democratic congressional leaders into the media spotlight. They had to solicit national media attention in order to counter the agenda-setting efforts and attempts to frame debate emanating from Republican administrations. The same holds true for Republican leaders in Congress today.

These findings fly in the face of the traditional distinction between "workhorses" and "showhorses" in Congress. Rather, there is strong evidence that the members who receive the most media attention are also the most effective members of Congress. Remember, the object of the media enterprise is to influence policy, not to receive media attention for its own sake (although many members enjoy the spotlight, too). Media entrepreneurs want to have an impact on policy, enhance their reputation, or be considered a "player" on an issue, just like the traditional perception of the "workhorses." It stands to reason that if they thought media attention would jeopardize their potential effectiveness, media entrepreneurs would look for alternative ways to establish their credibility in the Washington community.

One important implication of these findings is that, for all of the effort spent describing and analyzing the "new Congress," much of the old Congress still remains. Even though media entrepreneurs see the media as an important means to influence policy, they still understand the overriding value of constituent contacts, personal relationships, and the party leadership. Furthermore, the literacy case study provides evidence that a lot of policy is still made without a lot of media scrutiny. Furthermore, the members involved in this process were not particularly interested in generating a lot of media attention, except at the hearings stage.

Representative Tom Sawyer's role in passing the National Literacy Act demonstrates that it is still possible to take a low profile in Congress and achieve policy success. Likewise, the so-called "College of Cardinals"—the 13 Appropriations subcommittee chairmen—are notorious for avoiding the media spotlight. During his tenure as Appropriations Committee chairman, Representative David Obey (D-Wisconsin), however, seemed to be changing this tradition. As the former chairman of the Appropriations subcommittee dealing with foreign aid and foreign policy, Obey used his subcommittee to debate the appropriateness of American policy in various parts of the world in a very public way.

Context of the Media Enterprise

The media entrepreneur operates in a context in which Congress as an institution receives little attention on national or local television and faces declining amounts of coverage in the print media. As a result, understanding that the media enterprise is geared to a Washington audience is even more important. Comprised of thousands of politically oriented professionals, Washington is key to influencing policy by reaching various intermediate audiences to reach other members of Congress. In many ways, the public are irrelevant to this process.

It is also necessary to understand that soliciting media attention is not easy, nor is success guaranteed. Common Cause's success in generating media attention in campaign finance reform is dramatic evidence that interest groups can also successfully engage the media enterprise.

Added to this cacophony is the administration, which has its own public relations efforts, and various federal agencies, who wish to advertise their own achievements. A journalist's attention also may be distracted by other news outside Washington, such as natural disasters and international events. As a result, a media entrepreneur's attempts may very well fail to attract the media's attention.

Finally, the media entrepreneur also acts in the context of a member of Congress who has to communicate with his or her own constituents in order to increase support for reelection. As a result, media entrepreneurs do not consider the media enterprise a replacement for their efforts to communicate with their districts. Instead, media entrepreneurs see their constituents and the general public as an additional, important audience for their efforts to receive coverage in the national media, and they engage in the same efforts to reach their constituents as any other members. District newsletters and stories in the local media are just as important to the media entrepreneur as they are to any other member of Congress. Furthermore, there is evidence that media entrepreneurs are more in tune with their districts by their close monitoring of the district press.

Similarly, media entrepreneurs eschew the notion that because they receive a lot of national media attention, the district press is somehow beneath their notice. On the contrary, media entrepreneurs make an even greater attempt to stay in touch with their district, perhaps in order to ward off criticism of "going Washington" if they appear on the network news, but not in the morning paper. Furthermore, there is evidence that receiving favorable national press coverage can have positive benefits at home, as the local press take their cues from the national media. Senator Pete Domenici's experience in New Mexico is an excellent case of how favorable national attention stimulated favorable press coverage back home.

These results are important for several reasons. First, the overwhelming preponderance of the literature on the media and Congress concentrates on the efforts to reach constituents to the near exclusion of other efforts. There are several good reasons for this tendency. When examining the sheer volume of media-oriented activity in Congress, the bulk of press releases, interviews, and other efforts are geared toward the local press. Similarly, all members engage in constituent communications and local press relations, whereas only a few actively solicit national media attention. Therefore, the most inclusive study will examine the local press. Furthermore, by focusing on constituent communication, political scientists examine the larger connection to representative democracy. This research, however, is an attempt to explore how members of Congress use the media to influence the legislative process. Although the findings are tied in part to constituent communications, examining the members' relationship to the public is not the principal component of this research.

Second, the scholars considering the connection between press coverage and influencing policy have largely dismissed it. For example, Stephen Hess (1986) believes this maze is far too complex and uncertain to make the effort worthwhile. I disagree with Hess. Hess assumes that members of Congress can be reached only through their constituents. My research shows that media entrepreneurs see a wide variety of potential audiences inside the Washington community who provide cues to members of Congress. The route to cue givers is actually much less convoluted than Hess assumes. The complexity lies in the simultaneous way in which most of the action occurs. Absent strong and well-informed public opinion on any given issue, the media enterprise is an important way to reach other members through the policy conversation in the Washington community.

Furthermore, the success of these efforts cannot be easily measured solely through success on the floor. The object is to influence policy, which means a media entrepreneur simply wants to use the media to establish credibility in an issue area so that any inside strategies they employ later will be well received. Therefore, having one's name bandied about in Congress and in Washington serves an important purpose as well. Hess's model does not account for this phenomenon at all.

Third, although the relationships described in the preceding chapters are not strongly predictive, this research nonetheless remains an important first attempt to analyze these relationships in a systematic way. Furthermore, these patterns are not unimportant simply because they are not widely predictive. Political scientists have spent decades analyzing the complexities of the legislative process. This research helps explain some of the variation that traditional models of legislative behavior fail to include. Parsimony is a worthy goal, but at some point it fails to advance our knowledge because it misses a number of interesting and important phenomena.

Fourth, scholars also tend to dismiss the notion that members try to influence policy through the media because they believe these activities are limited to a very small population in Congress. Certainly the most aggressive members are atypical. Yet an important finding of this research is that there are many potential media entrepreneurs! The pool of media entrepreneurs comprises over 50 percent of the survey respondents. Recall that these respondents were identified by scoring an average answer of "agree" to four survey questions. Each survey question dealt with using the media in the context of influencing policy. They did not mention constituent communications, reelection, credit claiming, or any of the other myriad purposes publicity might serve.

Because media entrepreneurs consume more news than their counterparts, the media enterprise is an important tool in terms of coalition building because it reaches a lot of other potential media entrepreneurs. Because media entrepreneurs may comprise as much as 50 percent of the Congress, the media enterprise is an important way to reach people who may agree with one politically.

The importance of the media enterprise will only increase over time. Media entrepreneurs are a product of a generational shift taking place in Congress. As the older generation gives way to younger members who grew up in the television age, more members will be comfortable with soliciting media attention and will use it as a way to engage in the public policy debate. The relationships uncovered here stand to strengthen over time as the Newt Gingriches and Richard Gephardts become more the rule rather than the exception in Congress.

Finally, this research examines in depth the dynamics of the policy conversation in Washington for the first time. Previous work on the media, again understandably, has focused on the connection to the public as a whole. Even Polsby's (1981) and Heclo's (1977) classic descriptions of the Washington world are at best a cursory examinations. Here, I assumed that the public was irrelevant to the policy conversation ongoing within the issue networks in Washington. Although I learned that the public is not completely irrelevant, it is less important than has been previously discussed in political science literature. Similarly, the role of the media in reaching the Washington community may be a narrow question, but it remains important because the Washington community is comprised of individuals involved with politics and policymaking in some form. Therefore, understanding the role of the media in Washington lends insight into another part of the policy process inside the beltway.

Appendix I
Interviews Conducted
for This Research

Campaign Finance Reform

1. Chuck Alston, Reporter. *Congressional Quarterly Weekly Report.* March 5, 1991.
2. Chuck Babcock, Investigative Reporter. *Washington Post.* December 6, 1991.
3. Kim Bayliss, Legislative Director. Representative Mike Synar. March 1, 1991.
4. Senator David Boren. June 23, 1992.
5. Joe Craypa, Administrative Assistant. Representative David Obey. October 29, 1991.
6. John Deeken, Legislative Assistant. Senator David Boren. February 4, 1991.
7. Kevin Dempsey, Counsel. Senator John Danforth. November 4, 1991.
8. Fred Eiland, Press Officer. Federal Election Commission. December 6, 1991.

9. Sara Fritz, Reporter. *Los Angeles Times*. November 4, 1991.
10. Sharon Gang, Legislative Assistant. Representative Don Pease. November 2, 1991.
11. Karen Hobert, Field Organizer. Public Citizen. February 22, 1991.
12. Brooks Jackson, Investigative Reporter. Cable News Network (CNN). April 24, 1991.
13. Greg Kubiak, Former Legislative Assistant. Senator David Boren. April 25, 1991.
14. Susan Manes, Vice President for Issue Development. Common Cause. March 29, 1991.
15. Sheryl McCluney, Legislative Assistant. Representative Dan Glickman. March 1, 1991.
16. Ellen Miller, Executive Director. Center for Responsive Politics. March 21, 1991.
17. Perry Pokros, Staff Director. Task Force on Campaign Finance Reform, Representative Sam Gejdensen, Chairman. December 5, 1991.
18. Tamara Somerville, Legislative Assistant. Senator Mitch McConnell. April 28, 1991.
19. Steven Stockmeyer, Executive Vice President. National Association of Business Political Action Committees. November 3, 1991.
20. Herb Stone, Professional Staff Member. Subcommittee on Elections, House Committee on Administration, Representative Al Swift, Chairman. March 7, 1991.
21. Representative Mike Synar. July 29, 1991.
22. Fred Wertheimer, President. Common Cause. March 10, 1992.

Adult Literacy

23. Amanda Broun, Chief Education Counsel. Committee on Labor and Human Resources, Senator Edward Kennedy, Chairman. May 29, 1991.
24. Dr. Forrest Chisman, President. Southport Institute for Policy Analysis. May 29, 1991.
25. Sarah Platt Davis, Legislative Director. Representative Tom Sawyer. May 13, 1991.
26. Patricia Fahy, Former Staff Member. Senator Paul Simon. August 7, 1991.
27. Paul Feldman, Legislative Director. Representative David E. Price. January 15, 1991.
28. Andy Hartman, Minority Counsel. Committee on Education

and Labor, Representative William Goodling, Ranking
Minority Member. July 9, 1991.
29. Alice Johnson, Deputy to the AA. Senator Paul Simon. April
    29, 1991.
30. Robert Shireman, Chief Education Advisor. Subcommittee on
    Employment and Productivity, Committee on Labor and
    Human Resources, Senator Paul Simon, Chairman. April 29,
    1991.
31. Gayle Spangenberg, Executive Vice President. Business
    Coalition for Adult Literacy. July 17, 1991.
32. Renee Woodworth, Lobbyist. Southport Institute for Policy
    Analysis. July 9, 1991.
33. Ann Young, Professional Staff Member. Senate Select
    Committee on Education, Arts and the Humanities, Senator
    Claiborne Pell, Chairman. October 25, 1991.

Persian Gulf War Debate

34. Gayle Beagle, Administrative Assistant. Representative Henry
    Gonzales. January 22, 1991.
35. Robert B. Brauer, Special Counsel. Representative Ronald V.
    Dellums. March 22, 1991.
36. Charles Harman, Administrative Assistant. Senator Sam
    Nunn. January 23, 1991.
37. Steve Jarding, Press Secretary. Senator J. Robert Kerrey.
    September 18, 1991.
38. Senator J. Robert Kerrey. March 1, 1991.
39. Donna Martin, Professional Staff Member. Committee on
    Armed Services, Representative Barbara Boxer. March 1, 1991.
40. Representative Dave McCurdy. July 25, 1991.
41. Steve Patterson, Administrative Assistant. Representative
    Dave McCurdy. January 15, 1991.
42. Jerry Rabinowitz, Administrative Assistant. Representative
    Steven Solarz. February 12, 1991.
43. William Shore, Chief of Staff. Senator J. Robert Kerrey.
    January 15, 1991.
44. Senator Paul Wellstone, September 19, 1991.

AIDS Policy

45. Tom Brandt, Associate Director for External Affairs. National
    Commission on AIDS. March 23, 1992.

46. Carisa Cunningham, Press Liaison. AIDS Action Council. March 23, 1992.
47. Mike Frank, Legislative Counsel. Representative William Dannemeyer. August 27, 1991.
48. Tim McFeeley, Executive Director. Human Rights Action League. March 20, 1992.
49. Alexander Robinson, Legislative Counsel. American Civil Liberties Union AIDS Project. September 27, 1991.
50. Representative J. Roy Rowland. April 30, 1991.
51. Sheppard Smith, Americans for a Sound AIDS Policy. September 20, 1991.
52. James Stacey, Director of Media Services. American Medical Association. November 1, 1991.
53. Tim Westmoreland, Staff Director. Subcommittee on Health and the Environment, Committee on Energy and Commerce, Representative Henry Waxman, Chairman. March 9, 1992.
54. Robert J. Wilke, Jr., Legislative Assistant. Senator Jesse Helms. August 9, 1991.

Other Interviews

55. James Berard, Director of Communications. Representative Jim Oberstar. January 9, 1991.
56. Jeff Biggs, Press Secretary. Speaker Tom Foley. May 17, 1991. May 31, 1991.
57. Tony Blankley, Press Secretary. Representative Newt Gingrich, Minority Leader. May 20, 1991 and September 14, 1992.
58. Stan Cannon, Press Secretary. Senator Alan Simpson, Minority Whip. July 12, 1991.
59. Eleanor Clift, Congressional Correspondent. *Newsweek* Magazine. April 21, 1992.
60. Helen Dewar, Reporter. *The Washington Post.* May 7, 1991.
61. Diane Dewhirst, Press Secretary. Senator George Mitchell, Majority Leader. August 20, 1991.
62. David Dreyer, Director of Communications. Representative Richard Gephardt, Majority Leader. June 11, 1991.
63. David Fox, Former Press Secretary to Representative Lynn Martin; current Press Secretary to Representative Harold Rogers. September 14, 1992.
64. Bob Franken, Congressional Correspondent. Cable News Network (CNN). March 23, 1992.

65. Mike Freedman, Press Secretary. Representative David Bonior, Majority Whip. March 23, 1992.
66. Steve Gerstel, Congressional Correspondent. United Press International. March 16, 1992.
67. Hayes Gorey, Congressional Correspondent. *Time*. March 13, 1992.
68. James Glassman, Editor. *Roll Call*. August 8, 1991.
69. Mary Hager, Press Secretary. Representative William Gray, Majority Whip. May 10, 1991.
70. Merrill Hartson, Congressional Correspondent. The Associated Press. March 12, 1992.
71. Walt Riker, Press Secretary. Senator Robert Dole, Minority Leader. July 11, 1991.
72. Sabrina Sojourner, Press Secretary. Representative Maxine Waters. August 26, 1992.
73. Missy Tessier, Press Secretary. Representative Bob Michel, Minority Leader. May 20, 1991.
74. Representative James A. Traficant. October 1, 1991.
75. Nancy Travor, Congressional Correspondent. *Time*. March 16, 1992.
76. James Wooten, Chief Congressional Correspondent. ABC News. March 9, 1992.

Appendix II
Survey Instrument

USING THE MEDIA IN THE LEGISLATIVE PROCESS

A Survey of Congressional Offices

Thank you in advance for your cooperation. I am most interested in your **perceptions** and **opinions**, so please do not take a lot of time filling out this questionnaire. Your first response is often your best response. All thoughts and comments are welcome. Please feel free to attach any additional pages as necessary.

SECTION I.

Please indicate if you strongly agree, agree, disagree, or strongly disagree with the following statements.

1. Members of Congress—in both the House and the Senate—often solic-it media exposure (i.e. interviews, talk show appearances, op-eds, press releases, etc.) as a way to stimulate discussion about national policy pro-posals in Washington.

| Strongly Agree | Agree | Neither agree nor disagree | Disagree | Strongly Disagree | Don't Know |

2. Soliciting media exposure **is not** a particularly effective way to put an issue on the congressional agenda.

| Strongly Agree | Agree | Neither agree nor disagree | Disagree | Strongly Disagree | Don't Know |

3. Media exposure is an effective way to convince other legislators in both chambers to support policy proposals.

| Strongly Agree | Agree | Neither agree nor disagree | Disagree | Strongly Disagree | Don't Know |

4. Media exposure is an effective way to stimulate discussion on policy alternatives and issues among executive branch officials.

| Strongly Agree | Agree | Neither agree nor disagree | Disagree | Strongly Disagree | Don't Know |

SECTION II

5. Some observers have argued that the media have become quite impor-tant to members of Congress and Senators in terms of developing legis-lation and promoting party programs. In your opinion, how effectively do each of the following groups use the media?

Please evaluate each item according the following scale:

| 1 | 2 | 3 | 4 | 5 |
| Not Effectively | | | | Very Effectively |

   a. Your party leadership: 1   2   3   4   5
       Comments:
   b. Legislators with a national
       reputation: 1   2   3   4   5
       Comments:
   c. Committee Chairmen: 1   2   3   4   5
       Comments:

d.	Ranking Members:	1	2	3	4	5
	Comments:					
e.	Democrats:	1	2	3	4	5
	Comments:					
f.	Republicans:	1	2	3	4	5
	Comments:					
g.	Others:	1	2	3	4	5
	Comments:					

6. Many members of Congress use strategies such as writing op-ed articles and conducting interviews with reporters from the national media to publicize their ideas and policy positions. According to your experience, who are legislators trying to reach through these efforts?

Please evaluate each item according to the following scale:

1	2	3	4	5
Very Infrequently			Very Frequently	

a.	Colleagues in their own party:	1	2	3	4	5
	Comments:					
b.	Colleagues in the other party:	1	2	3	4	5
	Comments:					
c.	Congressional staff:	1	2	3	4	5
	Comments:					
d.	Their party leadership:	1	2	3	4	5
	Comments:					
e.	Executives in federal agencies:	1	2	3	4	5
	Comments:					
f.	White House Officials:	1	2	3	4	5
	Comments:					
g.	Interest Groups:	1	2	3	4	5
	Comments:					
h.	Academic "think tanks":	1	2	3	4	5
	Comments:					
i.	Other media:	1	2	3	4	5
	Comments:					
j.	Constituents:	1	2	3	4	5
	Comments:					
k.	The public outside the constituency:	1	2	3	4	5
	Comments:					

l. Others: 1   2   3   4   5
    Please Indicate:

7. The media may be used at various stages in the legislative process. When do you see members soliciting media attention for their policy proposals?

Please evaluate each item according to the following scale:
1   2   3   4   5
Very Infrequently   Very Frequently

a. To raise awareness of the
    problem (i.e., to place an
    issue on the national agenda): 1   2   3   4   5
    Who is the primary audience?
    Comments:
b. To frame the terms of debate
    (i.e., to push for specific policy
    alternatives or "spin control"): 1   2   3   4   5
    Who is the primary audience?
    Comments:
c. To respond to proposals from
    the White House: 1   2   3   4   5
    Who is the primary audience?
    Comments:
d. To respond to decisions and
    proposals from federal agencies: 1   2   3   4   5
    Who is the primary audience?
    Comments:
e. To move a bill through
    committee: 1   2   3   4   5
    Who is the primary audience?
    Comments:
f. To find support for a floor vote: 1   2   3   4   5
    Who is the primary audience?
    Comments:
g. To solicit support in the
    other chamber: 1   2   3   4   5
    Who is the primary audience?
    Comments:
h. To inform and influence
    interest groups: 1   2   3   4   5
    Who is the primary audience?
    Comments:

i. Other: 1   2   3   4   5
   Who is the primary audience?
   Comments:

SECTION III.

8. If you are seeking information regarding legislation, White House proposals and current issues being discussed on Capitol Hill, which media sources do you consult most frequently?

Please evaluate each item according to the following scale:

1	2	3	4	5
Very Infrequently				Very Frequently

i. Washington-based publications:

Congressional Quarterly Weekly Report:	1	2	3	4	5
National Journal:	1	2	3	4	5
Roll Call:	1	2	3	4	5
The Campaign Hotline:	1	2	3	4	5
"Faxed" news, such as The White House Bulletin:	1	2	3	4	5
Specialized trade publications and newsletters:	1	2	3	4	5
Examples:					

Overall use of Washington-based publications: **1   2   3   4   5**
   Comments:

ii. National newspapers and magazines:

Washington Post:	1	2	3	4	5
Wall Street Journal:	1	2	3	4	5
The New York Times:	1	2	3	4	5
The Washington Times:	1	2	3	4	5
The Christian Science Monitor:	1	2	3	4	5
The Los Angeles Times:	1	2	3	4	5
Newsweek:	1	2	3	4	5
Time:	1	2	3	4	5
U.S. News and World Report:	1	2	3	4	5
Other national newspapers and newsmagazines:	1	2	3	4	5
Please List:					

**Overall use of national newspapers
and newsmagazines**   **1   2   3   4   5**
    Comments:

iii. Broadcast media:
    National network news   1   2   3   4   5
    "MacNeil-Lehrer
    News Hour (PBS)   1   2   3   4   5
    "This Week with
    David Brinkley"   1   2   3   4   5
    Washington Week in Review"   1   2   3   4   5
    "Nightline"   1   2   3   4   5
    "Meet the Press"   1   2   3   4   5
    C-SPAN   1   2   3   4   5
    CNN   1   2   3   4   5
    National Public Radio   1   2   3   4   5
    Other broadcast media sources 1   2   3   4   5
        Please list:

**Overall use of broadcast
media sources:**   **1   2   3   4   5**
    Comments:

iv. Other media sources
    District/state media   1   2   3   4   5
    Other information sources   1   2   3   4   5
        Please list:

Overall use of other media sources: **1   2   3   4   5**
    Comments:

9. Comparatively speaking, how effective are the following approaches in generating support for policy proposals within Congress?

Please evaluate each item according to the following scale:
1   2   3   4   5
Not Effective   Very Effective

    a. Personal Contacts   1   2   3   4   5
    b. Party Leadership   1   2   3   4   5
    c. Television Interviews   1   2   3   4   5
    d. Op-ed Articles   1   2   3   4   5
    e. News Articles and
        Press Releases   1   2   3   4   5

f.	Interest Group Support	1	2	3	4	5
g.	Contacts from Political Action Committees	1	2	3	4	5
h.	Contacts from Constituents	1	2	3	4	5
i.	Contacts from Federal Agencies	1	2	3	4	5
j.	Contacts from the White House	1	2	3	4	5
k.	Other. Please indicate:	1	2	3	4	5

10. Comparatively speaking, how effective are the following approaches in generating support for policy proposals among political elites **inside Washington, but outside Congress?**

Please evaluate each item according to the following scale:

1	2	3	4	5
Not Effective				Very Effective

a.	Personal Contacts	1	2	3	4	5
b.	Party Leadership	1	2	3	4	5
c.	Television Interviews	1	2	3	4	5
d.	Op-ed Articles	1	2	3	4	5
e.	News Articles and Press Releases	1	2	3	4	5
f.	Endorsements from PACs or Interest Groups	1	2	3	4	5
g.	Grassroots Pressure	1	2	3	4	5
h.	Contacts from Federal Agencies	1	2	3	4	5
i.	Contacts from the White House	1	2	3	4	5
j.	Other. Please indicate:	1	2	3	4	5

11. According to your perspective, describe any differences you see between the House of Representatives and the Senate, and their relationships with the national media (both broadcast and print)?

12. According to your perspective, what differences, if any, do you see between Democrats and Republicans and they way they use the national media?

13. According to your perspective, do committee chairmen, ranking members, and party leaders use the media in different ways than do other members? What differences do you see in the way they deal with national media?

14. According to your perspective, are there any differences in the way any of the above groups deal with the *Washington-based* media as

opposed to the *national* media? (See Question 8)

15. What kinds of differences do you see between the way any of these groups deal with the *broadcast* media, as opposed to the *print* media?

16. In general, how would you characterize the relationship between the media and Congress?

SECTION IV:

17. Does your member consciously solicit national or Washington-based media attention for the purpose of attracting support for specific legislation?

Frequently   Occasionally   Rarely Never

   17a. **(If Rarely or Never)** What are your reasons for not routinely soliciting media attention?
   17b. **(If Frequently or Occasionally)** Under what circumstances does your office decide to use a media strategy?
   17c. **(If Frequently or Occasionally)** What other strategies did you use in addition to soliciting media attention?
   17d. **(If Frequently or Occasionally)** In general, how successful are these efforts to use the media?

18. From your experience, how successful are members' efforts to use the **national** media to raise awareness of an issue or shape the terms of policy debate in Washington? (Circle one)

Very	Occasionally	Rarely	No
Successful	Successful	Successful	Opinion

19. From your experience, how successful are members' efforts to use the **Washington-based** media (see Question 8) to raise awareness of an issue to share the terms of the policy debate in Washington?

Very	Occasionally	Rarely	No
Successful	Successful	Successful	Opinion

20. From your experience, how successful are members' efforts to use the national media to gain support for legislation?

Very	Occasionally	Rarely	No
Successful	Successful	Successful	Opinion

21. From your experience, how successful are members' efforts to use the **Washington-based** media to gain support for legislation?

| Very Successful | Occasionally Successful | Rarely Successful | No Opinion |

22. In general, how successful are attempts to use the media to gain support for policy alternatives? When are they not successful?

SECTION V: The following section requests some basic demographic information. Please remember that your responses will not be used to identify you or your member in any way.

23. What is your employer's party affiliation?

Democrat   Republican   Other

24. How long has your employer served in his/her current position?

25. In which chamber does your employer serve?
Senate   House of Representatives

26. Is your employer: (Check all that apply)

_____ a member of the party leadership
_____ a committee chair or ranking member
_____ a subcommittee chair or ranking member

27. How long have you worked in Congress? _____

28. How long have you worked for your current employer?

_____

29. How long have you served as Administrative Assistant/ Chief of Staff? _____

Thank you very much for your cooperation. I appreciate your time and effort. If you have any other comments you would like to add, please attach a separate sheet of paper. If you would like to receive a copy of the results of this survey, please include your name and address.

References

Alston, Chuck. 1989. "Common Cause: A Watchdog That Barks at Its Friends." *Congressional Quarterly Weekly Report*, 26 August, pp. 2204-2206.

Americans for a Sound AIDS Policy. 1991. "The Failure of Voluntary Testing." *AIDS/HIV News* 3(3): 1, 6.

Americans for a Sound AIDS Policy. 1992. "AIDS Epidemic SpreadsAmong Heterosexuals, Teens." *AIDS/HIV News* 4(1): 1, 5.

Barone, Michael and Grant Ujifusa. 1991. *The Almanac of American Politics: 1992*. Washington, DC: National Journal/Times Mirror.

Bennett, W. Lance. 1988. News: *The Politics of Illusion*, 2nd ed. New York: Longman.

Bergalis, Kimberly. 1991. "I Blame Every One of You Bastards." *Newsweek*, 1 July, p. 52.

Berry, Jeffrey M. 1989. *The Interest Group Society*, 2nd ed. Glenview, IL: Scott Foresman/Little Brown.

Bisnow, Mark. 1990. *In the Shadow of the Dome*. New York: William Morrow and Company.

Bonafede, Dom. 1982. "The Washington Press—Competing for Power with the Federal Government." *National Journal*, 17 April, pp. 664-674.

Campbell, James E., John R. Alford and Keith Henry. 1984. "Television Markets and Congressional Elections." *Legislative Studies Quarterly* IX(4): 665-678.

Cantor, Joseph E. 1989. "Campaign Financing in Federal Elections: A Guide to the Law and Its Operation." CRS Report for Congress. Washington, DC: Congressional Research Service. August 8.

Cantor, Joseph E. 1991. "Campaign Finance Legislation in the 102nd Congress." CRS Report for Congress. Washington, DC: Congressional Research Service. October 7.

Cantor, Joseph E. and Thomas M. Durbin. 1991. "Campaign Financing." CRS Issue Brief. Washington, DC: Congressional Research Service. January 4.

Carlson, Peter. 1990. "The Image Makers." *Washington Post Magazine*, 11 February, pp. 12-17, 30-35.

Cobb, Roger W. and Charles D. Elder. 1983. *Participation in American Politics: The Dynamics of Agenda-Building*, 2nd ed. Baltimore, MD: Johns Hopkins University Press.

Colby, David C. and Timothy E. Cook. 1991. "Epidemics and Agendas: The Politics of Nightly News Coverage of AIDS." *Journal of Health Politics, Policy and Law* 16(2): 215-249.

Common Cause. 1990. "Common Cause Urges Congress to Enact Real and Effective Campaign Finance Reforms." Press Release, January 25. Washington, DC: Common Cause.

Congressional Quarterly Weekly Report. 1990. "Bush Briefs Members on Gulf Policy; Democratic Leaders Voice Support," 1 September, pp. 2801-2802.

Cook, Rhodes, Ronald D. Elving and the CQ Research Staff. 1991. "Even Votes of Conscience Follow Party Lines." *Congressional Quarterly Weekly Report*, 19 January, pp. 190-195.

Cook, Timothy E. 1986. "House Members as Newsmakers: The Effects of Televising Congress." *Legislative Studies Quarterly* XI(2): 203-226.

Cook, Timothy E. 1989. *Making Laws and Making News: Media Strategies in the U.S. House of Representatives*. Washington, DC: The Brookings Institution.

Cunningham, Carisa. 1992. "Lynch Is Wrong: AIDS Is A Major News Story." *Washington Journalism Review* 14(1): 23.

Davidson, Roger H. and Walter J. Oleszek. 1981. *Congress and Its Members*. Washington, DC: Congressional Quarterly Press.

Doherty, Carroll J. 1990a. "Congress Worried About Oil, Threat to Saudi Arabia." *Congressional Quarterly Weekly Report*, 4 August. p. 2533.

Doherty, Carroll J. 1990b. "Gloves Come Off As Congress Swipes at Administration." *Congressional Quarterly Weekly Report*, 22 September, pp. 3029-3031.

Doherty, Carroll J. 1990c. "Consultation on the Gulf Crisis Is Hit-Or-Miss For Congress." *Congressional Quarterly Weekly Report*, 13 October, pp. 3440-3441.

Doherty, Carroll J. 1990d. "Both Chambers Craft Resolutions Backing Bush's Gulf Policy." *Congressional Quarterly Weekly Report*, 29 September, pp. 3140, 3142.

Doherty, Carroll J. 1990e. "Uncertain Congress Confronts President's Gulf Strategy." *Congressional Quarterly Weekly Report*, 17 November, pp. 3879-3882.

Doherty, Carroll J. 1990f. "Administration Makes Its Case But Fails to Sway Skeptics." *Congressional Quarterly Weekly Report*, 8 December, pp. 4082- 4085.

Doherty, Carroll J. 1990g. "Public Debate on Persian Gulf Poses Challenge for Members." *Congressional Quarterly Weekly Report*. 1 December, pp. 4004-4005.

Doherty, Carroll J. 1990h. "Members See Prospect of War Before Year Is Out." *Congressional Quarterly Weekly Report*, 27 October, p. 3630.

Doherty, Carroll J. 1990i. "Choice of Partners Questioned in Courtship of Support." *Congressional Quarterly Weekly Report*, 1 December, p. 4009.

Donovan, Beth. 1992. "Campaign Finance: Overhaul Plan Readied as Tool to Blunt Scandals' Effects." *Congressional Quarterly Weekly Report*, 4 April, pp. 861-863.

Drew, Elizabeth. 1983. *Politics and Money: The New Road to Corruption.* New York: Macmillan.

Duncan, Phil, ed. 1989. *Politics in America 1990: The 101st Congress.* Washington, DC: Congressional Quarterly Press.

Ehrenhalt, Alan. 1991. *The United States of Ambition: Politicians, Power and the Pursuit of Office.* New York: Random House.

Evans, Katherine Winton. 1981. "The Newsmaker: A Capitol Hill Pro Reveals His Secrets." *Washington Journalism Review*, 3: 28-33.

Fenno, Richard F., Jr. 1989. *The Making of a Senator: Dan Quayle.* Washington, DC: Congressional Quarterly Press.

Fenno, Richard F., Jr. 1991. *The Emergence of a Senate Leader: Pete Domenici and the Reagan Budget.* Washington, DC: Congressional Quarterly Press.

Foote, Joe S. 1991. "TV Savvy Congressmen Snatch News Coverage." Press Release from Southern Illinois University at Carbondale. August 28.

Fox, Harrison W., Jr. and Susan Webb Hammond. 1977. *Congressional Staffs: The Invisible Force in Lawmaking.* New York: The Free Press.

Fumento, Michael. 1990. *The Myth of Heterosexual AIDS.* New York: Basic Books.

Fumento, Michael. 1992. "Lynch is Right: Media Are On An AIDS Crusade." *Washington Journalism Review* 14(1): 22-23.

Gejdenson, Representative Sam. 1991. "House of Representatives Spending Limit and Election Reform Act of 1991: Statement of Introduction." Washington, DC: Committee on House Administration Task Force on Campaign Finance Reform. November 12.

Goldenberg, Edie N. and Michael W. Traugott. 1987. "Mass Media in U.S. Congressional Elections." *Legislative Studies Quarterly* XII(3): 317-339.

Grandy, William. 1991. "Poll: Most Want Tough AIDS Laws." *Chicago Tribune*, 6 May, p. A10.

Green, Michael. 1974. "Nobody Covers the House." In *Congress and the News Media*, ed. Robert O. Blanchard. New York: Hastings House Publishers.

Hardy, Ann M. 1990. "National Health Interview Survey Data on Adult Knowledge of AIDS in the United States." *Public Health Reports* 105(6): 629-634.

Heclo, Hugh. 1977. *A Government of Strangers*. Washington, DC: The Brookings Institution.

Heclo, Hugh. 1981. "Issue Networks and the Executive Establishment." In *The New American Political System*, ed. Anthony King. Washington, DC: The American Enterprise Institute. 87-124.

Helms, Senator Jesse. 1991. "Senate Passes Helms' Patient Protection Amendment." *Congressional Record* 137(110): S. 10353-10355.

Hess, Stephen. 1981. *The Washington Reporters*. Washington, DC: The Brookings Institution.

Hess, Stephen. 1986. *The Ultimate Insiders*. Washington, DC: The Brookings Institution.

Hess, Stephen. 1987. "Being Newsworthy." *Society* 24(2): 39-47.

Hess, Stephen. 1991. *Live From Capitol Hill! Studies of Congress and the Media*. Washington, DC: Brookings Institution.

Heymann, Philip B. 1987. *The Politics of Public Management.* New Haven, CT: Yale University Press.

Hinkley, Barbara. 1988. *Stability and Change in Congress*. New York: Harper and Row.

Hoff, Paul S. and Ken Bernstein. 1988. *Beyond the 30-Second Spot: Enhancing the Media's Role in Congressional Campaigns*. Washington, DC: The Center for Responsive Politics.

Hook, Janet. 1989. "The Turmoil and the Transition: Stage Set for New Speaker." *Congressional Quarterly Weekly Report*, 27 May, pp. 1225-1226.

Idelson, Heidi. 1991. "National Opinion Ambivalent As Winds Stir Gulf." *Congressional Quarterly Weekly Report*, 5 January, p. 14.

Jackson, Brooks. 1988. *Honest Graft: Big Money and the American Political Process*. New York: Alfred A. Knopf.

Jewell, Macolm E. and Samuel C. Patterson. 1986. *The Legislative Process in the United States*, 4th ed. New York: Random House.

Johnson, Judith A. 1991. "HIV Infected Health Care Workers: The Medical And Scientific Issues." CRS Report for Congress. Washington, DC: Congressional Research Service. August 21.

Johnson, Judith A. 1992. "AIDS and Other Diseases: Federal Spending and Morbidity and Mortality Statistics." CRS Report for Congress. Washington, DC: Congressional Research Service. March 4.

Kaid, Linda and Joe S. Foote. 1985. "How Network Television Coverage of the President and Congress Compare." *Journalism Quarterly* 62(1): 59-65.

Kedrowski, Karen M. 1987. "The Question of Literacy in Missouri: The Problems and Recommendations for Corporate Action." Unpublished report prepared for Southwestern Bell Telephone Company. St. Louis, MO.

Kerrey, Senator Robert. 1991. "Floor Statement of Senator Robert Kerrey." January 23.

King, Gary and Lyn Ragsdale. 1988. *The Elusive Executive: Discovering Statistical Pattersn in the Presidency.* Washington, DC: Congressional Quarterly Press.

Kingdon, John W. 1984. *Agendas, Alternatives and Public Choices.* Boston: Little Brown.

Kingdon, John W. 1989. *Congressmen's Voting Decisions,* 2nd ed. New York: Harper and Row.

Kozol, Jonathan. 1985. *Illiterate America.* Garden City, NY: Anchor Press/Doubleday.

Krauthammer, Charles. 1990. "AIDS: Getting More Than Its Share." *Time,* 25 June, p. 80.

Langbien, Laura I. and Lee Sigelman. 1989. "Show Horses, Work Horses and Dead Horses." *American Politics Quarterly* 17(1): 80-95.

Larher, M.P., J. Charrel, P. Enel, C. Manuel, D. Reviron, P. Auquier, and J.L. San Marco. 1991. "AIDS: A Storm Threatening Medical Confidentiality." *AIDS & Public Policy Journal* 6: 28-30.

Liebert, Larry. 1990. "Bush Faces War Standoff with Congress, Too." *Congressional Quarterly Weekly Report,* 22 December, p. 4202.

Light, Paul C. 1982. *The President's Agenda: Domestic Policy Choice from Kennedy to Carter.* Baltimore, MD: Johns Hopkins University Press.

Loomis, Burdett. 1988. *The New American Politician: Ambition, Entrepreneurship, and the Changing Face of Political Life.* New York: Basic Books.

Lynch, Daniel. 1992. "AIDS: The Number Eleven Killer." *Washington Journalism Review* 14(1): 19-21.

MacKuen, Michael Bruce and Steven Lane Coombs. 1981. *More than News: Media Power in Public Affairs.* Beverly Hills, CA: Sage.

Malbin, Michael. 1980. *Unelected Representatives: Congressional Staff and the Future of Representative Government.* New York: Basic Books.

Matlack, Carol. 1990. "Always on Sunday." *National Journal,* 24 November, pp. 2857-2860.

Matlack, Carol. 1991. "Washington's Leader of the PACs." *National Journal,* 14 December, p. 3037.

Matthews, Donald R. 1973. *U.S. Senators and Their World,* 2nd ed. New York: W.W. Norton.

McConnell, Senator Mitch. 1991a. "Campaign Finance Reform." Speech given before the Kentucky Center for Public Issues. March 28.

McKilip, Jack. 1991. "The Effect of Mandatory Premarital HIV Testing on

Marriage: The Case of Illinois." *American Journal of Public Health* 81(5): 650-653.

Merry, Robert W. 1991. "Sen. Paul Wellstone and Gadfly Politics." *Congressional Quarterly Weekly Report*, 2 February, p. 318.

Monk, John. 1994. "N.C. Clout Wanes in U.S. House: Democrats' Rejection Pushes Rose Farther into Background." *Charlotte Observer*, 1 December, pp. 1A, 18A.

New Republic, The. 1990. "Dying for Dollars" 203: 7-8.

Ornstein, Norman. 1989. "What TV News Doesn't Report About Congress—and Should." *TV Guide*, 21 October, pp. 11-12.

Ornstein, Norman J., Thomas E. Mann and Michael Malbin. 1990. *Vital Statistics on the Congress: 1989-1990*. Washington, DC: American Enterprise Institute.

Ornstein, Norman and Michael Robinson. 1986. "The Case of Our Disappearing Congress." *TV Guide*, 11 January, pp. 4-10.

Owens, John E. 1985. "Extreme Advocacy Leadership in the Pre-Reform House: Wright Patman and the House Banking and Currency Committee." *British Journal of Political Science* 15: 187-205.

Paletz, David L. and Robert M. Entman. 1981. *Media, Power, Politics*. New York: The Free Press.

Peters, Ronald M., Jr. 1990. *The American Speakership: The Office in Historical Perspective*. Baltimore, MD: Johns Hopkins University Press.

Polsby, Nelson, 1981. "The Washington Community, 1960-1980." In *The New Congress*, eds. Thomas E. Mann and Norman J. Ornstein. Washington, DC: The American Enterprise Institute.

Republican Study Committee. 1990. "Rep. Bill Dannemeyer (CA-39) Requests that RSC Members Support the Dannemeyer Amendment to HR 4785, The AIDS Prevention Act of 1990." June 6.

Rieselbach, Leroy N. 1986. *Congressional Reform*. Washington, DC: Congressional Quarterly Press.

Robinson, Michael J. and Maura E. Clancy. 1983. "King of the Hill." *Washington Journalism Quarterly* 5: 46-49.

Rossellini, Lynn. 1991. "Under the Senate's Skin." *U.S. News and World Report*, 24 June, pp. 33-34.

Sabato, Larry J. 1984. *PAC Power: Inside the World of Political Action Committees*. New York: W.W. Norton.

Sabato, Larry J. 1987. "Real and Imagined Corruption in Campaign Financing." In *Elections American Style*, ed. A. James Reichley. Washington, DC: The Brookings Institution.

Schattschneider, E.E. 1960. *The Semi-Sovereign People*. Hinsdale, IL: The Dryden Press.

Scheele, Henry Z. 1989. "Response to the Kennedy Administration: The Joint Senate-House Republican Leadership Press Conferences." *Presidential Studies Quarterly* 19(4): 825-846.

Schwartz, David. 1991. "U.S. Senate Gains a Controversial Voice." *Carolina Alumni Review* Summer: 29-35.

Shaw, Donald L. and Maxwell E. McCombs, eds. 1977. *The Emergence of American Political Issues: The Agenda-Setting Function of the Press*. St. Paul, MN: West.

Shilts, Randy. 1987. *And the Band Played On: Politics, People and the AIDS Epidemic*. New York: St. Martin's Press.

Shinn, Rinn-Sup. 1991. "Campaign Financing: National Public Opinion Polls." CRS Report for Congress. Washington, DC: Congressional Research Service. April 12.

Sinclair, Barbara. 1989. *The Transformation of the U.S. Senate*. Baltimore, MD: Johns Hopkins University Press.

Sorauf, Frank J. 1987. "Campaign Money and the Press: Three Soundings." *Political Science Quarterly* 102(1): 25-42.

Southport Institute for Policy Analysis. 1989. *Jump Start: The Federal Role in Literacy Policy*. Washington, DC: SIPA.

Stanfeld, Rochelle. 1990. "Floating Power Centers." *National Journal*, pp. 2915-2919.

Sullivan, John L., L. Earl Shaw, Gregory E. McAvoy, and David G. Barnum, "The Dimensions of Cue-Taking in the House of Representatives," *Journal of Politics* 55: 975-997.

Towell, Pat. 1991. "Aspin's Political Clout Grows As Nunn's Leverage Is Questioned." *Congressional Quarterly Weekly Report*, 23 March, pp. 756-757.

Troyer, Ronald J. 1990. "Accuracy in Academia: Claims-Making by a Professional Social Movement Organization." *Perspectives on Social Problems* (2): 119-142.

Trueheart, Charles. 1990. "Paul Wellstone: Odd Man In." *Washington Post*, 14 November, pp. B1, B2.

Twenhafel, David. 1991. "1991 U.S. Senate Employment Practices: A Study of Staff Salary, Tenure, Demographics and Benefits." Washington, DC: The Congressional Management Foundation.

United States House of Representatives, Committee on House Administration Task Force on Campaign Finance Reform. 1991a. "Hearings: March 22, April 18, 30, 1991." Washington, DC: Government Printing Office.

United States House of Representatives, Committee on House Administration. 1991b. "House of Representatives Campaign Spending Limit and Election Reform Act of 1991." Report No. 102-340. November 19. Washington, DC: Government Printing Office.

Yant, Martin. 1991. *Desert Mirage: The True Story of the Gulf War*. Buffalo, NY: Prometheus Books.

Yett, Sheldon. 1991. "Key Dates in the Gulf Crisis." *Congressional Quarterly Weekly Report*, 5 January, pp. 41-44.

Author Index

Subject Index